"If you are looking for a powerful devotional, you've found it! *DivorceCare* is *the* finest material I've found in working with those who have been impacted by a divorce. This book will provide help, hope, and healing for your life and family."

— DR. DENNIS RAINEY,
President, FamilyLife™

"*DivorceCare* is a wonderful combination of wise advice and assurances that God still loves you. This book is packed with a year's worth of healing and hope for anyone going through divorce."

— DR. TIM CLINTON,
President, American Association of
Christian Counselors (AACC)

"*DivorceCare: Hope, Help, and Healing During and After Your Divorce* will speed the recovery of those readers going through divorce and will redeem their catastrophe and turn it into a victory. You will find new strength in Jesus and a hope that will sustain you through your trials. I found it most uplifting and heartily endorse this excellent resource for those struggling through divorce themselves, no matter what stage they are in. It is also a great resource for counselors to recommend to clients. I know that all who read it will find the 'peace . . . which passeth all understanding' that God offers to all."

— DR. ARCHIBALD D. HART,
Author of *Helping Children Survive
Divorce* and *The Anxiety Cure*

"Those who have suffered the pain of divorce will welcome this book. The information, insights, and encouraging words will assist any reader in his or her journey of growth and recovery."

— H. NORMAN WRIGHT,
Author of *Recovering from the Losses
of Life* and *Crisis Counseling*

"This devotional book will serve as a personal counselor and daily source of encouragement and inspiration for the person who is re-emerging from the gray clouds of a failed relationship. I also recommend *DivorceCare* to those who have never experienced a divorce because its wisdom will serve as preventative medicine. Enjoy the crisp, scripturally sound, and practical wisdom of these pages."

— DR. MYLES E. MUNROE,
Author of *Single, Married, Separated,
and Life After Divorce*

"Divorce can so thoroughly shake a person's confidence that it creates a deep hunger for words of hope and affirmation. *DivorceCare: Hope, Help, and Healing During and After Your Divorce* is an encouraging book that offers guidance and wisdom for those choosing to grow in the midst of their trials. Reading each devotion will be akin to digesting nurturing food for the soul. You will be blessed by this wonderful book."

— DR. LES CARTER,
Author of *Grace and Divorce* and *The
Anger Trap*

"This devotional encourages, inspires, and brings hope to healing hearts. Daily you will be reminded that you are loved, cared for, and can face life with a renewed confidence that comes only from God."

— DR. LINDA MINTLE,
Author of *Divorce Proofing Your
Marriage* and *Breaking Free from
Anger and Unforgiveness*

"These pages are like a friend who provides words of comfort, hope, and direction during this unsettling and confusing time—just enough to carry you through another day. I longed for a book like this during my own separation and divorce."

— JAN NORTHINGTON,
Author of *Separated and Waiting*

"The devastation of separation and divorce is so catastrophic to your thinking and spiritual processes that you will need daily input to stay on the right path. The devotional book *DivorceCare* is designed to give you daily encouragement and to prevent you from doing more damage to yourself and making bad decisions that will scar your life further."

— DR. JIM A. TALLEY,
President, Relationship Resources,
and Author of *Reconcilable
Differences* and *Too Close Too Soon*

"I was touched by how this book skillfully leads a person crushed by a broken relationship to both wisdom and hope. If I could buy just one book for someone I love who is suffering from separation or divorce, this would be the book. I will be recommending this book to hundreds of hurting people."

— GARY RICHMOND,
Pastor to Single Parents,
First Evangelical Free Church of
Fullerton, California

"The best compliment a person can give is to speak another person's language. If you are suddenly alone and struggling emotionally, financially, or spiritually, this book speaks your language. It does so through short, easy reflections and friendly advice. *DivorceCare: Hope, Help, and Healing During and After Your Divorce* should be on every divorced person's nightstand. It is a lifeline—in any language."

— CYNTHIA YATES,
Speaker and Author of *Living Well on
One Income in a Two-Income World*

"Knowing personally how painful divorce can be, I found this book to be a great resource to help anyone stay spiritually focused during the loss of a relationship. Discover the healing power of God's Word in this daily devotional."

— ROB EAGAR,
Speaker and Author of *Dating with
Pure Passion*

"Reading *DivorceCare* is like sitting in a cozy living room with friends who have 'been there.' Each devotion reminds you of the reality that you are not alone—others have also cried out in loneliness and heartache and discovered the comforting touch of a compassionate God and kind friends. No matter what stage of divorce you find yourself in, this book will offer comfort and hope."

— ELSA KOK,
Author of *A Woman Who Hurts, A
God Who Heals* and *Settling for Less
Than God's Best? A Relationship
Checkup for Single Women*

"Hope is one of the greatest needs of a divorcing person—and this book comes through! With reassuring encouragement, this splendid devotional provides day-to-day insight on navigating the complex issues that surround separation or divorce. I highly recommend it to anyone seeking help."

— LAURA PETHERBRIDGE,
Author of *When Your Marriage Dies:
Answers to Questions About
Separation and Divorce*

"Many men and women struggle through the pain of divorce with little to no assistance. As a result, most still carry sadness and anger even ten to fifteen years after the divorce is finalized. Yet they fail to acknowledge these paralyzing emotions. This book is an excellent tool that can help divorced adults address their true feelings and make right decisions toward living the rest of their lives with joy, purpose, and the peace of God."

— ELEANOR REID,
Author of *Stop My Childhood from
Drowning: 39 Lessons from a Child
Experiencing Divorce*

"This book is the perfect companion to those who find themselves single again and looking for tangible help in bite-size pieces. You'll find encouragement and hope on every page."

— PAULA RINEHART,
Author of *Sex and the Soul of a
Woman*

DivorceCare

Hope, Help, and Healing During and After Your Divorce

Steve Grissom and Kathy Leonard

NELSON BOOKS
A Division of Thomas Nelson Publishers
Since 1798

www.thomasnelson.com

Published in Nashville, Tennessee, by Thomas Nelson, Inc.

Published in association with the literary agency of Sanford Communications, Inc., Portland, Oregon.

Nelson Books titles may be purchased in bulk for educational, business, fund-raising, or sales promotional use. For information, please e-mail SpecialMarkets@ThomasNelson.com.

Unless otherwise indicated, Scripture quotations used in this book are from the *Holy Bible, New International Version*®. Copyright © 1973, 1978, 1984 by International Bible Society. Used by permission of Zondervan Publishing House. All rights reserved.

Other Scripture references are from the following sources:

> *The Amplified Bible:* Old Testament. Copyright © 1962, 1964 by Zondervan Publishing House (used by permission); and from *The Amplified New Testament.* Copyright © 1958 by The Lockman Foundation (used by permission).

> *The Contemporary English Version.* Copyright © 1991, 1995 by the American Bible Society. Used by permission.

> *Holy Bible, New Living Translation.* Copyright © 1996. Used by permission of Tyndale House Publishers, Inc., Wheaton, Illinois 60189. All rights reserved.

> *The Message* by Eugene H. Peterson. Copyright © 1993, 1994, 1995, 1996, 2000, 2001, 2002. Used by permission of NavPress Publishing Group. All rights reserved.

> *The New American Standard Bible*®. Copyright © 1960, 1962, 1963, 1968, 1971, 1972, 1973, 1975, 1977, 1995 by The Lockman Foundation. Used by permission.

> *New King James Version*®. Copyright © 1982 by Thomas Nelson, Inc. Used by permission. All rights reserved.

Interior flower photo provided courtesy of Walter Petrie

Library of Congress Cataloging-in-Publication Data

Grissom, Steve.
    DivorceCare : hope, help, and healing during and after your divorce / Steve Grissom and Kathy Leonard.
      p. cm.
    Includes bibliographical references.
    ISBN 0-7852-1246-9 (pbk.)
    1. Divorced people—Prayer-books and devotions—English. 2. Divorce—Religious aspects—Christianity-Meditations. 3. Devotional calendars. I. Title: Divorce care. II. Leonard, Kathy. III. Title.
BV4596.D58G75 2005
242'.646—dc22   2005017669

Printed in the United States of America

05 06 07 08 09 RRD 5 4 3 2 1

Contents

Welcome

Your separation or divorce has brought you to a place you never hoped to be, and you wonder if you will ever be free from the deep pain and despair. Separation and divorce can bring confusing emotions, physical problems, financial difficulties, spiritual struggles, and losses that need to be grieved. You are not alone in this situation, and we want to assure you that full recovery is possible.

In this book you will meet men and women of all ages who have gone through separation and divorce and have come out victorious, hope-filled, and at peace. You will also learn practical steps for recovery from more than thirty professionals in areas related to divorce recovery. Best of all, you will find out how Jesus Christ can actively work in you to help you find true healing and live an abundant life.

These devotions are based on the DivorceCare® support group recovery program. DivorceCare® groups meet in more than 8,000 churches around the world, helping people recover from the devastating effects of separation and divorce. We encourage you to become part of a DivorceCare® program. To find a group meeting near you, visit www.divorcecare.org or call The Church Initiative at 1-800-489-7778.

Our prayers are with you this year as you walk forward toward joy, strength, and the healing that is available through Jesus Christ.

Meet the Experts

The following are the experts who contributed to this book. These Christian teachers, authors, and speakers are respected authorities on divorce topics. When referring to an expert in this book, his or her full name is used.

Dr. Robert Abarno is a Christian author, counselor, and clinical psychologist. He is the founder of Christ Centered Development, a teaching and equipping ministry in Wake Forest, North Carolina.

Kay Arthur of Precept Ministries in Chattanooga, Tennessee (www.precept.org), is a Bible teacher, the author of more than one hundred books and Bible studies, a radio and television hostess, and the principal spokesperson for the *International Inductive Study Bible*.

Dr. Bob Barnes is a popular conference speaker and author. He is the executive director of Sheridan House Family Ministries in Fort Lauderdale, Florida: a residential treatment program for teenage boys and girls, a marriage and family counseling center, and a social services center (www.sheridanhouse.org).

Sabrina D. Black is the director of Abundant Life Counseling Center in the Detroit area (www.sabrinablack.com). A national and international speaker, she is a member of the National Biblical Counselors Association and the American Association of Christian Counselors. She is the author of *Can Two Walk Together? Encouragement for Spiritually Unbalanced Marriages*, coauthor of *HELP! for Your Leadership* and *Prone to Wander*, and coeditor of *Counseling in African-American Communities*.

Dee Brestin is a conference speaker and the author of many Bible study guides for women (www.deebrestin.com). She and her late husband are the parents of five children, two of whom were adopted as older children from overseas orphanages.

Larry Burkett was cofounder of Crown Financial Ministries, the world's largest Christian financial counseling organization. Mr. Burkett hosted two daily radio programs, *Money Matters* and *How to Manage Your Money*, and authored several books, including *Family Financial Workbook* and *The Financial Guide for the Single Parent*.

Dr. Les Carter is a counselor at the Southlake Psychiatry and Counseling Clinic in Southlake, Texas, and is the author of *Grace and Divorce* and *The Anger Workbook* (www.drlescarter.com). Having been divorced himself, it is his desire to share God's healing truths with people in need. Known as "America's Anger Expert," Dr. Carter conducts anger management workshops across the nation.

Dr. Tim Clinton is an author and the president of the American Association of Christian Counselors (www.aacc.net). This organization exists to encourage excellence in Christian counseling.

Rob Eagar is the author of *Dating with Pure Passion*. Abandoned by his wife in his twenties, he discovered the joyful, healing power of a relationship with Christ. Today he inspires thousands of single adults each month through his speaking and writing (www.robeagar.com).

Doug Easterday has ministered in more than fifteen different nations on the topic of forgiveness and other subjects, teaching in Bible schools, camps, marriage conferences, and youth programs. He is on the pastoral staff at Christ's Center Church in Junction City, Oregon.

Dr. Tony Evans is the founder and president of the Urban Alternative. He is also the founder and pastor of the Oak Cliff Bible Fellowship in Dallas, Texas (www.tonyevans.org). Dr. Evans is an author and a regular speaker at crusades and Bible conferences in the United States and abroad.

Rev. Harold Graham is the director of Caring Ministries at Fellowship Missionary Church in Fort Wayne, Indiana. For more than thirteen years he has helped people go through the process of forgiving those who have hurt them.

Anne Graham Lotz is an author, speaker, and the president of AnGeL Ministries (www.angelministries.org). The daughter of Billy and Ruth Graham, Anne Lotz has hosted a series of *Just Give Me Jesus* revivals and Bible studies across the United States.

Dr. Archibald Hart is the senior professor of psychology and dean emeritus at Fuller Theological Seminary's Graduate School of Psychology in Pasadena, California, and a practicing clinical psychologist. Dr. Hart experienced the divorce of his parents when he was twelve years old and is the author of *Helping Children Survive Divorce* and numerous other books.

Wayne Hudson is an author, speaker, and teacher. With a passion for children of divorce, he is cofounder of the Jazz for Kids ministry. His primary focus is to those impacted by broken relationships. He is the author of *Many a Tear Has to Fall*, a resource for the divorced, as well as *Sometimes a Kid's Life Is Ruff Tuff Stuff!*, a children's book on divorce.

Bonnie Keen is a talented singer, songwriter, and group member, who has also experienced the trauma of divorce (www.bonniekeen.com). She is a speaker and has authored *Blessed Are the Desperate for They Will Find Hope*, *God Loves Messy People*, and *A Ladder Out of Depression*.

Dr. Craig Keener is the author of *And Marries Another* and other books. He is a professor of New Testament studies at Palmer Seminary in Wynnewood, Pennsylvania, a division of Eastern University (www.eastern.edu).

Mike Klumpp, after divorce, became a single dad of four children. His experiences inspired his book *The Single Dad's Survival Guide*. Remarried, parenting seven, and working on a volume for blended families, Mike also teaches karate and is the Student and Family Life Pastor for Grace Point Fellowship in Dripping Springs, Texas.

Warren Kniskern is a Christian attorney and Certified Family Mediator in Florida. Based on his own experience with divorce, he authored *When the Vow Breaks: A Survival and Recovery Guide for Christians Facing Divorce*. His current book, *Making a NEW Vow*, is a guidebook for a healthy remarriage.

Elsa Kok is a speaker, the editor of the *Single Parent Family* edition of *Focus on the Family* magazine, and the author of *A Woman Who Hurts, a God Who Heals* and *Settling for Less Than God's Best? A Relationship Checkup for Single Women* (www.elsakok.com). As a result of her own experiences, her sincere desire is to help those who are experiencing similar heartbreak and struggles.

Dr. Linda Mintle is a licensed clinical social worker with more than twenty years of experience, specializing in marriage and family therapy. She is the author of numerous articles and eleven books that include *Divorce Proofing Your Marriage* and *A Daughter's Journey Home*, is the resident expert of ABC Family Channel's *Living the Life*, and hosts her own Web site, www.drlindahelps.com.

Dr. Myles Munroe is the founder, president, and senior pastor of Bahamas Faith Ministries International (www.bfmmm.com), a church and international ministry organization based in Nassau, Bahamas. He travels internationally as a popular speaker and teacher, and he is the author of *Single, Married, Separated, and Life After Divorce* and numerous other books.

Jan Northington lives in Los Osos, California. She is a CLASS (Christian Leaders, Authors & Speakers Services) graduate and Certified Personality Trainer. Her passion is teaching and speaking. She has authored *Separated and Waiting* and has written numerous articles for the Christian marketplace.

Laura Petherbridge speaks at seminars, workshops, and retreats on spiritual growth, marriage, and divorce recovery (www.laurapetherbridge.com). She is the author of *When Your Marriage Dies: Answers to Questions About Separation and Divorce*. It is a frequently-asked-questions book geared for those going through separation and divorce.

Lou Priolo is the author of *The Heart of Anger, The Complete Husband, Teach Them Diligently*, and *Losing That Lovin' Feeling*. A noted lecturer and full-time biblical counselor for nineteen years, he currently serves as the director of biblical counseling at Eastwood Presbyterian Church in Montgomery, Alabama. He is an instructor at Birmingham Theological Seminary.

Dick Purnell is a writer and speaker (www.slr.org). He has been featured on national television and on radio programs, such as *America's Family Counselors, The Singles Connection,* and *Truths That Transform.* Single for forty-two years, he is sensitive to the concerns of singles and married couples because of his own experiences.

Dr. Dennis Rainey is the president and cofounder of FamilyLife™ (www.familylife.com), a division of Campus Crusade for Christ, and a graduate of Dallas Theological Seminary. He is the senior editor of the HomeBuilders Couples Series and a daily host of the radio program *FamilyLife Today.*

Linda Ranson Jacobs is the executive director of DivorceCare for Kids™ (www.DC4K.org) with The Church Initiative, Inc., of Wake Forest, North Carolina. She is one of the forefront leaders in the area of children, single-parent families, and divorce. She has extensive experience as an author, speaker, program developer, and consultant/trainer on children with emotional and behavioral issues. She created and developed the *DC4K*™ resources.

Eleanor Reid is the president and founder of Fruition, LLC, a corporate and personal strategy consulting firm. She is the author of several books, including *Stop My Childhood from Drowning: 39 Lessons from a Child Experiencing Divorce,* and she has prepared resources to help people prepare for and successfully undergo life transitions.

Gary Richmond is pastor to single parents at First Evangelical Free Church of Fullerton, California (www.fefcful.org). He counsels single parents and people experiencing divorce. He has also authored *Successful Single Parenting.*

Paula Rinehart has a private counseling practice in Raleigh, North Carolina. She is a frequent speaker at women's conferences in the United States and abroad. She is the author of five books, including *Strong Women, Soft Hearts* and *Sex and the Soul of a Woman.*

Doug Schmidt is the author of *The Prayer of Revenge: Forgiveness in the Face of Injustice*, a book about learning to forgive those who won't apologize or acknowledge that they've done anything wrong (www.dougschmidt.com). He has degrees in biblical studies and systematic theology from Wheaton College and Trinity Evangelical Divinity School.

Rose Sweet is an author, speaker, businesswoman, and conference leader (www.rosesweet.com). She is a member of the American Association of Christian Counselors and an active DivorceCare® leader in her church in California. Rose is the author of four books, including *Healing the Divorced Heart* and *Dear God, Send Me a Soul Mate*.

Dr. Jim A. Talley is an international author whose ten books are in six languages. He heads Relationship Resources, Inc., and is a marriage counselor in private practice in Oklahoma City, Oklahoma. He conducts a wide variety of seminars for singles on topics including dating, divorce recovery, and marriage reconciliation. Visit Dr. Talley's Web site at www.drtalley.com.

H. Norman Wright is a trauma therapist and the author of seventy books, including *Recovering from the Losses of Life* and *Crisis Counseling* (www.hnormanwright.com). He is on the faculty of Talbot Graduate School of Theology and on the executive board of the American Association of Christian Counselors.

Cynthia Yates is a gifted writer, speaker, humorist, and radio personality (www.cynthiayates.com). Having been divorced and left homeless and penniless with a young son, Cynthia has sincere empathy for and a desire to help others in need. Her books include *Living Well on One Income in a Two-Income World*, *Money and Me: A Woman's Guide to Financial Confidence*, and *1001 Bright Ideas to Stretch Your Dollars*.

Dr. Spiros Zodhiates is an authority on the Greek New Testament. He is the president of AMG (Advancing the Ministries of the Gospel) International (www.amginternational.org), an organization ministering in more than fifty countries. He is the author of numerous books, including *What About Divorce?* and *May I Divorce and Remarry?*

The following people contributed to this book by sharing their personal stories of separation, divorce, and recovery. We appreciate their courage, openness, and willingness to help others.

Alice	Lauren
Angie	Lee
Betsy	Linda
B.J.	Lisa
Bob	Loren
Bobby	Lynda
Cathy C.	Marc
Cathy D.	Margo
Cheryl	Marie
Christine	Melissa
Cindy	Muriel
Danny	Nancy
Dave	Nell Ann
Don	Odie
Ed	Patsy
Ginny	Phil
Greg	Priscilla
Harriet	Ron
Howard	Roy
James	Selma
Jeannette	Sherry
Jerry	Steve
Jim	Sue
Joanne	Susan
Joe	Teri
Joyce	Terry
Juana	Tim
Juaria	Todd
Kennie	Wallace
Kim	Wayne

What's Happening?

What's Happening?

Divorce is like a tornado—ripping through your life, threatening to destroy everything in its path. The emotional whirlwinds bring fear, confusion, and despair, affecting you, your children, family members, and friends. You will likely wonder, *Why did this storm hit my life, and why does it hurt so much?*

Dr. Jim A. Talley says, "The reality is that divorce is the most painful thing you can go through because it impacts so much of your life. There's no way around or easy way out. And everybody is looking for a painless way out of this whole situation."

It is easier to clean up the physical damage of a tornado than the emotional damage caused by divorce.

"I hated life," says Ginny. "I woke up every morning, and I absolutely hated it. I hated the pain that I woke up with and the pain that I went to sleep with."

You may wish you could get through the pain quicker, but healing is a process, a day-by-day, moment-by-moment process. In order to experience any level of recovery, you must see it through. There are no shortcuts. But take heart. In the coming days and weeks, you will see it is possible to heal and to look to the future with hope.

"'For I know the plans I have for you,' declares the LORD, 'plans to prosper you and not to harm you, plans to give you hope and a future'" (Jeremiah 29:11).

Dear Lord, my life is ripped apart, and I can't keep from focusing on the devastation and pain that seem to define my very being. Help me turn to You. No one else knows what I am going through. Amen.

Why Divorce Hurts So Much

"It's pretty natural to expect hurt when a mate leaves, but I was not prepared for the level of hurt or the level of pain I felt," says Steve.

The pain of divorce is much deeper and more soul wrenching than most people can imagine unless they have been through it themselves. Divorce can mean the end of your hopes and dreams, the end of your life as you have known it, a loss of control, and feelings of rejection, loneliness, and blame. There is anger, depression, helplessness, bitterness, resentment, feelings of worthlessness, and guilt. The list goes on and on.

"I was afraid that once I opened that door, the intensity of what I was feeling would break me into little pieces," says Marie. "I'd be scattered all over the floor in little tiny scraps, and I'd never be able to pull myself back together."

You will not be able to "hurry up and get over it." That is not possible. Instead, start by making a commitment to take a small step forward every day. Marie says, "Gradually, God has put the pieces back together, and the pieces that I don't have anymore, the severing of the part of me that was bonded with my husband, God has healed and replaced. He's in the process of finishing that up."

"I cry to you, O LORD; I say, 'You are my refuge, my portion in the land of the living.' Listen to my cry, for I am in desperate need; rescue me" (Psalm 142:5–6).

Lord and Savior, the intensity of my emotions is unbearable. Hold me in Your strong arms. Comfort me with the comfort that only comes from You, and guide me in taking one step forward each day. Amen.

The Level of Pain

"I thought, 'There's no way anyone can survive this kind of pain. You can't have this kind of pain and live,'" says Cathy. "It was the most excruciating pain I have ever experienced in my life. I kept thinking, *I'll soon die.* Then I realized I wasn't going to die, and I would pray: 'Lord, please take my life.'"

The level of pain you are feeling is beyond the comprehension of someone who has not been through divorce. People around you may mean well, but they cannot understand how deep the pain cuts and why it would have such an extreme effect on the physical, mental, emotional, and spiritual aspects of your life.

Anne Graham Lotz offers this reassurance: "When you're experiencing pain and difficulty—maybe the loss of a loved one or a divorce—it's a wonderful thing to know that God truly feels your pain. You may think God doesn't care, and maybe the pain has caused you to be hardened toward God, but God understands physical suffering firsthand. He, therefore, understands how to comfort you in your suffering."

Jesus knows how you feel. Although this may be difficult for you to believe, the Bible assures you it is true:

"In all their suffering he [Jesus] also suffered, and he personally rescued them. In his love and mercy he redeemed them. He lifted them up and carried them through all the years" (Isaiah 63:9 NLT).

Jesus, You know exactly how I feel. Please rescue me.
Amen.

Alienation: What Is It?

Merriam-Webster's dictionary defines *alienation* as "a withdrawing or separation of a person or a person's affections from a position of former attachment." In separation and divorce, you are alienated not only from your former mate, but also from relatives, friends, and sometimes from the church.

Dr. Myles Munroe says, "When a person gets divorced, you often see the opposite of what happens in a physical death. Your family may back away from you, seeing you as a failure, a loser. Some people in the church may back away from you. Society backs off from you; they see you as someone whose life didn't work. When you divorce, you end up lonely, isolated, rejected, and dejected, which adds to the trauma.

"Being divorced is bad enough, but to have your family or your church turn against you, that makes the hurt even worse. A person who has been divorced ends up in a state that God never intended, and that is the state of isolation."

God does not intend for you to be alienated from other people, and He certainly does not intend for you to be apart from Him. God loves you unconditionally. While your family and friends are wrong to alienate you, separation from God only occurs when you back away from Him.

Keep in mind that while you may feel alienated from some people in the church, your best opportunity to find help and support is in a local church family.

"Do not be afraid or terrified because of them, for the Lord your God goes with you; he will never leave you nor forsake you" (Deuteronomy 31:6).

Faithful God, forgive me for thinking that You, too, have rejected me. Lord, I open the door of my heart to You today. Please come in and love me. Amen.

The Church Can Help You

The church, as God intended, provides supportive hands, wise minds, and loving hearts to help those who are hurting and in need. The driving force and the solid foundation of the church is Jesus Christ, who loves you dearly and without conditions. Even if some people in your church have pulled away from you, help is still available there.

"When you are going through a divorce, you feel like you are wearing the scarlet letter and everyone is shying away from you," says Warren Kniskern. To some extent that's true, but the worst thing to do is to withdraw from the people of God.

"This is a time more than any other time that you need to be with the people of God and receive their encouragement. Keep your focus on Christ instead of on your problems, or else you're going to sink just as surely as Peter sank when he walked on the water to Jesus."

In the Bible, Peter was on a boat one stormy night, and he looked up and saw Jesus walking on the raging sea. Jesus asked Peter to come to Him. At first Peter jumped up with joyful assurance and started across the water to Jesus. Then he became afraid, focusing on his inadequacies instead of on Christ's sufficiency.

"When he saw the wind, he was afraid and, beginning to sink, cried out, 'Lord, save me!'

"Immediately Jesus reached out his hand and caught him. 'You of little faith,' he said, 'why did you doubt?' And when they climbed into the boat, the wind died down" (Matthew 14:30–32).

Lord, give me the courage to seek help in the church and to keep my focus on You and not me. Grant me the faith to persevere. Amen.

Not Sure About Church?

Many people look everywhere else for help before they go to the church, or they just don't give the church a chance. Perhaps you have had a bad experience there. Do not give up. The church is not a building, a social gathering, or a clique. The church is a group of people whose lives have been changed because of Jesus. They are not perfect people, but their love and commitment to Jesus is the reason they gather together. There is room for you there. Find a church where the people love Jesus, and they will love you too.

"I'm not a big joiner of any group," says Joanne. "I like to do things by myself. I'm a very stubborn person. But the warmth that I felt from being back in church and learning to develop a more active relationship with my God was a special thing in that time of my life."

God promises in the Bible that He will supply all your needs. These needs include physical, emotional, and spiritual needs. Give God a chance to use the people in His church to help you.

"Let us not give up meeting together, as some are in the habit of doing, but let us encourage one another—and all the more as you see the Day approaching" (Hebrews 10:25).

Jesus, I hesitate to seek help from people in the church for a number of reasons. Please open my heart to see and to accept the love they have for me that I might not have noticed before. Amen.

Coping with Feelings of Isolation

Laura Petherbridge says, "I would go to church on Sunday morning and I would think, *Everybody has their wonderful little Ozzie and Harriet families, and I don't belong here anymore. I'm sitting in the corner of the pew drowning in sorrow. On the outside I might not look like I'm struggling, but inside I'm dying. I feel very distant from everyone. I can't connect with people anymore because they do not understand my pain.*"

This is a normal reaction for a person going through separation or divorce. You are not alone in these feelings, so do not let your confusing emotions worry you. If you would like to find a place where people truly understand how you feel and what you are going through, consider connecting with a DivorceCare® group or another Christian divorce recovery support group.[1] In this type of group, you will not only find people to connect with, but you will also learn about a God who can be trusted no matter how difficult or dark your circumstances.

"'Everyone who calls, "Help, God!"' gets help.' But how can people call for help if they don't know who to trust? And how can they know who to trust if they haven't heard of the One who can be trusted? And how can they hear if nobody tells them?" (Romans 10:13–14 MSG).

Dear God, help! I feel so alone and helpless. Lead me to a support and recovery group where I can build friendships with people who understand what I am going through and where I can learn to put my trust in You. Amen.

---

1. DivorceCare® is a support and recovery program offered in churches around the world. To find the group nearest you, call 1-800-489-7778 or go to www.divorcecare.org.

Pointed in the Right Direction

"I pondered the direction of my life, and I turned to follow your statutes" (Psalm 119:59 NLT).

The first step you need to take is to point yourself in the right direction. That direction is toward God. This may seem to be a pat answer, too simplistic for the complexity of your emotions. But it is true. God alone can save you and give your life meaning and purpose and energy again.

"When you finally reach the bottom and when you finally get to the point where everything else is exhausted and your very essence is gone and everything that you had on earth is gone and torn apart, there's only one way to go," says Don. "I learned very quickly that Jesus Christ is the only solution and the only way."

Anne Graham Lotz says, "In the middle of your problems, in the middle of the hurricanes and the storms that come into your life and turn everything topsy-turvy, you need to keep your focus on Him. On the days when you lose focus, remember that He stays focused on you."

You may be thinking, *God sure isn't helping me*, but have you *asked* God for His help, and do you trust that God's answer and timing are best? Each day give your burdens and your requests to God, and focus on His loving-kindness. He will not fail you.

"Let the morning bring me word of your unfailing love, for I have put my trust in you. Show me the way I should go, for to you I lift up my soul" (Psalm 143:8).

Living God, I turn to You. I have reached my lowest point, and there is nowhere else to go but in the direction of You. Save me, Jesus. Amen.

Energy Distribution

Ideally, the amount of energy you expend each day is equally balanced across the physical, emotional, mental, and spiritual aspects of your life. But during and after a separation or divorce, your energy distribution is much different. As much as 85 percent of your energy can be diverted to dealing with the emotional upheaval, leaving only 15 percent to deal with all your physical, mental, and spiritual demands.

"Emotionally you're spinning," says Dr. Jim A. Talley. "You are going round and round. It's like you are running your engine wide open, but you're in neutral and not going anywhere, yet you can't shut the motor off. Eighty-five percent of your energy is being consumed in the whole emotional area. That leaves you 5 percent mental, 5 percent spiritual, and 5 percent physical. Mental difficulties include the inability to make decisions. Physically, you are totally exhausted. Spiritually, you have a loss of faith; you are not sure God exists, and you're not sure if you even care if He exists."

The emotional turmoil, the mental fog, the total loss of energy, and the questioning of God are to be expected. You don't desire any of it, but you have it, and your feelings and thoughts are natural.

"I am worn out from groaning; all night long I flood my bed with weeping and drench my couch with tears. My eyes grow weak with sorrow; they fail because of all my foes. Away from me, all you who do evil, for the LORD has heard my weeping. The LORD has heard my cry for mercy; the LORD accepts my prayer" (Psalm 6:6–9).

God, I'm wiped out. Help me to acknowledge that my feelings are completely normal, and give me the energy to turn to You for help. Amen.

Imbalanced Energy Distribution

When your energy distribution is imbalanced to such an extreme for an extended period of time, it is inevitable that you will experience an energy collapse.

"I was to the point of exhaustion," admits Cheryl. "I couldn't do anything. I couldn't go to work for a few days. I couldn't function. I was just a zombie. But it was after that time I finally realized I needed to deal with everything that was going on. I had to pull myself together and deal with the issues at hand."

You will likely experience an energy collapse, but you will also begin to move back to a balanced state again. Nothing happens quickly in the divorce recovery process. The journey is mostly uphill, but there are things you can do and information you can gain that will aid you in your recovery process and bring you to a level of peace and healing. Each day, turn to God and call out to Him in prayer, asking Him to supply you with the energy to get through the day.

"Be merciful to me, O LORD, for I am in distress; my eyes grow weak with sorrow, my soul and my body with grief. My life is consumed by anguish and my years by groaning; my strength fails because of my affliction, and my bones grow weak" (Psalm 31:9–10).

Lord, I have no energy. Every part of my life seems to be collapsing. I am crying out to You because I have no one else to cry to. Hear my prayer. Amen.

Feeling Guilty About Lack of Balance

Your energy imbalance affects every aspect of your life. You may feel guilty because you lack the spiritual energy to relate to God or because you lack the physical energy to care for your children or to keep up with family and friends. Please don't.

Dr. Jim A. Talley says, "You need to be aware that these things are normal and to be expected, that you will recover, and that things will be fine. It's a matter of going through the process and allowing God to help you stabilize yourself. Put yourself back on the right track, and allow God to walk through this process with you. It is not a quick fix.

"The painful reality is you have two choices as you walk through this process: You can either have extreme pain by doing it the right way or excruciating pain by doing it the wrong way. There is no pain-free way out."

Do not feel guilty if you are not living up to your own expectations of how you should act in regard to your spiritual, emotional, physical, or mental responses. Regaining a balance is not possible right now. Just take one forward step at a time.

"When I am afraid, I will trust in you. In God, whose word I praise, in God I trust; I will not be afraid. What can mortal man do to me?" (Psalm 56:3–4).

Lord God, I choose to walk this journey with You, realizing that my pain is going to be a way of life for a while. But not forever. Amen.

Search for Stability

After you experience separation or divorce, it is natural to want to try to stabilize your life and regain a feeling of personal security. Unfortunately, some people get so focused on finding that lost sense of security that they are willing to look just about anywhere.

"There's a whole industry evolved to provide excitement strong enough to divert the pain," says Dr. Jim A. Talley. "People in divorce are just looking for something to absorb some of that energy and some of that pain in their lives, and they tend to look in the wrong areas."

Roy says, "You can get consumed with your work. You can medicate the pain with drugs or alcohol. There are a lot of things you can do to try to live with the fallout of the divorce, but I don't think you are ever going to be released without coming to know God through His Son, Jesus Christ."

Don't fall into the "do what feels good" trap. You need to be free from this pain, not imprisoned by it. True security and true freedom are found in a relationship with Jesus Christ, and this relationship is available to everyone who believes.

"Jesus replied, 'I tell you the truth, everyone who sins is a slave to sin. Now a slave has no permanent place in the family, but a son belongs to it forever. So if the Son sets you free, you will be free indeed'" (John 8:34–36).

Lord God, I am sometimes tempted to ask, "Who cares?" and then go out and do something to numb the pain for a while. Please protect me from that temptation, and guide me to do what pleases You. Amen.

Stabilizing Your Life: How Long Will It Take?

Each person's recovery experience is unique, and there is no guarantee on the amount of time it will take until you feel whole again. Although you cannot be certain about the date, you can be certain about the healing, and in order to heal, you must take some specific steps. The first step, as we have said before, is to point yourself in the right direction. Second, make a commitment to moving forward. Third, acknowledge that what you are experiencing is normal. The fourth step is to understand that you must go through the recovery process.

"Let the pain run its course," says Rob Eagar. "As humans, we are so focused on wanting to feel good all the time. Then when hurt and pain come into our lives, we do anything to get rid of it. Understand that it is going to hurt for a while. Having that realization helped me to face my pain and to be able to say, 'Okay, this is how it's going to be.'"

An important part of your healing is based on your understanding that recovery is a process, and it is a process you must go through, despite the pain.

"Give me understanding that I may live" (Psalm 119:144).

Lord, I did not choose this pain, and I am so tired of it. Help me understand that there are no shortcuts in divorce recovery. Help me realize that I must walk this journey of healing no matter how long it takes. Amen.

Fishing in the Desert

Where have you been looking for stability? Think carefully about the places and people you have gone to for feelings of assurance or acceptance. You may have searched in places you never thought you'd visit. In a desperate attempt to ease the pain, you may be doing things that part of you finds repulsive.

"The process of alienation that occurs during divorce destroys your moral value system, and you end up doing things that you never thought you'd do in your whole life," says Dr. Jim A. Talley.

It is not uncommon for people to fall into alcohol, sex, drugs, meanness, or rage, seeking anything or anyone that will make them feel good, at least for a moment.

"Finding true love in a bar," says Dr. Talley, "is like finding fish in the desert. You tend to go to the wrong places first and finally end up in the right places."

Your moral value system may be buried, but it is still intact. It is never too late to change your ways. Start by nurturing your spiritual life. Open up the Bible. Visit a church. If that church does not embrace you, visit another. Cry out to God.

Pray this prayer with the psalmist:

"In you, O LORD, I have taken refuge; let me never be put to shame; deliver me in your righteousness. Turn your ear to me, come quickly to my rescue; be my rock of refuge, a strong fortress to save me. Since you are my rock and my fortress, for the sake of your name lead and guide me. Free me from the trap that is set for me, for you are my refuge. Into your hands I commit my spirit; redeem me, O LORD, the God of truth" (Psalm 31:1–5). Amen.

The Impact of a New Relationship

Dr. Jim A. Talley says, "Another relationship is like Novocain for the heart. It is the easiest, quickest, slickest way to do away with the pain. But it's sort of like having a broken foot. You can take a shot of Novocain in your foot after you break it, and you can still walk. You can keep right on walking. You can look around and say, 'I'm fine. Really, I'm fine.'

"One day you look down, and you see these white bones sticking through the skin of your foot, and you realize that you've done a lot more damage to yourself with the Novocain than if you had put a cast around it, protected it, and put some structure to it."

You need to protect your heart, and you need structure so that your heart is supported and strong on its own. Getting involved in a new relationship will only damage a heart that is not fully healed.

To find structure and support for your heart, start with prayer, daily prayer. Then read God's Word. It is also helpful to find a mature Christian friend who will pray with you and who can answer questions you may have about the Bible. Learn to strengthen your heart God's way.

"For the eyes of the LORD range throughout the earth to strengthen those whose hearts are fully committed to him" (2 Chronicles 16:9).

Lord Jesus, I cannot do this alone. Help me realize it is not a relationship with another person that I need, but a relationship with You. I commit myself today to daily prayer and to learning more about You in Your Word. Lead me, Holy God. Amen.

Embrace Your Singleness

A person helped get you into this situation. Do not think that another person will help get you out—no matter how right he or she may seem for you.

"After people get divorced, they rush into a new relationship because they hurt," explains Dr. Myles Munroe. "They believe the secret to relieving the hurt is a new relationship, which is the worst thing a person can do. If you get remarried and you're still hurting, you are taking your hurt into another relationship, and that is going to become the foundation of the relationship, which is faulty."

When you are making decisions regarding a new relationship, do not make any decisions based on your feelings. Feelings are temporal and not always rational. Be wise, and take the time to grow and to build your life on a strong foundation.

"You must gain custody of yourself," continues Dr. Munroe. "You must begin to rebuild your life and embrace your singleness again. Use that experience to analyze your own weaknesses, the areas in your life where you were not able to cope in the first relationship. Then strengthen those areas, get knowledge, get teaching, and get information. Rebuild yourself first because your future relationship is only as good as what you bring to it."

The Bible says you should not depend on humans—yourself or other people—to be strong for you. You must depend only on God.

"This is what the LORD says: 'Cursed is the one who trusts in man, who depends on flesh for his strength and whose heart turns away from the LORD'" (Jeremiah 17:5).

Dear God, I want to feel strong and in control of my life again. Please help me to realize that human strength always fails, but strength that is based in You will last forever. Amen.

Face Reality

"The reality is you have to take things the way they are, not the way you want them to be," says Dr. Jim A. Talley. "You have to face the fact that if you're single and you're divorced, you really are single and divorced."

You may not want to be single, but reality does not cater to a person's desires. Do not pretend you are still married if you are not. Be honest with yourself and start thinking about what kind of a single person God would want you to be.

"When a break in the marriage takes place," says Eleanor Reid, "you have to build yourself back up, strengthen yourself in the Word of God, and then begin to focus on your new life and the new path that you have as a single individual."

Be honest with God if you are having trouble facing the reality of your circumstances. He knows everything about you, so pour out the truth of your situation and your deepest feelings to Him. He promises healing.

"O LORD, you have searched me and you know me. You know when I sit and when I rise; you perceive my thoughts from afar. You discern my going out and my lying down; you are familiar with all my ways. Before a word is on my tongue you know it completely, O LORD" (Psalm 139:1–4).

Lord God, when I am tempted to deny the reality of my situation, help me to be truthful with myself and others. Amen.

Daily Choices

"Pain can drive you to a sense of hopelessness and despair or it can drive you to God. It's your choice," says Jan Northington.

"When you are in the midst of a situation like separation or divorce, you tend to think there are few choices available to you. In reality there are a million choices available to you, and the choices you make will ultimately be those that have an effect on both your immediate and your future actions."

Think about decisions you have already made that are positive. One positive action you have chosen is to search for comfort and answers through this book. Perhaps you have gone to church, talked to a wise friend or counselor, prayed, or started reading the Bible. Each day you make choices about work, finances, transportation, food, and your children. You choose what type of attitude to have as new situations arise. You choose whether or not to lash out at someone when you are angry.

Some days the choices you make may seem too small to make a difference. But if you change your course only a few compass degrees, the longer you move in that direction, the more you will see the impact of that decision.

Many times you make wrong choices, and that can bring you down. At the same time, though, you are making right choices, and they will have a positive effect. God knows your motivations, and He knows your heart. Pray today that you will make God-pleasing choices, decisions that bring you closer to Him.

"Why don't you choose to be led by the Spirit?" (Galatians 5:18 MSG).

Holy Spirit, lead me on the path that leads to life, peace, and hope. I pray that today I will make choices that are pleasing to You. Amen.

Can You Heal from Divorce Without Christ?

This question was asked to professionals in the divorce recovery field and to people who have been through divorce: Can a person heal from divorce without Jesus Christ?

"Bottom line—without Jesus Christ you never have total healing," says Dr. Archibald Hart.

Dr. Linda Mintle says, "Because of Jesus Christ, you can be free from any symptom, not just recovered, but totally transformed and free. That is a promise."

Marc speaks from his own experience: "Only His healing grace can heal that wound in your heart. Jesus is the only way to get through this experience. He was my only way. That's for sure."

"I know one woman who has been through four divorces," says James. "She says time has healed her, but when I look at her life and see her reactions to things, I see such hurt and unforgiveness. To me, only Christ can heal it."

Howard says, "I wouldn't say that only Christians recover, but how much do you want to recover? How well do you want to be? Do you want to use a walker, or do you want to walk? Do you want to walk, or do you want to run? Do you want to run, or do you want to soar? God wants the heights for you."

Yes, God wants the heights for you.

"Even youths grow tired and weary, and young men stumble and fall; but those who hope in the LORD will renew their strength. They will soar on wings like eagles; they will run and not grow weary, they will walk and not be faint" (Isaiah 40:30–31).

Almighty God, I will never be healed without You. I don't want to be calloused and hardened. I want to soar on wings like eagles, just as You promised. Amen.

Help Through the Holy Spirit

Do not think you need to find the strength and have the ability to stabilize your life by yourself; that would be impossible. You need the help of the Holy Spirit to regain a proper balance in your life.

The Holy Spirit is God living within the heart of a believer. A believer is a person who believes that Jesus Christ is God and that He came to earth and paid the penalty for sin by dying on the cross; He defeated death and lives today so that people might come to know Him personally and live forever in heaven with Him. A believer recognizes that he or she is a sinner and seeks God's forgiveness for those sins.

"For all have sinned and fall short of the glory of God" (Romans 3:23).

If you believe and have expressed that Jesus is Savior of your life, then the Holy Spirit dwells in you and is daily at work in you. You must lean on Him to help you develop and work through a self-stabilization plan.

"The Holy Spirit . . . will teach you all things and will remind you of everything I have said to you" (John 14:26).

If you do not have a personal relationship with Jesus but would like to, please pray this prayer to invite Him into your life:

Dear Lord, I know I have done things that are wrong. Please forgive me. I believe You are God and that You died on the cross to save me from the effects of my sins. I receive You as the center of my life, and I give You control of it. Thank You for giving me the gift of eternal life. In Jesus' name I pray. Amen.[2]

---

2. If you have prayed that prayer for the first time, congratulations! We encourage you to tell a friend and to find a mature believer who can help you develop a Bible reading plan and who can answer questions you may have. If you are not sure how to find a mature believer or a good Bible study, visit your local church or call The Church Initiative at 1-800-489-7778 for help in directing you to a church.

Spiritual Stabilization

Your recovery process will be much smoother if you work on stabilizing your spiritual life.

"Your spiritual life gives you the power to overcome the emotional energy that's being drained from you. It gives you an outside energy source to draw upon," says Dr. Jim A. Talley.

The following suggestions will help you strengthen your spiritual life:

- Renew or begin a personal relationship with Jesus Christ
- Learn about Jesus through prayer and Bible study
- Belong to a church family
- Meet regularly with a mature Christian who can mentor you and be a role model for you

Yesterday's devotion talked about how to have a personal relationship with Jesus. In order to build that relationship, you must talk to Him and learn more about Him. Prayer could be simply defined as "talking to God." Tell Him you need Him. Tell Him your fears, your worries, and your frustrations. Be honest. Tell Him how glad you are that He is in control of your life. Spend time with Him, and allow Him to speak to your heart.

You can learn more about who Jesus is, about prayer, about healing, and about living a life that is pleasing to Him by reading the Bible. If you are not sure where to start reading, begin with the book of John, Psalms, or Proverbs.

"And He opened their understanding, that they might comprehend the Scriptures" (Luke 24:45 NKJV).

Jesus, I believe in You, and I love You. Help me to read the Bible and learn more about You. Amen.

Emotional Stabilization

Stabilizing emotionally is a difficult, but important, part of your healing. Remember, about 85 percent of all your available energy is being consumed by your emotions.

"The answer to emotional instability is friendship," says Dr. Jim A. Talley. "Opposite-sex friends lead you down the road to relationships. Same-sex friends provide you emotional stability. My advice for the emotionalist is to stop the wild ups and downs and to concentrate on building quality, intimate friendships with the same sex in order to have real emotional stability."

Laura Petherbridge says, "Same-sex friendships can keep you from making poor choices. They build you up. They teach you what's good about yourself, how you can grow, and how you can be all that God created you to be."

Building friendships is a practical, doable step, but do not think it is an easy, quick thing to do. Friendship takes time and energy; it requires you to be a giver and a listener, not just a taker and a talker. Friendship involves personal sacrifice, but the rewards are tremendous.

"Two are better than one, because they have a good return for their work: If one falls down, his friend can help him up. But pity the man who falls and has no one to help him up!" (Ecclesiastes 4:9–10).

Father God, guide me today to a friend. Motivate me to pick up the phone and call someone just for the sake of getting together, talking, listening, and building our friendship. Amen.

Spiritual Support

You need to build a spiritual support system to help you get through the tough times.

Marie says, "When I was a new Christian, there was a woman in my church who was my spiritual mother and my mentor. I would talk to her about everything that was going on, and she'd say, 'Whenever you feel that emotion or when you feel like you cannot pray, turn to the Psalms and read them out loud.'"

A person of the same sex who is a mature believer in Christ can guide you in building a relationship with Jesus and will help you find spiritual answers to your questions. He or she will encourage you, listen to you, and offer biblical advice.

In the Bible, Paul was a spiritual mentor for Timothy. Paul guided him to become a spiritual leader, teaching and admonishing him about how to walk as a follower of Christ.

Paul said to Timothy: "Don't let anyone look down on you because you are young, but set an example for the believers in speech, in life, in love, in faith and in purity. Until I come, devote yourself to the public reading of Scripture, to preaching and to teaching . . . Be diligent in these matters; give yourself wholly to them, so that everyone may see your progress. Watch your life and doctrine closely. Persevere in them, because if you do, you will save both yourself and your hearers" (1 Timothy 4:12–13, 15–16).

God will provide you with a spiritual mentor too. Just ask Him! He wants you to learn more about Him and to grow spiritually.

Lord, I need someone to come alongside me and to help me grow spiritually. Lead me to that person. Amen.

Divorce Recovery Support Groups

"I didn't belong anywhere," says Cathy, "and that is the most horrible feeling in the world, to go places where you used to belong and you don't belong anymore. Even with my family I didn't feel like I belonged because they couldn't understand what I was going through. I got the same lines of 'Oh, just get up and get over it,' 'It'll be okay,' 'You still have us,' and 'You have your kids.' That was supposed to make it better. I couldn't make them understand what I was feeling inside, and it hurt so much.

"I got in a divorce recovery group, and it became my family. This was a place I belonged where I could tell people how I felt and they understood. They became my family because of that shared pain."

Many churches offer divorce recovery support groups. These groups provide a safe place where you can share your hurts, your concerns, and your fears with other people who are in the divorce process. These people can best relate to what you are going through, and the facilitators of these support groups, who have typically been through divorce themselves, are in a position to give you spiritual guidance.

A DivorceCare® group or another Christian divorce recovery support group can be the "family" you need during this time of aloneness.

"God sets the lonely in families, he leads forth the prisoners with singing; but the rebellious live in a sun-scorched land" (Psalm 68:6).

Lord and Savior, I need family. Lead me to be a part of God's family. Amen.

Rebuild Your Family Support System

Although there may be some people in your family who do not want to rebuild a relationship with you, do not let those people stop you from seeking out the rest of your family. You need their loving support.

Dr. Jim A. Talley suggests, "Go back to your parents and rebuild that initial relationship with your mother or father or a friend or grandparent. It takes time. I've encouraged a single mom to go to a family reunion all the way across the country with her son, to visit the family and introduce her child to the whole family structure that he's had no availability to because his father didn't want anything to do with her family.

"Constructing a family genealogy is another fun thing to do. That's an activity that forces you to increase your mental capacity because it's hard work. It doesn't allow you to spin in that pool of emotional pity all the time."

During divorce, the thought of working to rebuild relationships or going out of your way to do anything seems exhausting and impossible. You will not rebuild your life in a day or a week or even a year, but you can always take small steps forward. What step will you take today?

"Go home to your family and tell them how much the Lord has done for you, and how he has had mercy on you" (Mark 5:19).

Lord God, rejection from family cuts deep. Give me the opportunity and the courage to make things right with those estranged from me. Amen.

Relating to Those Close to You

Divorce affects everyone close to you—your children, parents, relatives, and friends.

Your loved ones will have different responses throughout the divorce process, depending on their relationship with you and with your former spouse. They may feel sadness, disappointment, resentment, or anger. Their responses to you can vary from offering encouragement and support to showing meanness and blame. They might avoid you out of embarrassment or discomfort.

Sabrina D. Black says it is important to preserve the relationships with your loved ones to the best of your ability. She says, "Family members will often send mixed messages. You need to make sure you are being prayerful before God as you communicate with them. You need to keep in mind that the relationship is the most important thing. The goal is to love the other person, and as you are loving the person, you need to be honest with him or her."

God wants you to love people even when they have been unlovable, even when they have spoken against you, hurt you, or blamed you. This kind of love can be difficult because you won't feel like loving certain people. Ask God to help you with this. As a human, you cannot do it on your own, but with the help of the Holy Spirit you can learn to love with a godly love regardless of another person's response to you.

"Most important of all, continue to show deep love for each other, for love covers a multitude of sins" (1 Peter 4:8 NLT).

Loving Father, help me to remember that I am not the only one struggling with difficult emotions as a result of the divorce. When family members and friends hurt or reject me, teach me to love them and to be honest with them about my emotions. Amen.

Resetting Your Expectations

You have certain expectations in your daily life. Expectations of yourself, your children, your family members, your friends, and your former spouse. Until you stop and think about it, you may not realize just how high your standards are for yourself and for those around you. To move forward into the future, you need to learn to reset your expectations.

Consider how much you are asking of yourself and how much you can actually handle. Also, do you expect more from others than is realistic under the circumstances of your divorce? If you find yourself getting upset because someone does not live up to a certain expectation of yours, then maybe it's time to back off and reset that expectation.

Dr. Jim A. Talley says, "You expected somebody to do something. That person didn't do it, and you get mad. What makes you even madder is that person doesn't seem to give a rip that he or she didn't do it. Now you're really hurt, and you begin to boil on the inside. You shift at that point to real bitterness. You have to go back and reset your expectations to what you can control and deal with. You can't force other people into your expectations."

Reset your standards to a place where you can function, and examine your motivation for having that expectation in the first place.

"People may think they are doing what is right, but the LORD examines the heart" (Proverbs 21:2 NLT).

Heavenly Father, sometimes I expect too much and for the wrong reasons. Show me how to reset those expectations to a healthy and productive level. Amen.

Seeking Approval from Others

Harriet says, "The realization came to me a couple of weeks ago that I have been living out everybody else's expectations for me. It's human nature that my friends want me to heal, and I had tried over time to convince them I was okay. I realize now that I was trying to get their stamp of approval that I was okay and that I was healing. I did this by buying into their expected response of 'I don't love my husband anymore.' What I didn't reckon with is the fact that there is nothing wrong with me still loving my husband. In fact, a year later, a year after we've separated, I still love my husband very much."

You cannot make decisions based on the approval of others. You will only add to your stress and fatigue if you try to live up to the expectations of others. Reset your own expectations to a level you can cope with, and focus your energy on keeping within your own standards. This will help to free you emotionally.

The Lord's expectations of you are pure and simple:

"He has showed you, O man, what is good. And what does the LORD require of you? To act justly and to love mercy and to walk humbly with your God" (Micah 6:8).

Lord and Savior, help me to realize that I do not need to live up to anyone's expectations but Yours. Your expectations are refreshing and easy—to act justly, love mercy, and walk humbly with You. Amen.

Expecting Too Much Progress Too Quickly?

"If you're a marathon runner," says Dr. Jim A. Talley, "and you have open heart surgery, how long do you think it's going to be before you can jog again? How long before you can run a mile? How long before you can run a marathon? When you put it in physical terms, people know it may take four or five years for recovery.

"Divorce is open-heart surgery, emotionally. Some people are not willing to give it enough time, and their expectations for recovery are too fast. When you get up and go faster than you're supposed to and you push your healing cycle too quickly, you have to do it over again and you get a relapse. What would normally take five years is going to take six or seven because you've done more damage to yourself in the process."

Relax. Breathe deeply. You have just had open-heart surgery and the prognosis is good. You will recover, but be prepared for therapeutic exercises, time for rest, getting back into work slowly, and for other people to think you look healthy on the outside when you still have a lot of healing left to do on the inside.

"He heals the brokenhearted and binds up their wounds . . . Great is our Lord and mighty in power; his understanding has no limit" (Psalm 147:3, 5).

Healing God, forgive me for trying to recover too quickly. Please bind up my wounded heart and give me the wisdom to take things slowly. Amen.

Hope Is Found in God

"Are you feeling like an absolute, total failure, my friend, because of divorce?" asks Kay Arthur.

"Oh, precious one, God has help. God has answers. God has healing. If you listen carefully and believe God, you are going to find the answer to your situation."

No matter what your circumstances are, you can experience healing and hope through Jesus Christ. The Bible teaches about a just and sovereign God, who is in control of all things and who can bring good out of all situations. Most important, God is a loving God, and He loves you just as you are. He loves you regardless of what you have said, done, or felt. You can never do anything that will cause Him to love you less. Turn to Him today and be renewed in His love.

Can anything ever separate us from Christ's love? Does it mean he no longer loves us if we have trouble or calamity, or are persecuted, or are hungry or cold or in danger or threatened with death? . . .

I am convinced that nothing can ever separate us from his love. Death can't, and life can't. The angels can't, and the demons can't. Our fears for today, our worries about tomorrow, and even the powers of hell can't keep God's love away. Whether we are high above the sky or in the deepest ocean, nothing in all creation will ever be able to separate us from the love of God that is revealed in Christ Jesus our Lord. (Romans 8:35, 38–39 NLT)

Jesus, thank You for loving me. It is through Your love that I will be healed and whole again someday. Amen.

The Road to Healing

Finding Help

When human life is threatened by serious injury, a medical system is activated to provide help. Patients are sped to an emergency room to stabilize their condition and to get a diagnosis of what is wrong. Recovery might take months or years, but a health care system is in place to help the patients each step of the way.

The emotional damage from divorce can be just as traumatic, just as devastating, as physical injury.

"I didn't sleep at night," says Sherry, "and all these infomercials come on at three and four o'clock in the morning about anxiety. I knew exactly what it was because my heart would be racing so hard that I thought I was going to have a heart attack. Then I started praying to have a heart attack."

The help system for divorce trauma is not as apparent. There is no hospital emergency room to go to. Yet, if you read God's words in the Bible, you will find that a different kind of help system, or emergency room, exists, and it's up to you to discover more about the healing offered there. Just as God restored and healed the nation of Israel in the Bible, He promises to heal your wounds as well. Can you trust the promises of God?

"'I will restore you to health and heal your wounds,' declares the LORD, 'because you are called an outcast, Zion for whom no one cares'" (Jeremiah 30:17).

Lord God, You are known as the Great Physician, and through You I will find healing. I understand that it will take time, but, because of who You are, the healing will be full and complete. Amen.

When a Marriage Breaks Apart

When a couple marries, they are no longer two individuals. They become what the Bible calls "one flesh." Genesis 2:24 puts it this way: "For this reason a man will leave his father and mother and be united to his wife, and they will become one flesh."

Unfortunately, people make decisions that lead to the breaking of marriage bonds. To better understand the extreme pain of separation and divorce, think about what happens when a marriage bond comes apart. The married couple does not revert to being two individuals again. Instead, they become two parts of the same one-flesh marriage, torn away, with huge, gaping emotional wounds.

Dr. Myles Munroe shares: "People will say, 'My husband and I separated.' That's not true. You tore, and that's where the hurt is. You actually tear, and parts of you go with the other person. That's why breaking a relationship is so difficult because you lose a part of yourself forever."

Don says, "There wasn't an aspect of my life that wasn't torn and ripped. There was pain in parts of my body that I didn't even know pain could reach."

Jesus describes this one-flesh relationship:

"So they are no longer two, but one. Therefore what God has joined together, let man not separate" (Mark 10:8–9).

Dear God, what happened to my marriage? Place Your healing touch on my gaping wounds. Save me, Lord. Amen.

Traumas of Separation: A Broken Heart

Dr. Myles Munroe describes three traumas of separation: a broken heart, a broken spirit, and a painful soul.

A person's heart is broken when the bonds of a relationship are broken.

"A broken heart," explains Dr. Myles Munroe, "is actually the tearing of those bonds; it's like ripping a part of your life away and leaving these webs hanging and bleeding. A broken heart is so terrible that, according to the Word of God, Jesus Himself has to fix it."

God sent His Son, Jesus, to earth to fulfill a purpose. That purpose is to draw people to Himself and to save them from sin, death, and brokenness. Jesus came to earth to preach and teach and to minister to the needs of everyone He met. Jesus made it clear that He would be available to meet the needs of every person from that day forward.

A healing relationship with Jesus is available today for everyone who believes, regardless of what that person has done in the past. He alone can heal your broken heart. Read these words spoken by Jesus, and claim His promise for yourself:

"The Spirit of the LORD is upon Me, because . . . He has sent Me to heal the brokenhearted, to proclaim liberty to the captives and recovery of sight to the blind, to set at liberty those who are oppressed" (Luke 4:18 NKJV).

Jesus, You bring healing, freedom, and sight. I need all three. Help me to know You more intimately. Amen.

Traumas of Separation: A Broken Spirit

"A broken spirit who can bear it?" (Proverbs 18:14 NASB).

The Bible says that no person can bear it when his or her spirit is broken. Not only is it impossible to bear, but it is also impossible for a person to mend. God alone can mend a broken spirit.

"A broken spirit comes from a broken heart," says Dr. Myles Munroe. "When you have had your soul torn, it affects your entire life. It causes you to have a depressed spirit. The trauma of a broken spirit is very real, and it is almost hellish in the sense that no one can save you from it. God is the only One who can repair a spirit."

Dr. Linda Mintle says, "Nothing in God's economy is beyond repair. God does His best work with broken pieces. If you look in the Bible, He takes people who are broken and wounded, and He restores them and uses them mightily. With faith and a belief in Jesus Christ, you can be totally transformed and free. That is a promise."

God promises to save anyone whose spirit is broken and bruised. Turn to Him for healing and renewal.

"The LORD is close to the brokenhearted and saves those who are crushed in spirit" (Psalm 34:18).

God, I know You are near even when I don't feel Your presence. Forgive me for turning away from You. You know I cannot bear my broken spirit alone. Please save me as You have promised in Your Word, the Bible. Amen.

Traumas of Separation: A Painful Soul

A "painful soul" is what's left of your soul after it has been torn apart. Here is what a painful soul feels like:

"It felt like all of my blood had turned to ice," shares Susan. "My heart was racing. I thought that I was going to get sick. I remember having this feeling that a big hole had opened up underneath me and that I was sinking down into it, and I couldn't find my way back up."

James says, "I felt like my heart and my soul had been pulled out."

God can and will heal you. Your painful soul can be mended. The Bible says, "He restores my soul" (Psalm 23:3). But how? Psalm 19:7 says, "The law of the LORD is perfect, reviving the soul." God's words in the Bible will revive your soul. Make a commitment to read the Bible each day.

Proverbs 3:8 says that wisdom will bring "healing to your body and refreshment to your bones" (NASB). Wisdom comes from seeking God, learning more about Him, and surrendering fully to Him. Proverbs 24:14 says that "wisdom is sweet to your soul; if you find it, there is a future hope for you, and your hope will not be cut off."

The Bible has much to say about souls. If you look in a concordance (similar to an index in the back of many Bibles) for the word *soul*, you will find several interesting and encouraging Scriptures. Draw close to God in His Word to gain wisdom and receive healing for your soul.

What is it that your soul desires for fulfillment?

"My soul thirsts for God, for the living God. When can I go and meet with God?" (Psalm 42:2).

Yes, Lord, my soul thirsts for You. I want to meet with You. Amen.

The Losses in Your Divorce

To help you understand why you hurt so deeply, it's important to understand what you have lost in the breakup of your marriage. Yes, you have lost a mate, but you've also lost dreams, friends, relatives, money, a daily helpmate, and sometimes personal or professional status; you may have losses associated with your children. H. Norman Wright says, "Each day you will discover new losses that you never planned on."

Recovery involves being aware of your losses. Mr. Wright continues, "If you've experienced a number of crises or ongoing losses in your life, this is another loss. If you've not yet recovered from those other losses, this could take you longer to recover from because you're trying to balance several losses at the same time."

Your past losses directly affect how you cope with your current losses and the level of your pain. This activity can help you to recognize and deal with your past and current losses.

1. Think of past losses: friends, jobs, pets, family members.

2. Write down these losses and read them out loud.

3. Once you have written down past losses, move on to recent losses. Some suggestions are listed above: daily helper, financial support, status, and time with children. What can you add to the list? Be specific—cook, housekeeper, driver, bill-payer, gardener, lover, friend, house, car, responsibilities.

4. Read your recent losses out loud.

"Surely my soul remembers and is bowed down within me" (Lamentations 3:20 NASB).

Lord, I know that recognizing losses is a step in the recovery process. Help me take the time to do the activity above. Amen.

The Initial Response to Loss: Shock

H. Norman Wright identifies six aspects of loss that you will likely experience during the separation or divorce process. The first is shock. "The very first response that you go through in any kind of loss or crisis is shock. It's a feeling of numbness, and it protects you from the sharpness of the pain that you're going to experience."

Susan shares, "I remember the night he told me he was leaving me. I was too shocked to cry. I walked around in shock for about six weeks. I don't know when it hit me."

Harriet says, "When I found out he was having an affair, the shock must have taken over right away because there was a sense of unrealness."

The sense of numbness or incomprehension is your body's natural defense mechanism to protect you from the reality of the situation. Yes, you do have to face that reality at some point, but during the initial days of trauma, your body is specially designed to let you deal with only a small number of things at a time.

God created you to be a complex, unique individual. The Bible says you are "fearfully and wonderfully made" (Psalm 139:14). God takes care of you in ways that you don't even realize. If you are in shock right now, it is good for two reasons. One, your body is protecting you. Two, you have begun the first stage of loss, which means you have already started on the road to healing.

"I praise you because I am fearfully and wonderfully made; your works are wonderful, I know that full well" (Psalm 139:14).

Heavenly Father, I know You are taking care of me. Lead me on this healing journey one step at a time. Amen.

The Grief Response

Where there is death, there is grief. You have experienced the death of your relationship, and once the initial shock wears off, you must grieve.

Jan Northington shares, "I grieved my hopes and my dreams for the future. I had always dreamed of a family. I was going to raise my children with the love of a mom and a dad, and my kids were always going to see their mom and dad love each other. I grieved the loss of my newly remodeled home that I had to sell and leave, along with my neighbors, my church family, my job, and my coworkers. I had to grieve the standard of living that I had become accustomed to. I also had to grieve the dream that one day I would be a stay-at-home mom because suddenly it looked like that would never ever happen. Not only did I grieve the loss of my husband's love, but I had to grieve the loss of the close connection I once shared with his family."

You have so much to grieve. Don't try to tough it out and ignore this step in the recovery process. Healing comes from acknowledging and releasing your emotions.

In the Bible, people grieved freely, loudly, and without embarrassment.

"The king's sons came in, wailing loudly. The king, too, and all his servants wept very bitterly" (2 Samuel 13:36).

"While Ezra was praying and confessing, weeping and throwing himself down before the house of God, a large crowd of Israelites—men, women and children—gathered around him. They too wept bitterly" (Ezra 10:1).

"Wail and cry out!" (Jeremiah 48:20).

Lord God, may I grieve loudly and fully for my many losses. Give me the opportunity to express my emotions freely. Amen.

Grief Is Legitimate

Grief can be described as an overwhelming, unpredictable mass of emotions that bombard you and threaten to take over your life for an extended period of time. These emotions are your body's natural response to the loss and pain that occur in a divorce.

You will hinder your healing if you try to suppress the emotions of grief. Your losses are legitimate and must be faced. Many people say that the loss associated with divorce is worse than the loss of a spouse through death:

"In death there is closure because the person has died," says Dr. Linda Mintle. "In divorce, your ex-spouse is still out there. And, if you've had children with that person, chances are you will meet again under any number of circumstances, such as graduations, weddings, the birth of a grandchild, or at other significant events in your life. This kind of open-ended, ongoing relationship makes closure more difficult."

Wayne says, "Divorce is worse than death because in divorce that person chose to leave you. In death so many times the person did not choose to leave, and you know that he or she died loving you; whereas in divorce it's not like that. Your ex-spouse is gone, and he or she wanted to leave."

In divorce, you are mourning the death of a relationship that is no longer available to you, even though the people involved are still here. This is so difficult!

"Trust in him at all times, O people; pour out your hearts to him, for God is our refuge" (Psalm 62:8).

Jesus, I need to express my emotions. I need to let them hit me, and then face them. Help me to do this in a way that's healthy! Amen.

Anger and Blame

"Anger is a defense mechanism where you take whatever is bothering you and is wrong within you, and you project it on another person and blame him or her for it. Frequently the other person accepts the blame, which satisfies you temporarily but doesn't solve the problem," says Dr. Robert Abarno.

Blame is a natural reaction to your loss. You feel as though you need to blame someone: your former spouse, God, yourself, friends, or the person with whom your spouse had an affair.

"The other woman became more and more of a scapegoat in my mind because it was easy for me to hate her," says Harriet. "So I heaped coals on her head. She might as well have been a witch riding a broomstick because in my mind she grew worse, with a forked tail and cloven hooves."

The problem with blame, though, is what it leads to. Blame and anger work together to produce resentment. When you fuel your anger with accusations and the self-justified shifting of responsibility, you will begin to burn with resentment. From resentment comes bitterness. Bitterness is a steady disease that eats you from the inside out, but seldom affects the object of your bitterness.

"Resentment kills a fool" (Job 5:2).

"Don't you realize that this will end in bitterness?" (2 Samuel 2:26).

Lord, what can I learn from my feelings of blame? Help me to keep my feelings in perspective and to accept my own responsibility for the situation. I want to learn something about myself and not be blind to opportunities for personal and spiritual growth. Amen.

Saying Good-Bye to Your Losses

People in grief must learn to say good-bye to what they have lost. Saying good-bye is not a onetime experience, but there will come a day when final good-byes are said.

H. Norman Wright offers practical advice to help you say good-bye to your losses: "You have to work through your feelings—especially anger. Write a 'non-mailed' angry letter, and pour out your heart in it. Then sit with an empty chair placed in front of you, put the person's name there, and read the letter out loud.

"Another idea is to write a letter of forgiveness. It might be, 'Dear So-and-So, I forgive you for the way you betrayed me.' Then write the first rebuttal that comes to mind. Keep doing this, whether it's ten or twenty times, until you come to the place where there are no more rebuttals and you can say, 'I forgive you for . . .'"

Mr. Wright continues, "It's when the good-byes are said that you can turn the corner and move ahead."

You may not want to say good-bye, but this is necessary at some point in your recovery process. Saying good-bye does not mean you are closing yourself off from the other person. You are saying good-bye to what you have lost, to the things of the past, and to a relationship that is over. You are experiencing closure to the grief, blame, anger, and emotions that are behind you. A new way of living is before you that may or may not include your former spouse.

"Therefore, if anyone is in Christ, he is a new creation; the old has gone, the new has come!" (2 Corinthians 5:17).

Lord, a new way of living is before me. My life will be filled with new joys and experiences. Teach me to say good-bye to the old. Amen.

The Goal of Grieving: Rebuilding and Resolution

If you work through the process of grief, you will come to the point of rebuilding and resolution. Then your focus will shift from the past to the future.

"Rebuilding and resolution almost go hand in hand," explains H. Norman Wright. "They occur when you are starting to look forward to your life again in a new way and you are more forward looking than backward looking. You have a sense of hope that, yes, there is meaning in life, that you can go on with your life, and in spite of the fact that you are caring for the three children by yourself and you're exhausted most of the time—there is hope. You have a sense of direction for your future."

With God, there is always hope. There is always rebuilding and resolution. He will restore your life, and you will have joy in your heart again. God's promises are for you.

He sent His Son, Jesus . . .

"To comfort all who mourn, and provide for those who grieve in Zion—to bestow on them a crown of beauty instead of ashes, the oil of gladness instead of mourning, and a garment of praise instead of a spirit of despair. They will be called oaks of righteousness, a planting of the LORD for the display of his splendor" (Isaiah 61:2–3).

Thank You, God, for sending Jesus to be my hope and direction in this mixed-up life. Amen.

Face Your Problems

One of the first responses you may have had during the divorce process was denial, but the time of denial has to come to an end. Be honest with yourself. Face your problems. This process is threefold.

1. Recognize/define your problems.
2. Admit your problems to yourself and to others.
3. Take steps to deal with your problems in a healthy manner.

Dr. Linda Mintle says, "Some people know they're emotionally stuck and that they're not moving on from the intense emotions of the divorce. Yet, they don't want to face their problems; they don't want to deal with the emotions. They know that facing their feelings is going to feel really bad. Many people don't want to face those bad feelings, and they don't want to do the work. They don't want to look at their baggage or their unhealthy patterns in relationships. Remember that you have to feel bad before you feel better."

You are making your life even more difficult if you refuse to confront the reality of your situation. We understand that this is much easier said than done, though! Facing your problems is especially difficult because, first of all, you don't want them to be true, and second, you are just plain exhausted. Now is the time to depend on the Lord's strength.

"But the Lord stood at my side and gave me strength" (2 Timothy 4:17).

"The name of the LORD is a strong tower; the righteous run to it and are safe" (Proverbs 18:10).

Father God, You are my strength. Enable me to admit and face my problems and then to deal with them. I know You are always by my side. Thank You. Amen.

Let Go of the Pain

"When Jesus saw him lying there and learned that he had been in this condition for a long time, he asked him, 'Do you want to get well?'" (John 5:6).

Are you purposely hanging on to pain, anger, or blame? Are you living off of those emotions? Perhaps you feel that your negative emotions bring you satisfaction or a feeling of control. Do you sometimes think it feels good to get angry at your ex-spouse or to share stories that highlight your ex-spouse's faults? Let go of the negativity that you are clinging to. You don't want your new identity to be grounded in bitterness and resentment.

You must build a new, solid foundation for your life. This foundation must be different, stronger, and deeper than your last. If you build your life in Jesus Christ, you will not be shaken.

"Therefore everyone who hears these words of mine and puts them into practice is like a wise man who built his house on the rock. The rain came down, the streams rose, and the winds blew and beat against that house; yet it did not fall, because it had its foundation on the rock. But everyone who hears these words of mine and does not put them into practice is like a foolish man who built his house on sand. The rain came down, the streams rose, and the winds blew and beat against that house, and it fell with a great crash" (Matthew 7:24–27).

Lord Jesus, I want my life to be so firmly ensconced in You that no storm can knock it down. Amen.

New Directions for Emotional Investments

Emotional investments. You have probably not considered that phrase before. You have invested time, money, emotions, and more in your former spouse. Your initial reaction might be "I've lost it all!" Your investments are not lost. They just need to be directed to new outlets because they are no longer profitable in the current areas.

Take care, though. You do not want to put your investments in another relationship right now. That would be an unwise choice at this point in your healing process.

New directions for your emotional investments can include building same-sex friendships, getting a pet, taking classes, journaling, pursuing a new hobby, and attending a divorce recovery support group.

Cindy shares, "The first time I attended a divorce recovery group, I thought, *What am I doing here? I don't need a support group.* But I did, and the support group gave me a safe place. In the beginning I was afraid that if I opened my mouth, I'd start crying, and I wasn't comfortable sharing my situation. But I saw other people sharing their stories, and we all started to become friends and nurtured each other and supported each other. It meant a lot."

You may feel that a support group isn't for you, but we encourage you to try it for a few weeks. The healing rewards of a biblically-based support group can be tremendous.

"Though one may be overpowered, two can defend themselves. A cord of three strands is not quickly broken" (Ecclesiastes 4:12).

Almighty God, I have emotions that need to be invested someplace new. Help me to choose a new outlet and to follow through on this decision. Amen.

Practical Advice for Your Friends

Friends often mean well and sincerely want to help, but they don't know how. This can bring added stress and pain to you. H. Norman Wright had a person come to him with this dilemma:

"I'm going through a divorce. Recently, I ran into seven of my friends throughout the course of the day, and every friend asked, 'What's going on? Tell me about it,' so I went through the whole story with each one. By the end of that day I felt terrible. The reason was that with every friend, I went through the situation and experienced the pain again, so I was more depressed at the end of the day. What can I do about this?"

Mr. Wright suggests: "Write a letter to your friends describing what is going on and what you are feeling. Write down the best way for your friends to respond because sometimes they give you unsolicited, undesired, inappropriate advice, and that's not what you need. As you meet your friends or fellow employees, instead of having to go through it again and again, give them the letter. Your friends will be appreciative because often they don't know how to act. You will get a greater amount of healthy support."

Consider writing a letter of this type not only to help your friends, but also to help you. Even if you never end up handing out a copy, the exercise will help you recognize what it is that you expect and need from your friends.

"A friend loves at all times" (Proverbs 17:17 NKJV).

Jesus, thank You for friends who love me even when I'm not being very lovable. Amen.

What Is Recovery?

If recovering from loss, from the pain in your life, is one of your goals, it is important to define *recovery*.

"You're running along and you trip and you hit the ground. Recovery can mean just getting up and moving on," says H. Norman Wright.

Dr. Robert Abarno says, "I think recovery means that you're aware of your losses. The awareness that you never want to experience that pain again is a positive thing. Recovery is turning back to Jesus. He redeems you from your sins. He sets you free. He gives you new life in Him. That's the only way I know that you can recover. There is no other way."

Recovery occurs on many levels. It involves forward movement, and that movement is usually slow and painful. Recovery involves an awareness of your losses, an acknowledgment that you must grieve, and the difficult process of grieving your losses. Recovery is complete only through Jesus Christ, who gave His life on the cross to save you.

Receiving God's comfort and restoration begins with turning to Him and turning away from your sins. Pray that God will reveal to you any sinful areas of your life that you need to address.

"But he was pierced for our transgressions, he was crushed for our iniquities; the punishment that brought us peace was upon him, and by his wounds we are healed" (Isaiah 53:5).

Jesus, thank You for Your healing sacrifice. Forgive me for my sins of selfishness and defeatism. You love me so much that it is hard for me to fully comprehend. Thank You for enabling me to experience full recovery in You. Amen.

Recovery Is a Choice

You may not have had a choice in your losses, but you do have a choice in your recovery. You can choose what attitude you will have about your experiences. There are two basic attitudes to choose from. The first is one of bitterness and defeat—emotions that can stay with you for the rest of your life. The second attitude is one where you choose to work through your feelings and learn how to be a better person.

Which attitude will you choose? Bitterness and defeat, or working through your problems and learning from them?

"That's when I realized either I had to choose to die or I had to choose to come through this," says Sue. "It probably would have been easier to die, except for the responsibility of four children. So at that point I said, 'I have to make it,' and I started the uphill battle."

Don says, "I had to get myself out of that pity pot and really focus on where my life needed to be, on the kids and on repairing my life the way that Jesus Christ says to."

Jesus suffered tremendously during His life on earth, but He always chose to see it through because He knew the rewards of moving forward.

"Therefore, since Christ suffered in his body, arm yourselves also with the same attitude, because he who has suffered in his body is done with sin. As a result, he does not live the rest of his earthly life for evil human desires, but rather for the will of God" (1 Peter 4:1–2).

Lord God, I know it is Your will that I choose to take positive actions in my life, actions that will take me forward and lead me closer to You. Amen.

How Do You Know If You've Recovered?

Anytime you do not feel anger, blame, self-pity, bitterness, or resentment, then you are experiencing recovery. If you think of your former spouse less often than you used to, this is a sign of recovery. If you are living in the present more than you are dwelling in the past, you are recovering. When you look back and see where you have been, that means you are in a position of recovery. The peace of Christ indicates recovery.

"I look back and think, *Wow, I'm not in that hole anymore. I'm almost to the rim. I'm peeping over the edge here,*" says Howard.

"You have peace," says Dr. Robert Abarno. "That's the way you know you are in the center of God's directive will. God's peace passes all understanding."

Gary Richmond shares a story that a friend told him: "Gary, last night I was watching television, and I laughed right out loud. I said to myself, *How can I be laughing? I'm being divorced.*" Gary's response to his friend was "This is a sign that you're healing. Let it happen."

Recovery does not mean you will not feel pain again. Painful moments will occur unexpectedly for several years. Be aware that this will happen, and when those painful moments hit you, be prepared to deal with them by countering them with prayer, Scripture, positive memories, or reaffirming statements. You can always look back and see how far you've come.

"Then maidens will dance and be glad, young men and old as well. I will turn their mourning into gladness; I will give them comfort and joy instead of sorrow" (Jeremiah 31:13).

Thank You, Lord, for signs of recovery in my life. Thank You for smiles, laughter, and new, good memories. Amen.

Jesus' Role in Your Recovery

A relationship with Jesus Christ is the foundation for healing.

"The presence of Christ gives you a greater depth of meaning to life, of feeling loved," says H. Norman Wright. "When somebody rejects you, you can turn to the Scriptures. You can read what it says there and realize that in spite of what's happened, God's love is so great that if you had been the only person ever created here on earth, He still would have sent His Son, Jesus, to die for you. That means you are really special. You are loved."

Marie shares, "I believe that a broken heart can be mended only by the Person who made it. I wasn't truly happy before I knew Christ, before I accepted Jesus as my personal Savior. I was spinning around on the merry-go-round, but I wasn't really having a good time. Now He's all that I need. It's an absolute fact of my life, and I wouldn't have it any other way."

Todd says, "Even when you don't feel that God is there, He is. There are going to be periods where you feel so dry and you feel like He's not there. He'll never, ever leave you, and you have to trust that."

Having a personal relationship with Jesus Christ is essential to your healing.

"Yet to all who received him, to those who believed in his name, he gave the right to become children of God" (John 1:12).

Lord Jesus, the merry-go-round that I've been riding has not been fun. As a matter of fact, it makes me sick to my stomach. But I believe in Your presence and in Your healing. I'm riding with You now. Amen.

A Relationship with Christ

If having a relationship with Jesus Christ is the key to having God's presence in your life, then it's important to understand how to have such a relationship. This is the most important step you can take to experience personal healing.

"The most important decision anybody will ever make is to have a relationship with Jesus Christ," shared Larry Burkett. "That relationship, I'll guarantee you, will never fail you. Even though the other relationship has failed, the relationship with Jesus Christ will never fail. He's faithful even though all of us are unfaithful. He says, 'I will still be faithful to you.'"

Danny says, "Give Him a chance. Seek God. Seek Christ. He'll prove to you that He's sufficient. It's hard to explain how that relationship works, and sometimes He feels so far away. But He's right beside you, and for the person who doesn't believe in Christ as Savior, I would say give it a chance. Find out for yourself."

The Bible says that "if you confess with your mouth, 'Jesus is Lord,' and believe in your heart that God raised him from the dead, you will be saved" (Romans 10:9). It also says that "everyone who calls on the name of the Lord will be saved" (Romans 10:13).

If you would like to have a saving, healing relationship with Jesus Christ, pray these words with a sincere heart:

Jesus, I want You to be Lord of my life. I believe that You died and rose from the dead to save me from my sins. Forgive me for my sins, and thank You for giving me the chance to start a new life in You. Amen.

Restoration

If you were taken to a hospital with a serious injury, you would want the best doctors, the best specialists, and the best care you could get to help you recover. While there, you might have to make some hard choices. The doctors might tell you that it takes painful surgery to help in your healing. That's a choice you'd likely agree to.

This scenario can be compared to your divorce situation. You did not choose to be injured through divorce, but it happened. Now, you want the best care possible in your recovery. The best restorative care may involve pain, rest, rehabilitation, and a long recovery time.

"Healing is never instantaneous," says Rose Sweet. "It happens in layers. The first thing is you wake up some day and you feel a little bit better, maybe not as depressed. You're able to get through the day without crying or thinking about your ex. Then the next day, you might feel bad again. Take one day at a time."

"Give yourself a season of time to recuperate," says Paula Rinehart. "Deliberately build into each week something that feels generally replenishing—it might be going to a museum once a week or having coffee with a friend. Do not go from one day to the next on automatic pilot, but intentionally recuperate."

God is the Great Physician. He will restore you if you choose to accept His care.

"Do you not know? Have you not heard? The LORD is the everlasting God, the Creator of the ends of the earth. He will not grow tired or weary, and his understanding no one can fathom. He gives strength to the weary and increases the power of the weak" (Isaiah 40:28–29).

Great Physician, I accept Your care. Guide me through this painful recovery process. Amen.

Facing Your Anger

Anger in Divorce

Anger can root deeply, grow quickly, and choke out your emotional health. Unless you cut away at your anger and learn to express it in a healthy manner, it can cause great harm to you and to others around you.

"I wanted to hurt him as badly as he hurt me," shares Joanne. "My anger was big, and it was black. It made me want to kill him. I knew I wouldn't, but I wanted to. I had enough knowledge to know that my anger was going to eventually eat me alive. Acid corrodes, as people say. That's when I knew that I had to direct my anger or learn to control it or dissipate it."

You may feel guilty about the extreme thoughts your anger is leading you to have. Be assured that these thoughts are normal for a person who is going through a divorce.

Howard shares, "I had tremendous guilt over some feelings I had, just awful and violent things I wanted to do to get even. It was such a relief to know that the things I'm feeling—the depression, the suicidal thoughts, the anger, and the violent thoughts—are something common to this situation, something that can be faced and overcome."

If you are in a divorce, you will at some point feel anger. The extent of that anger will vary from person to person, but God commands everyone to be wise in anger.

"A fool gives full vent to his anger, but a wise man keeps himself under control" (Proverbs 29:11).

Almighty God, the force of my anger is unbelievable. Sometimes it takes over, and all I see is red-hot rage. I pray for wise, safe anger. Hear my prayer. Amen.

Why Is the Anger So Deep?

Because . . .

 You loved your spouse with all your heart.

 You gave so much of yourself to him/her.

 You worked at the relationship.

 You trusted your spouse.

 You were faithful.

 You went to church, believed in God, and tried to live right.

 You thought you'd be together forever.

"You never think that you're going to get kicked in the teeth, but stuff happens, and you do," says Joanne.

"Your feelings are going to be overpowering sometimes, but I think people are much worse off if they don't let those feelings rage through their bodies. You have to rage, pounding your fists. You have to scream, whine, moan, and complain to your nearest and dearest friends; you have to do whatever you can to let it pass through your system."

Divorce brings an abrupt end to things that you thought were good, right, and secure in your life. Now you aren't sure which parts of your married life were real and which parts were only illusions. You are not wrong to feel anger. Justified anger can be a good and necessary response.

Jesus showed righteous anger when He saw people buying and selling their goods in the temple, making a profit from religious activities rather than revering God.

"Jesus entered the temple area and drove out all who were buying and selling there. He overturned the tables of the money changers and the benches of those selling doves. 'It is written,' he said to them, 'My house will be called a house of prayer,' but you are making it a 'den of robbers'" (Matthew 21:12–13).

Lord God, I am so angry. I am furious at my former spouse, at myself, and at other people involved. I want to scream! Show me how to express my anger. Amen.

Angry with God

"At first I was very angry with God," says Sherry. "I thought, *God, I've always gone to church. I did everything right. I tried to do all the things You wanted. I went to Sunday school. I taught classes. Then You let this happen to me.*"

It is natural to feel angry with God. Do not feel guilty about your anger. Instead, express your feelings straight to God. Rant and rave and cry out to Him, but then realize that He is God. He loves you very much, and He is not the one to blame for your circumstances.

In the Bible, Job was a righteous man who underwent great pain, loss, and suffering. Job was not afraid to express his confusion and despair to God. At one point he said, "I loathe my own life; I will give full vent to my complaint; I will speak in the bitterness of my soul. I will say to God, 'Do not condemn me; let me know why Thou dost contend with me. Is it right for Thee indeed to oppress, to reject the labor of Thy hands, and to look favorably on the schemes of the wicked? . . . According to Thy knowledge I am indeed not guilty; yet there is no deliverance from Thy hand'" (Job 10:1–3, 7 NASB).

Although Job did not understand why he had to live through this horrific pain, he did not waver in his faith. Job later said:

"Though He [God] slay me, yet will I trust Him" (Job 13:15 NKJV).

Holy God, help me to have the faith of Job. Amen.

Defining Anger

Dr. Les Carter says that having anger means standing up for your own worth, needs, and convictions.

"You don't get angry when folks are kind, pleasant, or understanding. Anger shows up when someone has rejected you or is being uncooperative, or when a person is being critical, harsh, or difficult to get along with. When anger appears on the scene, it arouses your sense of self-preservation.

"You want to preserve one of three things. You want to preserve your worth as a human being; your anger can be your way of wishing to say, 'Please, show me some respect, will you?' Anger can be your way of preserving your basic needs: 'Recognize that I have needs, and acknowledge them, please.' Or anger can be a way that you stand up for your deepest convictions. It is your way of saying, 'I believe in things, and I don't want to back away from them.'"

You will feel anger at some point in your divorce. Do not try to deny or suppress this emotion. God does not condemn you for your anger when it is justified. God Himself is described as "slow to anger"—not "never angry."

"And he passed in front of Moses, proclaiming, 'The LORD, the LORD, the compassionate and gracious God, slow to anger, abounding in love and faithfulness'" (Exodus 34:6).

Lord God, sometimes my anger is justifiable; sometimes it's not. Help me to be slow to anger, like You. Amen.

Anger: The Emotion of Self-Preservation

Has your former spouse threatened your sense of self-worth?

Sue says, "Probably the worst day was when I confronted him and said, 'I could jump out of the second-story window and splatter myself on the street, and I think you would probably be happy.' There was no response from him except for, 'That's not true.' By the expression on his face, I could tell his heart; there really were no feelings there."

Does your former spouse acknowledge your needs?

Harriet says, "It dawned on me one day. Why should he change? Why should he get rid of the other woman? He had the best of both worlds. He had a loving wife, who kept his home clean and neat and entertained well; she had a good job and a beautiful son and was well respected in the community. Then he had his other life with his mistress. He was like a cat with a great big bowl of cream in front of him."

Has your former spouse flagrantly ignored your convictions?

When your self-worth is threatened or your convictions are being trampled on, you will want to lash out. Anger deriving from self-preservation can be justified as long as you are expressing it in a way that is healthy. Start by bringing your anger to God. He can handle it.

"Casting all your anxiety on Him, because He cares for you" (1 Peter 5:7 NASB).

Lord God, I am hurt, angry, and confused. I don't like this feeling of worthlessness and rejection. I know You are the God of peace. Teach me how to accept and assimilate that inner peace. It seems so far away sometimes. Amen.

Is Anger Bad or Sinful?

Most people are quick to point out the negative aspects of anger, but being angry is not always bad. Some people have been taught that anger is sinful, that it is not pleasing to God. Anger itself is not a sin; it is a natural, God-given response.

Ephesians 4:26–27 says, "Be angry, and yet do not sin; do not let the sun go down on your anger, and do not give the devil an opportunity" (NASB). God tells us in this verse to go ahead and get angry, but He also tells us not to sin in our anger.

"There may be times when the anger can be fully appropriate," says Dr. Les Carter. "There may be times when the anger is necessary or required. It all depends on why you're angry, what you're doing with your anger, and what the purpose of it is. You need to be judicious in your use of anger."

The Scriptures teach much about God's character, and there are several instances in the Bible when God is angered.

"The LORD's anger burned against Israel and he made them wander in the desert forty years, until the whole generation of those who had done evil in his sight was gone" (Numbers 32:13).

"If you violate the covenant of the LORD your God, which he commanded you, and go and serve other gods and bow down to them, the LORD's anger will burn against you, and you will quickly perish from the good land he has given you" (Joshua 23:16).

Lord God, in my anger, give me wisdom. Help me to be sure my anger is appropriate so that I do not respond to a situation in error. Forgive me for when I have been angry and have sinned as a result. Amen.

When Is Anger a Sin?

If God says to be angry but not to sin, how do you know when your anger has crossed the line of sin?

Anger is sinful when it rises up quickly, taking over rational thought. Ecclesiastes 7:9 says, "Do not be quickly provoked in your spirit, for anger resides in the lap of fools."

Betsy says, "I saw his car, and I took a big rock and I smashed it through the windshield, and that was just a release of the anger. It was humiliating. It was a big mistake. I shouldn't have done that."

Juaria shares from her experience: "When you've been abused, you sometimes lie in bed and think about how you can get that person back. I remember one time thinking that I would wait until my husband was sleeping and boil some hot water and get him back for good. That was the wrong thing to do. Prayerfully, I considered my thoughts, and God really convicted me and made me understand that it's not for me to get him back. God is the One who has control over that."

Anger is a sin when it is accompanied by bitterness, blame, and unforgiveness. "Get rid of all bitterness, rage and anger" (Ephesians 4:31).

Anger is wrong when it stirs up arguments and produces controversy. "An angry man stirs up dissension, and a hot-tempered one commits many sins" (Proverbs 29:22).

Anger must not be stored up within you for any extended period of time. "Do not let the sun go down while you are still angry" (Ephesians 4:26).

Righteous Lord, forgive me for letting my anger get out of control. Please refresh my spirit, and give me the strength to walk rightly with You. Amen.

Let It Out

"It's okay to be angry at God when you've been divorced," says Dr. Myles Munroe. "Go to God. Shout at Him. Tell Him you hate it. Tell Him how you feel. God's not upset. He wants you to release that anger, to Him. That's why the Bible says, 'Be angry and sin not.' God wants you to tell Him how you feel so lonely and how you got the bad end of the deal. Lock yourself up in your bedroom and scream at God. You've got to let it out."

This deliberate act of expressing anger in a safe place should be done in private, just between you and God. Use it as a time to really talk out your issues with God. You never have to worry about saying the wrong thing with God.

If you are a parent, you will need to be wise in how you release your anger. Choose a time and place when your children are not present. You don't want to scare them!

It may help to have a regularly scheduled time when you close the door and release your anger in shouts and tears. This will help you train yourself to express anger at appropriate times and in appropriate places; the best time is not when you are immediately reacting to someone's words or actions. As weeks and months go by, and you have spent regular time with God expressing your emotions, you will find that the worst of your anger has been effectively spent.

"Cry out from anguish of heart and wail in brokenness of spirit" (Isaiah 65:14).

"Therefore groan, son of man! Groan before them with broken heart and bitter grief" (Ezekiel 21:6).

O God, I am crying and groaning all the time. Help me to release my angry emotions. Amen.

Straight Talk with God

In the Bible, David was a warrior and king who often wrote songs and prayers to God. He was never afraid to pour out his heart to the Lord. David expressed his deep pain, frustration, hurt, shame, and confusion, but he always ended his cries of despair by declaring that God is good, He is still in control, and He is worthy to be praised and honored.

In this psalm, note how David did not monitor his words when talking to God. He was not worried that he would shock or offend God. He said exactly what he was feeling.

O my God, I cry out by day, but you do not answer . . . All who see me mock me; they hurl insults, shaking their heads . . . I am poured out like water, and all my bones are out of joint. My heart has turned to wax; it has melted away within me. My strength is dried up like a potsherd, and my tongue sticks to the roof of my mouth . . . I can count all my bones; people stare and gloat over me . . .

But you, O Lord, be not far off; O my Strength, come quickly to help me. Deliver my life . . . Rescue me . . . save me . . . For he has not despised or disdained the suffering of the afflicted one; he has not hidden his face from him but has listened to his cry for help . . . They who seek the Lord will praise him." (Psalm 22:2, 7, 14–15, 17, 19–21, 24, 26)

Wow, Lord. I can relate to that pain. Help me relate to the strong faith as well. Amen.

Source of Anger: Overdependence on Others

By identifying the causes of your anger, you will be better prepared to handle your anger when it arises. Anger can stem from several sources. One source is an overdependence on other people.

You were born dependent on others for many things, including affirmation and love. As you grew, you learned that some people are dependable and some are not. You may also have discovered that too much dependence on another person can be unhealthy. In a divorce situation, one spouse will sometimes depend too much on the other to meet his or her emotional needs, and this can result in great frustration and anger for both.

You do not need to depend on your former spouse for your emotional well-being. Depend on God. He knows that you need love, affirmation, and a human touch. He will make sure that you get it and that it comes from the right source.

"This is what the LORD says: 'Cursed is the one who trusts in man, who depends on flesh for his strength and whose heart turns away from the LORD . . . But blessed is the man who trusts in the LORD, whose confidence is in him. He will be like a tree planted by the water that sends out its roots by the stream. It does not fear when heat comes; its leaves are always green. It has no worries in a year of drought and never fails to bear fruit'" (Jeremiah 17:5, 7–8).

Lord God, You are my confidence and my assurance. Help me to depend on You and not my former spouse. Amen.

Self-Worth

On a scale of 1 to 10, with 1 being "no confidence in myself whatsoever" and 10 being "completely confident in myself," rate your current level of self-worth:

1 2 3 4 5 6 7 8 9 10

This number has likely lowered since the divorce process began. Having your self-worth threatened by another individual, especially someone you trusted, can be debilitating. Your mind probably plays tricks on you, and that is Satan's influence.

"Satan was involved in this process," says Rob Eagar. "He would whisper thoughts into my mind, such as *This is the end of the world. This is your last chance at love. You have no hope in life anymore.* Thoughts like that weighed me down.

"I learned that I have to renew my mind with the truth, which is in God's Word. I realized that there is hope, that God loves me, and my self-esteem is not based on whether another person loves me or rejects me. My self-esteem is based on the love that Christ has for me."

You are the one who is in charge of what you think about. When thoughts come into your mind that are negative and bring you down, you must renew your mind by replacing the bad thoughts with good ones immediately. This will help build your self-esteem.

God's Word tells us to keep our minds focused on things that are right and good.

"Finally, brothers, whatever is true, whatever is noble, whatever is right, whatever is pure, whatever is lovely, whatever is admirable— if anything is excellent or praiseworthy—think about such things" (Philippians 4:8).

Jesus, You love me so much that You died on the cross to save me from sin and death. I want to focus on Your love and find my strength and self-worth in You. Amen.

Source of Anger:
Others Are Trying to Control You

When you feel you are in control of a given situation, you have a sense of security. When others try to take over that control, you instinctively rebel.

Dr. Les Carter gives this example: "Enter into your life someone who says, 'I don't like the way you do things. We're going to do things my way.'

"That happens frequently in a divorce. Another person may start making decisions that directly affect you, that are way out of bounds from what you believe. He or she may say things about you behind your back. You feel like you're constantly scrambling, trying to figure out what to say in rebuttal. You feel controlled.

"When that occurs, your natural desire is to want to recapture control. You can find yourself in a power play: *You've got control over me. I want to prove I can have control back over you.* Before you know it, you get pulled into frustrating circumstances, the net result being anger.

"If you want to let go of some of the anger, then let go of it by realizing you can't control other people. You may not like what they have to say or how they are acting, but that's not something you can control."

You are always the one who controls how you react to a situation. Your attitude, your words, and your actions are all the results of decisions made by you. Focus on controlling yourself, and walk on a higher plane than those who are negative, petty, or domineering.

"From the ends of the earth I call to you [God], I call as my heart grows faint; lead me to the rock that is higher than I" (Psalm 61:2).

Lord, lead me to a higher realm where You dwell. Amen.

Source of Anger: Mythical Thinking

Holding on to idealistic views of life can be a source of anger for you. Perhaps you have been holding on to dreams, which are now only myths. By clinging to what you can no longer have, you are feeding your frustration.

"My white picket fence was falling down, and I had four children who needed two parents, and one was emotionally not there," says Sue.

Everyone has ideals and expectations of life. When some of your beliefs prove false, you are confused and despairing. In order to protect yourself, you hold on to whatever shreds are left of that ideal, and you begin to feel angry because what you had believed in with all your heart is falling apart around you. You are angry with the person who helped destroy your dreams, and you are angry with yourself for believing those dreams in the first place.

Dr. Les Carter says, "Mythical thinking is a refusal to acknowledge ugly truth. Ugly truth tends not to find its way in all these fairy tales."

One fantastic characteristic of God is that He *is* truth. When God promises you a dream or an ideal to look forward to, you can believe that it will come to pass. Search God's Word to find His promises to you. Trust Him because He will never let you down.

"Trust in the LORD with all your heart and lean not on your own understanding; in all your ways acknowledge him, and he will make your paths straight" (Proverbs 3:5–6).

You, O Lord, are the God of truth. You cannot deny Yourself. You always keep Your promises. I believe in the reality of You, Jesus. Amen.

Source of Anger: Self-Inflicted

Some anger can be self-inflicted, brought on by your own actions and wrong decisions.

"You want to feel loved and accepted," says Dr. Les Carter. "As a result, you may find yourself more susceptible to sexual acting out, or maybe you have started hanging around a more unsavory crowd and engaging in social activities you might never have done before. These actions result in 'self-inflicted wounds,' which can later cause you to feel anger because you have a neediness that is pushing you to live in ways that you normally wouldn't choose."

When you give in to sexual or other temptations, your pain is numbed for a short time, but you remember what you did for a long time, and it can make you angry. If you have already given in to temptation and are feeling guilty or angry, stop. There is no need to dwell on what has been done. Turn to God for forgiveness, and forgive yourself.

When you ask God to forgive a sin, He forgives you thoroughly. This is extremely difficult for our human nature to comprehend, as we like to remember and rehash things in our minds. God's Word says there is "no condemnation" for those who seek forgiveness through Jesus Christ. You must be an imitator of Christ and stop blaming yourself when you have already been forgiven. God is not pleased with self-condemnation because that is not how He taught us to behave.

"Therefore, there is now no condemnation for those who are in Christ Jesus, because through Christ Jesus the law of the Spirit of life set me free from the law of sin and death" (Romans 8:1–2).

Dear Lord, please forgive my sins in the name of Jesus Christ. Help me develop a plan to keep me from future temptation. Amen.

Source of Anger: Pride

Divorce hurts your pride, and wounded pride can lead to anger. You may be angry with your former spouse:

- For not trying hard enough to make the marriage work
- For making it public that he or she is rejecting you
- For seeming to disregard what was good in the marriage
- For making you look foolish because you didn't know what was going on
- For putting you in an awkward social position

"You plan to spend fifty years with a person," says James, "and the next thing you know life is cut out from underneath you. I would say the anger comes from wanting vindication, wanting justification, and wanting to prove to other people that it was a good marriage."

You naturally want to be accepted. You want other people to approve of and respect you. But in divorce, egos get bruised. You are forced into socially uncomfortable positions. Past friendships no longer fit. Your life and your problems are suddenly exposed and seem to be an open forum for other people to discuss and offer their advice and opinions on. You wonder just how much friends, family, or coworkers have known about the situation all along.

It is okay to want to be accepted, but know that divorce does result in hurt pride. Do not be concerned about what people are saying or thinking about you, and don't let your pride be a source of uncontrolled anger at your former spouse.

"When pride comes, then comes shame; but with the humble *is* wisdom" (Proverbs 11:2 NKJV).

Heavenly Father, teach me to control my anger in humility. Amen.

Source of Anger: Fear

What fears do you have as a result of your divorce?

Sue shares, "I felt desperate and extremely fearful. Satan would always try to attack me with fear. Fear that I couldn't make it on my own. Fear that my former husband was going to take the children. Fear that I would not ever be emotionally well again."

Fear can be a source of anger, and fear is triggered when a person feels threatened emotionally.

"Fear can cause you to have a great sense of agitation," says Dr. Les Carter. "Consider a dog, for example, that barks at somebody on the other side of the fence. The bark sounds like the dog is angry, but in fact, it may be that the dog is kind of afraid and is just trying to make it sound like it's stronger than it really is."

You don't have to be strong or confident or self-sufficient. God wants you to depend on His strength, and He will be victorious through you. Try depending on God today. When fear threatens to come into your mind, choose a Bible verse to repeat again and again. Claim that verse, and watch God work. You might want to pick one of the verses below, or you can look in a concordance for the word *fear* and find another Scripture that might be meaningful to you.

"In all these things we are more than conquerors through him who loved us" (Romans 8:37).

"But he said to me, 'My grace is sufficient for you, for my power is made perfect in weakness.' Therefore I will boast all the more gladly about my weaknesses, so that Christ's power may rest on me" (2 Corinthians 12:9).

Jesus, thank You for Your grace—Your undeserved, free gift of love to me. Amen.

Source of Anger: Loneliness

Loneliness is an expected response when going through a divorce, but you might be surprised to learn that loneliness can contribute to anger. You may be feeding your anger with thoughts that you are lonely because no one understands you or no one wants to be with you. You are angry because you are alone, and why should you have to be alone?

Dr. Les Carter explains, "The longer you are disconnected from other people or the more you feel misunderstood, a powerful sense of anger can come in." Dr. Carter says to be careful not to allow any of your emotions, including loneliness and anger, to build up to such a high pitch that they become out of control and harmful.

Be aware that your loneliness can lead to anger. When you are overwhelmed with loneliness, make it a habit to call or visit a friend or relative, and be honest with them about your feelings.

Rob Eagar says, "When you're experiencing pain or deep rejection, it is okay to ask for help. It was a big thing for me to realize it's okay to tell my friends or my family: 'I am hurting right now. I need your help.' Don't try to be an island or live in a cave. Get out and get involved, and let people know that you could really use their support and involvement right now."

Turn to the Lord, who is always with you, and choose not to let your emotions build up to a breaking point.

"Be sure of this: I am with you always, even to the end of the age" (Matthew 28:20 NLT).

Lord, You are always with me. I want to feel Your arms around me. Fill the deepest part of my lonely soul. Amen.

Source of Anger: Feelings of Inferiority

Dr. Les Carter says, "Anger is closely tied to your sense of well-being as a person and closely tied to your feeling of worthiness. The less worthy you feel, the more likely you are to try to compensate for that by laying into someone, by blaming or accusing him or her, and that's where your inferiority feelings can show themselves as anger."

Rose Sweet says, "In divorce you are forced to realize that some people may never love you. You had better find someone who always did love you and always will love you. That's only one Person—that's God.

"If you feel like you're a failure, you're forgetting God. You are looking at yourself either through your own human eyes or other people's eyes. You have to quit doing that. Realize that you are so precious and so loved and that you are not alone. He wants to help you. He wants to heal you. You may have failed, but you are not a failure."

Your identity and your self-esteem are found in a relationship with the Lord. Build your life's center on a solid foundation. Having a strong foundation will enable you to sustain whatever troubles come your way.

"We are hard pressed on every side, but not crushed; perplexed, but not in despair; persecuted, but not abandoned; struck down, but not destroyed" (2 Corinthians 4:8–9).

Lord, I am hard pressed, confused, persecuted, and I've fallen on my backside, but with You, I will stand again, and I'll stand strong. Amen.

Dealing with Anger

Over the next few days, we will look at ways to deal with anger. Some of these responses are healthy, and some are unhealthy. Harriet has chosen a healthy response to anger. She shares, "I am building a relationship with my heavenly Father like I never dreamed possible. I have realized through all of this that I can talk real straight with God because He already knows who I am. He already knows the thoughts and the feelings that are in the deep recesses of my mind and my heart.

"Do you know what it feels like to be able to say, 'God, I really hate my husband's guts, and I hate his mistress, and I wish that his major body parts would fall off'? I am able to speak honestly with the one Person who has the power to help me to grow beyond that. I know I have nothing to hide from my precious Father because He already knows me."

We cannot emphasize enough the importance of talking honestly with God and building a relationship with Him. God knows you intimately, more than any person ever will. Talk with Him daily as you go about your business at home, at work, and at night in bed. He is always available to listen, and He wants to hear from you.

"Pray continually" (1 Thessalonians 5:17).

Holy God, You know everything I am thinking and feeling. I want daily conversations with You to be a lifelong habit. Thank You for listening to me and for loving me. Amen.

Don't Stuff It

Some people deal with anger by suppressing it. They may do this because they have been taught it is wrong to express emotions that might cause conflict. Others want to appear successful at coping. Some just don't realize they have a lifetime habit of pushing down trouble-some emotions.

"When I first got involved in a divorce recovery program, I didn't realize I was suppressing anger," admits Joe. "I thought that it was a sin to be angry, and I didn't want to displease the Lord in any way; then I realized that the Lord gives us justifiable anger. It's healthy to be angry."

Susan says, "At first I suppressed my anger because I was raised to believe that anger was not an appropriate way to express your frustra-tions. Then finally it broke. It came flying out. I had emotions and feel-ings that I never had experienced before, and they surprised me. I didn't realize that I could have that much rage and frustration inside my body."

Psalm 18 describes circumstances in which God showed righteous anger at David's enemies for what they were doing to David.

"The earth trembled and quaked, and the foundations of the mountains shook; they trembled because he [God] was angry. Smoke rose from his nostrils; consuming fire came from his mouth, burn-ing coals blazed out of it . . . Out of the brightness of his presence clouds advanced, with hailstones and bolts of lightning. The LORD thundered from heaven; the voice of the Most High resounded" (Psalm 18:7–8, 12–13).

Most High God, teach me how to recognize my anger and to express—not suppress—it. Amen.

Out-of-Control Anger

While some people suppress their anger, others express it openly and aggressively.

"I went by my husband's office that day to get my frustration out. I took a rock and smashed it through the windshield of his car. Then I got in my car, and I drove off," says Betsy.

Angie says, "My coping mechanism when I'm hurt is to lash out. I remember my ex calling several times, and I would just rage at him. I can't believe the things I actually said; I'd just completely cuss him out and tell him what a horrible person he was. That was very hurtful. That was very damaging."

The problem with aggression is that it often leads to sin. If your anger is justified, then practice expressing it in a neutral, safe setting alone or with someone who will not fuel your anger but will just listen. If an unexpected situation occurs that ignites your anger, decide right now that you will hold your tongue and wait for an appropriate moment and mind-set to release it.

"The acts of the sinful nature are obvious: sexual immorality, impurity and debauchery; idolatry and witchcraft; hatred, discord, jealousy, fits of rage, selfish ambition, dissensions, factions and envy; drunkenness, orgies, and the like. I warn you, as I did before, that those who live like this will not inherit the kingdom of God.

"But the fruit of the Spirit is love, joy, peace, patience, kindness, goodness, faithfulness, gentleness and self-control. Against such things there is no law. Those who belong to Christ Jesus have crucified the sinful nature with its passions and desires" (Galatians 5:19–24).

Holy Spirit, I pray that my life brings forth good "fruit."
Please give me peace, patience, gentleness, and self-
control. Amen.

Silent Anger

Some people have a passive-aggressive approach to anger. They act out their anger through practices such as silence, stubbornness, or procrastination. This is not a healthy release of anger.

Dr. Les Carter explains, "You may do many evasive things to create irritability in that other person. How many of you have been frustrated in an interaction, and you may be prone to giving the silent treatment or going into another room and saying nothing? Or I wonder how many times you may know someone wants you to do something and you procrastinate; you put things off, and you refuse to be cooperative. It's a form of expressing anger. You're trying to take care of yourself, of your turf so to speak, but you're doing it at the expense of someone else."

Any time you express anger in a way that is unhealthy, you are not resolving your anger, and you are ultimately hurting only yourself.

Dr. Carter continues, "I've seen many individuals who have gone through the difficulties of divorce, who really don't work through it mainly because they continue to cling to unhealthy forms of anger."

People who have a passive-aggressive approach to anger may not realize they are angry, or they may feel they are handling their anger well. After reading the descriptions above, consider if this is a response you have had; it is important in the divorce process to find one area at a time where problems can be addressed and healing can take place.

"But they did not listen or pay attention; instead, they followed the stubborn inclinations of their evil hearts. They went backward and not forward" (Jeremiah 7:24).

Lord God, give me the sense to move forward in wisdom and not just react without thinking beyond the moment. Amen.

Give Anger a Voice

One healthy way to deal with anger is the assertive approach. An assertion is a positive and often forceful declaration. This is different from aggression.

Dr. Les Carter says, "There are times when somebody has violated your worth or your convictions, and you need to stand up for it. Not in a selfish way, but in a responsible way. Sometimes people ask me, 'Do I have a right to be angry?' I'll say, 'Let's take the word *right* and throw it away. That implies what's best for me and me alone. It can be a selfish word. Let's put the word *responsibility* in its place and ask it again: 'Do I have a responsibility to be angry?' Now, many times, the answer is no, not really. Other times the answer is yes, it would be an act of responsibility.

"Sometimes you do need to stand up for what's right and let someone know he or she violated your convictions. Sometimes you need to communicate in firm, unbending ways as to how you want to be respected. This can be done while also showing respect to the other person. It's a form of anger where you're seeking to solve problems and to preserve what's right, and you're trying to do so in a way that's going to be beneficial to all."

In the Bible, Paul was a man who spoke assertively. He encouraged the believers to speak out for what they believed and not let others trample on their words, hearts, and convictions. When your anger is justified, speak with the authority of the Lord.

"Encourage and rebuke with all authority. Do not let anyone despise you" (Titus 2:15).

Lord of All, I am angry, but I want to express my anger in a way that is right and good. Do not let me release my anger in selfishness. Amen.

Drop It

"There are times when you may have legitimate desires to be assertive," says Dr. Les Carter, "but the person on the receiving end is just not going to hear it. That happens many, many times in divorce cases. Rather than going to the suppression of anger, there needs to be a willingness at those times to say, 'Let's leave the anger alone. I'm finished with it. It's in God's hands.'"

Lisa says, "The sooner you're able to let go of that anger and let God clean out the inside of you, the sooner you will be free of it, and it won't hold you back like a ball and chain. When you're able to let go of that through God's help, then you'll be able to move forward with your life."

Dropping anger does not mean suppressing it. It is an acknowledgment that anger, at this point, is no longer useful. It is a willingness to forgive and be forgiven.

"Never pay back evil for evil to anyone. Respect what is right in the sight of all men. If possible, so far as it depends on you, be at peace with all men. Never take your own revenge, beloved, but leave room for the wrath of God, for it is written, 'Vengeance is mine, I will repay,' says the Lord" (Romans 12:17–19 NASB).

Lord, I give my anger to You. The wisest choice at this time seems to be for me to drop my anger. Help me replace that emotion with one that pleases You. Amen.

Reducing Anger

Reducing your anger is not an easy process. Here are some practical ideas of ways to deal with your anger.

- Call a friend, or write in a journal. Cindy says, "I've got a whole journal of awful things I have felt and thought. That helped."

- Monitor your negative words and attitudes. "I had one person who called his ex-spouse the dictator," says Dr. Les Carter, "and I said, 'Every time you refer to her in that negative way, it just keeps the anger alive a little bit more.' You need to let go of little things like that."

- Read the Bible. "Every minute I could I was reading the Bible, and there was a peace that started coming about," says Sherry.

- Be thankful for what is good in your life. "I knew that God was saying, 'You can be angry at what happened, but the rest of your life is pretty good. You've got a lot to be thankful for,'" says Cindy.

- Have an accountability partner. Dr. Les Carter says, "Share what you're feeling so you can learn to get beyond it. Express the areas you need to forgive. Share the things you need to accept that aren't going to change. As you talk openly, you tend to take ownership of the solutions you're discussing."

"I want men everywhere to lift up holy hands in prayer, without anger or disputing" (1 Timothy 2:8).

Holy Lord, thank You for the people who have gone through this before me and are willing to share their advice. Thank You that I am not alone. Amen.

Making Amends

"Fools mock at making amends for sin, but goodwill is found among the upright" (Proverbs 14:9).

You should seek to put things right with the person who has made you angry.

"Not because it's fair, not because you're hoping the other person is going to reciprocate, but you want to make amends simply for the fact that you know it's healthy for you," says Dr. Les Carter.

In any conflict, one person is not 100 percent at fault, so even if you feel your former spouse is always the one who starts the arguments or causes the problems, think about times when your reaction did not help the situation.

Whatever has been negative in your words, attitudes, and responses, make the sincere attempt to change your ways and amend the wrongness. Approach your former spouse with the willingness to be appropriate from now on and not hold grudges or be hurtful or speak angry words. Be sure that you are being respectful and keeping your focus on God when you do this.

Your former spouse might not believe you or might not be interested in making amends. If this happens, do not become frustrated; just tell your former spouse you are sorry he or she feels that way. Choose to move forward in healing regardless of what the other person does or says.

"Reject the wrong and choose the right" (Isaiah 7:15).

Lord God, I want to make amends with a sincere heart that is free from bitterness and blame. Amen.

Forgiveness and Anger

Forgiveness is a sign of true healing, and it is one of the most difficult things to do in a divorce situation. Forgiveness also takes time.

Forgiveness might be easier if you approach it in steps. The first step could be to seek forgiveness for hurtful things you have said or done in anger. Go to your former spouse and ask forgiveness for specific words or incidents. Then, forgive yourself for those things.

"I truly worked on trying to forgive myself," says Susan, "but I think I tried too fast to cover up the anger that I felt. It was a very, very deep cut. What ended up happening is that with each little brush I would have with my ex regarding finances, or any little hurt that would happen to my children or to me, he would scrape that surface off again, and I hadn't really cleaned the wound out yet. I never truly let all the anger and the frustration come out."

If you are struggling to repent of your hurtful words and spiteful actions, perhaps you, too, still have anger that needs to be released and not harbored. Continue to find ways to express your anger in a productive, healthy way. Then, confess any out-of-control anger to God, to the person it was directed against, and to yourself.

"Therefore confess your sins to each other and pray for each other so that you may be healed" (James 5:16).

"Blessed is he whose transgressions are forgiven, whose sins are covered" (Psalm 32:1).

Faithful Lord, forgive me for letting anger take control again. Forgive me for holding on to anger when I should be releasing it. Help me to forgive myself. Amen.

When Your Anger Hurts Others

Proverbs 18:21 says, "The tongue has the power of life and death, and those who love it will eat its fruit."

"Words hurt," says Dr. Linda Mintle, "and they hurt deeply. Proverbs 18:21 tells us that the power of life and death is in the tongue. You can devastate people by your words." You must take responsibility for your words and understand the deep and lasting harm that can occur when you speak without thinking.

Are you sometimes shocked and disappointed by the angry words that pop out of your mouth? Perhaps you cringe as you think of a particular moment when you were raging uncontrollably. By now you are probably aware of the damage your anger has inflicted on yourself and on those around you.

"Confession, repentance, and forgiveness are the only ways to deal with anger. You have to confess and repent of sins you have committed as a result of your anger. You have to move back toward God and seek forgiveness from God, yourself, and the other person," says Dr. Robert Abarno.

God will forgive you—just ask in Jesus' name.

"Then I acknowledged my sin to you and did not cover up my iniquity. I said, 'I will confess my transgressions to the LORD'—and you forgave the guilt of my sin" (Psalm 32:5).

"I confess my iniquity; I am troubled by my sin" (Psalm 38:18).

Lord, forgive me. Thank You that when I confess my sins to You, You not only forgive, but You remember them no more (Isaiah 43:25). Amen.

Rationalizing Anger

You can prolong your anger by rationalizing it or blaming others for it rather than accepting full responsibility for your part. To rationalize something means "to cause it to seem reasonable," when it may not be reasonable at all.

Listen to some rationalizations:

- "It's not my fault I am angry."
- "My former spouse deserves my anger after what he or she did to me."
- "Why should I bother when my former spouse isn't even trying?"
- "I have had such a hard life."
- "Anger is a habit of mine. I wouldn't know how else to respond."

When you rationalize your anger, you are telling yourself that you have the right to be angry. Focusing on your rights results in self-centered thinking and not God-centered thinking. Choose to act in wisdom, not to act with self-righteous anger.

The book of Proverbs contains instructions on how to think and act wisely. A good suggestion is to read one chapter of Proverbs each day.

"The proverbs of Solomon son of David, king of Israel: for attaining wisdom and discipline; for understanding words of insight; for acquiring a disciplined and prudent life, doing what is right and just and fair; for giving prudence to the simple, knowledge and discretion to the young—let the wise listen and add to their learning, and let the discerning get guidance . . . The fear of the LORD is the beginning of knowledge, but fools despise wisdom and discipline" (Proverbs 1:1–5, 7).

Righteous Lord, please look at my heart, and reveal to me the truth about the reasons behind my anger. Each day I will commit to reading from Proverbs to gain godly wisdom. Amen.

Facing Your Depression

Understanding Your Depression

Depression is a natural reaction to profound loss. A person going through a divorce will likely experience some form of depression. Although depression is often associated with feelings of deep sadness, depression can take other forms as well.

Joyce shares, "I would go to work every day and put on a happy, smiling face, but as soon as I put the key in the door to my apartment, I would literally slide down the wall and cry.

"Then, I would crawl as a child to the bedroom and leave things as they were until the next morning—not wanting to eat, not wanting to be bothered. Family and friends would call me to make sure I was okay, and I would lie there listening to their calls. I didn't want to talk to anyone. I wanted to be alone.

"The depression began to show on the outside. People would ask me, 'Why are you losing so much weight? You don't seem to care about yourself as you used to.' I didn't want to do any activities, things that at one point I liked to do. I wanted to come home and sleep."

Depression is a normal and even necessary reaction to your loss. You are not alone in these behaviors and actions. You will learn in the next few weeks different signs of depression, how to deal with it, how to learn from it, and how to overcome it.

"Come quickly, LORD, and answer me, for my depression deepens. Don't turn away from me, or I will die" (Psalm 143:7 NLT).

Lord God, I am depressed inside and out, but I choose to work through this no matter how hard it gets because You are by my side. Amen.

Depression: What Does It Look Like?

Jim shares, "I turned everything inward and became very quiet. I wouldn't call the church; I never asked for help. I stayed home a lot and kept the house dark."

Joanne says, "The first two months I couldn't breathe. I cried when I got up in the morning; I cried all day; I cried when I went to bed at night. I didn't care how I looked or what I said."

"I didn't want to think I was depressed because to me, that's a sign of weakness," says Marie. "I really thought I was coping well. I didn't allow myself to feel anything. I would push myself at work, working late, night after night. I wasn't dealing with the reality that I was depressed."

In the Bible, David felt emotionally as if he were in a "slimy pit" full of "mud and mire." While in this emotional state, David "waited patiently for the LORD." Not only was he patient in his depression, but he was also vocal in it. He cried out to the Lord. As a result, God lifted him up and put his feet on solid ground. God put a new song in David's mouth. God will do the same for you if you trust in Him.

"I waited patiently for the LORD; he turned to me and heard my cry. He lifted me out of the slimy pit, out of the mud and mire; he set my feet on a rock and gave me a firm place to stand. He put a new song in my mouth, a hymn of praise to our God" (Psalm 40:1–3).

Lord, I am so depressed. My life no longer has meaning or joy, and sometimes I just don't care. I cry to You, God. Lift me out of this pit. Put my feet on solid ground. Please put a new song in my heart. Amen.

Depression Is a Healing Emotion

Most people would not consider depression a healing emotion. Dr. Archibald Hart explains how this can be true:

"Every depression will pass. If you do the right things, you can shorten it; you can bring healing; and you can grow. If you do the right things, this could be one of the most wonderful things that has ever happened to you. I work with a lot of depressed people. When they are over it, they all say to me, 'I'm a better person because of it. Somehow through this pain, I have found a new me, and God has become more precious than ever before.'"

Ginny shares, "The most important things I've learned are (1) God never leaves us, (2) we are all sinners, and (3) God wants to be there; we just have to ask Him.

"When you go through hard times, God isn't testing you to be faithful to Him; He's proving His faithfulness to you. I wouldn't trade what I've been through for anything. As much as I've hated going through it, it has given me the relationship with God that I didn't have before. There's such peace in that."

As you go through each day, look to the future expectantly to see how God will use the depression in your life.

"Thanksgivings will pour out of the windows; laughter will spill through the doors. Things will get better and better. Depression days are over. They'll thrive, they'll flourish. The days of contempt will be over" (Jeremiah 30:19 MSG).

Almighty God, forgive me for trying to work through the depression on my own. Use this awful depression to bring about something good in my life. Amen.

Concrete and Abstract Losses

Your depression is directly related to the losses you have experienced as a result of your divorce. There are two main types of losses: concrete and abstract. Concrete losses are measurable, such as the loss of income, a spouse, or your car. Abstract losses cannot be measured. These losses include the loss of self-esteem, dreams, or affection. Both types of losses are important and need to be grieved.

The greater your losses, the greater the depression.

"You will only grieve something that means something to you," says Bonnie Keen. "Grief is actually a way of honoring what your marriage meant. I did believe in my marriage. I did believe that I would stay married forever, and this is now a death. This is a grieving time."

Rose Sweet encourages you to express your grief: "You have to mourn all of your losses. Mourning is such an important part of the cleansing process. In the Bible, people would go out and mourn and wail and weep. We don't do that anymore. We stuff everything, and we try to smile for the camera. We forget that mourning is part of God's design for us to get all those negative feelings and energies out so that we can heal completely."

Allow yourself to grieve and to be depressed. You have sustained a major loss. Let your body do what it was designed to do.

"God blesses those who mourn, for they will be comforted" (Matthew 5:4 NLT).

Father, help me to recognize both my concrete losses and my abstract losses. Then, help me grieve. Amen.

Symptoms of Depression

It is possible to be depressed and not know it.

"Many people are depressed and don't know it," says Dr. Archibald Hart, "because they think that when people are depressed, they are crying all the time and wallowing in self-pity. Perhaps what you are feeling is a profound state of lethargy, no energy and no interest."

The symptoms of depression vary from person to person. In the next few days we will be discussing several different signs of depression. These symptoms include feelings of disconnectedness, sadness, hopelessness, guilt, indifference, and worthlessness. Other symptoms are headaches, changes in sleeping and eating patterns, and low energy. You may also be entertaining thoughts of suicide or have noticed an impact on your spiritual life.

You have ample reason to be depressed as you move through the divorce process. Remember that your depression is not only necessary, but it can be productive in your forward movement toward healing. Dr. Hart says, "Depression is a unique state of the body and mind in which you experience sadness and low energy as a way of preparing the body to do something significant."

"So the king asked me, 'Why does your face look so sad when you are not ill? This can be nothing but sadness of heart'" (Nehemiah 2:2).

Lord, help me to embrace my depression as a step in the healing process. Help me to understand that I can learn from this depression and that You have something significant planned for me as a result of my growth. Amen.

Disconnectedness

One sign of depression is a feeling of disconnectedness. You no longer feel that you are connected to other people. You aren't sure if you know how to connect with people anymore.

Not being able to relate to others is a serious loss, but it is a loss you can grieve and then remedy. Express your feelings of disconnectedness to God and then to another person: "I feel alone. No one understands me. I feel uncomfortable around people. Other people feel uncomfortable around me. I'm just bringing everyone down."

After you have acknowledged, expressed, and grieved your emotions, you must take steps to build friendships again. You need your family and friends to make it through this tough time.

James shares his experience: "I was driving home one day, and I told God that I wouldn't mind spending time with friends—maybe see a movie, watch a video, or get a pizza. That was my prayer.

"I went home, and soon after, there was a knock on my door. The two friends at my doorstep, who had been to my house only twice in about six months, said, 'James, we're going to pick up videos and get a pizza.' So here it was, not fifteen minutes later, and I received answers to all three prayers. That is not a coincidence. God was visible. He said, 'James, I am always here. You just gotta see Me.'"

Remember, at this stage in your healing, it is important to focus on friendships with people of the same sex. You need more time to heal before you become romantically involved.

"By yourself you're unprotected. With a friend you can face the worst" (Ecclesiastes 4:12 MSG).

Lord God, I need to express my needs to You. Help me to get up, get out of the house, and spend time with people. Amen.

Profound Sense of Sadness

"I have great sorrow and unceasing anguish in my heart" (Romans 9:2).

Another symptom of depression is a profound sense of sadness in your life.

"There's an emptiness in you. You feel like a big hole has suddenly developed in the center of your being. Persistent sadness is there all the time," says Dr. Archibald Hart.

Cindy says, "If I opened my mouth, I would start sobbing because I was so sad. I had lost a tremendous amount of weight. My hair fell out by the handfuls. Sadness had taken over my whole being."

Jesus was called a "man of sorrows." It may seem impossible that Jesus could know how you feel, but He does. He, too, was "despised and rejected" by people, and He was "familiar with suffering." Call on God in your sadness as One who knows every fear, hurt, pain, and disappointment hidden in your heart. Jesus can be the light in your darkness.

"He had no beauty or majesty to attract us to him, nothing in his appearance that we should desire him. He was despised and rejected by men, a man of sorrows, and familiar with suffering. Like one from whom men hide their faces he was despised, and we esteemed him not. Surely he took up our infirmities and carried our sorrows, yet we considered him stricken by God, smitten by him, and afflicted" (Isaiah 53:2–4).

Jesus, You know my pain. You were pierced by rejection and shame. You are God. Shine Your light in my darkness, and show me the way out. Amen.

Hopelessness and Pessimism

"Why did I ever come out of the womb to see trouble and sorrow and to end my days in shame?" (Jeremiah 20:18).

Good question. Maybe you have asked God a similar question.

There are times when hopelessness and pessimism may overwhelm you.

"You have a negative view of the past, of the present, and of the future. You feel that nothing is going to get better—that it's terrible now and it's going to stay this way the rest of your life," says Dr. Archibald Hart.

Hopelessness and pessimism are symptoms of depression, but depression will not last forever, even though it may sometimes feel like it. If you feel that you have no hope and if your words and thoughts are marked by negativity, tell God. Ask hard questions like Jeremiah did. State specifically why you feel hopeless and why you feel pessimistic. God answered Jeremiah's question with words of hope and promises of joy. Be honest with God, and watch what He can do.

The Lord declares, "They will come and shout for joy on the heights of Zion; they will rejoice in the bounty of the LORD—the grain, the new wine and the oil, the young of the flocks and herds. They will be like a well-watered garden, and they will sorrow no more. Then maidens will dance and be glad, young men and old as well. I will turn their mourning into gladness; I will give them comfort and joy instead of sorrow" (Jeremiah 31:12–13).

Lord God, this is why I feel hopeless . . . and this is why I am pessimistic . . . Please turn my mourning into joy. Amen.

Guilt, Worthlessness, and Helplessness

"Guilt is a common sign of depression. You blame yourself for what has happened," says Dr. Archibald Hart.

"Divorce," says Bonnie Keen, "is a hammer blow to your self-esteem."

Ron shares, "I was just helpless."

Guilt, worthlessness, and helplessness may be an integral part of your daily life now. The emotions themselves are not wrong, but the questions you need to ask yourself are *Where will I let these emotions lead me? Will I let these feelings bring me down, or will I choose to keep my eyes on Jesus no matter what?* Jesus loves you regardless of what you have done, what you look like on the outside, or what you look like on the inside. You can never do anything that will cause Him to love you less. That is amazing. That is God.

Jan Northington explains, "Pain can drive you to a sense of hopelessness and despair or it can drive you to God. It's your choice. You may think there are few choices available to you, but in reality there are a million choices available."

Selma shares, "As long as I could keep my eyes on Jesus, I was fine. He loves me regardless of what has happened in the past and regardless of what I've done. Knowing that just gave me the strength to go on." Never forget how much Jesus loves you.

"Let us fix our eyes on Jesus, the author and perfecter of our faith, who for the joy set before him endured the cross, scorning its shame, and sat down at the right hand of the throne of God" (Hebrews 12:2).

Heavenly Father, when I choose to focus on You, I realize I am worthwhile and strong. Thank You for filling my future with hope and gladness. Amen.

No Longer Enjoying Favorite Activities

Bonnie Keen is an accomplished recording artist, songwriter, speaker, and author. Her desire is to bring God's message of love to people everywhere. Despite her God-given love of music, there was a time in Bonnie's life when she struggled to make it through a concert due to the depression she was feeling from her divorce.

She says, "I was a total wreck. I cried and cried. I would cry until it was time to go onstage and sing. I would sing, and then I'd sit down and cry again. I could not figure out what was happening to me. There was no joy in what I usually loved doing."

If you no longer enjoy the things you used to enjoy, it's another sign that you are experiencing depression. Bonnie experienced some dark times, just as you are, but she kept her eyes on Jesus Christ and placed her faith in Him. God saw her through, and today she ministers to those who are hurting, who don't feel God's love, and who desperately need His comfort.

"My heart is steadfast, O God, my heart is steadfast; I will sing and make music" (Psalm 57:7).

"Don't be afraid, for I am with you. Do not be dismayed, for I am your God. I will strengthen you. I will help you. I will uphold you with my victorious right hand" (Isaiah 41:10 NLT).

Faithful God, even though I don't feel like doing anything, I know that I need to get up and do something. Lead me back to an old hobby or activity, or perhaps I could try something new. Amen.

Disturbed Sleep Patterns

A change or disturbance in your sleep patterns is another sign of depression. Some people cannot sleep at all, and some people sleep almost all the time.

"I couldn't eat. I couldn't sleep. I was just a basket case," says Cheryl.

Bonnie Keen says, "I was up for almost two solid weeks without sleeping. I remember I could sleep two hours at a time and then I would just be awake."

Laura Petherbridge shares: "I literally slept all the time. I was absolutely exhausted." If you are a person who is reacting to your situation by sleeping a great deal, be aware that sleep can become an addictive behavior, which is unhealthy. Force yourself to exercise, to get out, and to be with other people. Get on a schedule that incorporates a healthy amount of sleep, and pray for the energy to stay awake when you should be awake!

The Bible offers several promises that have to do with sleep. Choose one of these promises to claim today. God loves you, and He wants your sleep to be peaceful and refreshing.

"He gives His beloved sleep" (Psalm 127:2 NKJV).

"I will lie down and sleep in peace, for you alone, O Lord, make me dwell in safety" (Psalm 4:8).

"When you lie down, you will not be afraid; when you lie down, your sleep will be sweet" (Proverbs 3:24).

Dear God, I know that You love me so much. Please calm my troubled thoughts and heart so that I can have a good night's sleep. Amen.

A Change in Eating Habits

Your depression can show itself through a change in your eating habits. Many people in divorce either experience an extreme lack of appetite or the desire to binge. Both habits are unhealthy.

"Realizing that my marriage had fallen apart, the first way it manifested itself was I lost the will to eat. In fact, I lost eighteen pounds in two and a half weeks," says Rob Eagar.

Dave says, "I was nauseous and had diarrhea and couldn't keep anything down. Nothing tasted good. I was forcing myself to eat and drink."

"Nine months ago," says Odie, "I was eighty pounds heavier, due to the stress of my divorce. I woke up one day, and I said, 'This is God's temple. I'm destroying it.'"

When you eat, choose to eat healthy foods. A poor diet affects a person emotionally as well as physically. Now is a good time to choose to put whole grains, water, proteins, and vitamin-rich vegetables in your body and start new, wise habits.

"Do you not know that your body is a temple of the Holy Spirit, who is in you, whom you have received from God? You are not your own; you were bought at a price. Therefore honor God with your body" (1 Corinthians 6:19–20).

Lord, I know that healthy eating will bring benefits in other areas of my life as well. Help me choose to do what is right with food and remember to honor You with my body. Amen.

Substantial Loss of Energy

A substantial loss of energy is a sign of depression that often accompanies divorce.

"You have no energy. You can't lift anything. You feel like you're lazy. Even if the house caught on fire, you don't think you could get up and leave," says Dr. Archibald Hart.

Bonnie Keen shares, "For me, to get up, get out of bed, and get the kids ready for school was like climbing a mountain. Depression can make you feel like you can't do anything. Go to the grocery store? I can't possibly do that."

Bonnie discovered that when she did get up and perform a simple task or get out of the house for a while, it really helped. Every small step you take will help on your road to recovery.

Getting out into the sunshine is one practical step that will help increase your energy level. Talk to your doctor or a nutritionist about which foods and vitamins your body needs more of at this time; a simple change in diet can do wonders for your energy level. Exercise, even ten minutes per day, will increase your energy. Make a point to talk with someone about your physical struggles as well as your emotional and spiritual struggles. Stay in constant communication with God. Post Bible verses throughout your house and car to keep yourself energized spiritually.

"My soul is weary with sorrow; strengthen me according to your word" (Psalm 119:28).

Lord God, help me to read the Bible and be strengthened by Your Word so that I can take a step forward today. Amen.

Entertaining Thoughts of Suicide

Your depression may be so deep that you begin to think about suicide. Having recurrent thoughts of death is common in depression.

"That feeling is normal," says Dr. Archibald Hart. "To feel that is not a problem. To take it further than that feeling is a problem. Put those thoughts out of your mind. If you are afraid that you might do something serious, find a friend, find someone, go to your church leader, go to counseling—talk to somebody about your feelings because you need to set up some accountability for that."

If your depression is deep or it is prolonged, we encourage you to get help. If you are considering suicide at this very moment, then call 911, or call someone who will come get you or stay with you until you can find professional help.

Do not feel ashamed about your feelings of suicide. Separation and divorce are serious crises, and sometimes you will need to see a doctor for help.

"We were under great pressure, far beyond our ability to endure, so that we despaired even of life. Indeed, in our hearts we felt the sentence of death. But this happened that we might not rely on ourselves but on God . . . He will deliver us. On him we have set our hope that he will continue to deliver us" (2 Corinthians 1:8–10).

Lord God, when I am at my lowest point, may I always call someone to help me up. Lead me to find professional Christian help for my depression. Help me to talk about my feelings to other people. Amen.

Inability to Concentrate

Depression can result in an inability to concentrate or remember things.

"I couldn't concentrate," says Dave. "I'd be driving home and I'd miss my turn. All of a sudden I'd look up, and I would be four or five blocks past where I was supposed to turn."

Marie says, "I had to remind myself how to do basic things. I remember several times when I would do things like start the coffeemaker but not put the water in. I got to the point where I left a list of instructions next to the coffeemaker."

"At work," says Rob Eagar, "I was reduced to a man who mindlessly stared at the wall all day."

Marie continues, "I remember staggering out of bed and standing there in the bathroom just staring at myself for about two or three minutes and then saying, 'Okay, turn on the taps. Pick up your toothbrush.' After I would say the instruction, I would do the thing."

Follow Marie's advice and say out loud the things you need to do. It is also a good idea to get a pad of paper and start writing things down both at home and at work.

"My child, listen to me and treasure my instructions. Tune your ears to wisdom, and concentrate on understanding. Cry out for insight and understanding" (Proverbs 2:1–3 NLT).

Lord, I will start by concentrating on You. Please give me the ability to focus on the tasks that need to get done at home and at work. Thank You for being a constant help. Amen.

Headaches, Plus

The symptoms of depression overlap each other. One symptom can be the direct cause or result of another. For instance, if you do not get enough sleep or if your eating habits are erratic, you could suffer from severe headaches.

Rose Sweet says, "Your physical health is deeply affected by divorce. When you have an open wound that you haven't healed, you are constantly tired. You have headaches, backaches, depression, crying fits, weight gain, weight loss, and other physical problems that make it even worse." Fatigue, chest pain, abdominal pain, migraines, and heart palpitations are other common disturbances for people in separation or divorce.

Take a moment to think about the symptoms of depression in your life. The first step in dealing with any type of problem is to recognize what that problem is. Once you have recognized the symptoms of your depression, focus on overcoming the symptoms you have more control over; for instance, poor eating habits. Eating right will help you to sleep, which, in turn, will keep you from having headaches or stomachaches. Eliminating stressors one at a time will help control your depression.

The writer of this psalm was afflicted by multiple problems. Pray this prayer with the psalmist as he turned to God with hope:

"Turn to me and be gracious to me, for I am lonely and afflicted. The troubles of my heart have multiplied; free me from my anguish . . . Guard my life and rescue me; let me not be put to shame, for I take refuge in you. May integrity and uprightness protect me, because my hope is in you" (Psalm 25:16–17, 20–21). Amen.

Spiritual Life Affected

In your depression, you may feel far from God. Although your inner spirit longs for God, your emotions can pull you in the opposite direction. Perhaps you feel it is useless to pray, that God isn't near, or that your depression indicates a lack of faith. Untrue!

"Depression does not define your state of faith," says Bonnie Keen. "My doctor had to talk to me about that quite a bit. I thought if I just had enough faith in God, I wouldn't be depressed. He said that if you're in a depression and you need to get help, it does not mean that you're not a person of faith. It means for this season of time, however short or long it is, you might need help physically. You might need to get a doctor to help you get through that time. I did."

Right now your spiritual life is being affected by the divorce, and things are confusing and hard. Your relationship with God, though, is not based on feelings. It is based on truth. Cling to the truth during this season of depression, and know that God is with you and that your prayers are always heard.

"If you have faith as small as a mustard seed, you can say to this mountain, 'Move from here to there' and it will move. Nothing will be impossible for you" (Matthew 17:20).

Lord God, help me to pray even when I don't feel like it. My spirit longs to be in fellowship with Your Spirit. I do not want my emotions to dictate my spirituality. Amen.

Is Depression a Sin?

"God is in the process of helping me be a little easier on myself," says Marie, "and accepting things I once thought were negatives, like depression. It's okay to be depressed. How can you not be depressed? You sustained a major hit emotionally. Depression is not necessarily a bad thing. It's a symptom. To me it represented a signal to take an honest look at what I was going through, to feel all of the feelings, and to look at the issues."

Some people think depression is a sin.

"Depression itself is not a sin," explains Dr. Archibald Hart. "Depression is a natural response to loss. Your behavior may be sinful, but the depression is never sinful."

In the Bible, the prophet Elijah felt so depressed at one point that he wanted to end his life. "[Elijah] came to a broom tree, sat down under it and prayed that he might die. 'I have had enough, LORD,' he said. 'Take my life; I am no better than my ancestors.' Then he lay down under the tree and fell asleep" (1 Kings 19:4–5). But God had other plans for Elijah. God first cared for Elijah's physical needs and then directed Elijah along a new path for his life.

Jesus was the perfect man (without sin), yet Jesus, too, felt depressed at times.

"Then Jesus went with them to a place called Gethsemane, and He told His disciples, Sit down here while I go over yonder and pray. And taking with Him Peter and the two sons of Zebedee, He began to show grief and distress of mind and was deeply depressed. Then He said to them, My soul is very sad and deeply grieved, so that I am almost dying of sorrow" (Matthew 26:36–38 AMP).

Jesus, You know my sorrow and grief. Forgive me for condemning myself and thinking I am doing something wrong. Amen.

Dealing with Depression: Identify the Loss

Let's look at some positive steps you can take to deal with your depression. The first step is to identify your losses.

"The divorce represents many, many losses," says Dr. Archibald Hart, "so you've got to try to identify the most significant loss first. Deal with that, then move to the next significant loss. You may find that you've got quite a bit of work to do as you cycle through the various losses, but you have to identify the loss because you cannot grieve a loss that you don't know."

Beyond the loss of a spouse, you have to grieve many other significant losses. Perhaps you were forced to move from your home. Your ex-spouse may have gained custody of your children. Friends you had as a couple may pull back from you. Perhaps you haven't balanced a checkbook for years because your former spouse took care of finances; this, too, is a loss. You might not know how to cook meals or shop for a good vehicle since you lost the person who normally handled these things for you. Your list of losses can go on and on.

If you do not know what you are depressed about, then you cannot expect to get over it. It may help to write down each specific loss. Have a list that you can add to and subtract from as needed. Over the next three days we will discuss what to do with the losses you have identified today.

"I will never forget this awful time, as I grieve over my loss" (Lamentations 3:20 NLT).

Holy God, help me to identify my losses so I can grieve each one. Amen.

Dealing with Depression: Accept the Loss

"I'm a fixer; I'm a problem solver," says Cathy. "That's what I do for a living—solve people's problems. Now, for the first time in my life, something had come up that I couldn't handle. There was no way I could fix it."

You are not going to "fix" what you lost. Neither will you "solve" your depression. Instead, you must accept it.

Dr. Archibald Hart says, "You have to move toward accepting the loss. Many people perpetuate their depression because they won't let go of a loss. The purpose of depression is to bring you to the place of letting go. In order to get to the place of letting go, you have to come to accept the reality of the loss."

Go down your list of losses. Say these words out loud for each loss, "I have lost this. I accept that this is no longer a reality for my life." Accept that you have lost each one. Every day you may need to pray that God will show you a new loss that you had not thought of before. Be thorough in your grieving, and be sure to face one loss at a time, taking as much time as you need for each loss. Some losses will be more difficult to accept than others.

"I cry out, 'My splendor is gone! Everything I had hoped for from the LORD is lost!'" (Lamentations 3:18 NLT).

Lord, my hope is now in You. You are the faithful and loving God. In You, I will find everything I need. Fill me, Lord. Amen.

Dealing with Depression:
Put the Loss in Perspective

After you have identified and accepted a loss, you must then put the loss in perspective. Seek to understand how your losses fit into the whole scheme of life. This will help you to let them go.

After Job experienced deep suffering and severe losses, he finally realized that God is supreme and His ways are perfect. Job said to God: "I know that you can do all things; no plan of yours can be thwarted. You asked, 'Who is this that obscures my counsel without knowledge?' Surely I spoke of things I did not understand, things too wonderful for me to know" (Job 42:2–3).

Dr. Archibald Hart says, "This is where I think Christian believers have the edge when it comes to dealing with depression because God gives us a framework in which we can put all our losses. The apostle Paul writes in Philippians about counting all things as loss for the excellency of knowing Christ Jesus my Lord."

When you are able to look at a loss from the perspective of Christ, you will begin to experience the release of that loss.

"I consider everything a loss compared to the surpassing greatness of knowing Christ Jesus my Lord, for whose sake I have lost all things. I consider them rubbish, that I may gain Christ . . . I want to know Christ and the power of his resurrection and the fellowship of sharing in his sufferings, becoming like him in his death, and so, somehow, to attain to the resurrection from the dead" (Philippians 3:8, 10–11).

Lord Jesus, I want to know You more. Give me Your perspective on my losses so I can experience the greatness that Paul spoke of. Amen.

Dealing with Depression: Learn from the Depression

Your depression will begin to lift as you release your losses, but there is a final step in dealing with depression:

"You should never go through a depression without learning from it," says Dr. Archibald Hart. "Depressions tell you something about yourself, like a mirror to the inner values that you hold. By appropriately pausing at the end of the process to learn what you can about yourself, this is where the healing comes about in depression. You should be a better person after the depression than you were before."

The Bible says that sorrow is better than laughter. Why would that be true? Because when you are hurting and in distress, you are more apt to examine your heart and your motivations. You know your spirit is grieving, and you have the opportunity to deal with the root cause of the pain. It is far better to grieve and learn than to be happy but a fool. What have you learned from your depression and grief that you can use to reinvest in a better future? What wisdom have you gained?

"Sorrow is better than laughter, for sadness has a refining influence on us. A wise person thinks much about death, while the fool thinks only about having a good time" (Ecclesiastes 7:3–4 NLT).

Lord, what can I learn in my depression? What can I learn about myself, others, and You that will result in a fuller life for me? Teach me, Holy Spirit. Amen.

Develop a Strategy

By having a plan, you will find it easier to overcome depression.

Dr. Archibald Hart says, "You need to have a strategy for coping. You need to understand what you're doing and why you're doing it. You know, for example, that you don't have the energy to do things, yet there are things that have to be done. There are kids who need to be taken care of or a job you have to go to, so you need a strategy for dealing with that. Write it down. Take a notebook and write (1) wash dishes or wash clothes, (2) [next task]. Your memory is impaired, so you can't rely on memory."

Dr. Hart says that if you do not have a strategy in place, you will likely add to your own confusion and stress.

In the Bible, when Elijah was depressed, God gave him a strategy to deal with it. God's first instructions were, "Get up and eat." First things first. You have to take care of the basics in your life. Then you can formulate a plan to move forward from there.

"An angel touched him and told him, 'Get up and eat!' He looked around and saw some bread baked on hot stones and a jar of water! So he ate and drank and lay down again. Then the angel of the Lord came again and touched him and said, 'Get up and eat some more, for there is a long journey ahead of you.' So he got up and ate and drank, and the food gave him . . . strength" (1 Kings 19:5–8 NLT).

Strong Lord, I need a plan, and I probably need to write it down! With a strategy in place, I will be able to tackle my responsibilities. Thanks for Your help, Lord. Amen.

Accept Yourself As You Are

One step in managing your depression is to accept yourself as you are and to accept God's love.

"If you have thought of yourself solely as a wife or husband, and you lose that," says Dr. Linda Mintle, "sometimes you don't even know who you are. You have to learn that you are more than just a relationship . . . and you must ultimately define yourself in Christ. He delights in you; He has created you in a good way; His gifts are in you."

Marie shares, "I didn't feel so miserable. I didn't feel so lonely. I didn't feel ugly or worthless anymore. God had reminded me: 'I made you. I love you. My love for you doesn't have anything to do with your husband. I love you regardless of what has happened. Let me be your God.'"

Jeremiah 31:3 says that "The LORD appeared to us . . . saying: 'I have loved you with an everlasting love; I have drawn you with loving-kindness.'"

You don't need to clean yourself up to have a relationship with God. When Jesus came to earth, He spent His time loving, caring for, teaching, and healing those who were sick and hurting—physically, spiritually, and emotionally. He isn't looking for people who "have it all together" or who appear good and holy on the outside. He is looking for people who realize they cannot face life without Him. He wants you to come to Him just the way you are.

"Jesus said to them, 'It is not the healthy who need a doctor, but the sick. I have not come to call the righteous, but sinners'" (Mark 2:17).

Thank You, Lord, that You have chosen me to be Your special child; that You have created me to be valuable, lovely, and talented in my own way; that You love me with an everlasting love. Amen.

Catch Negative Thoughts

Another important suggestion in overcoming depression is to catch your negative thoughts as they occur.

"Much of depression is fed, fueled, and maintained by excessive negative thinking: *I don't think I can do this. I don't think this is going to work,*" says Dr. Archibald Hart. "You need to challenge those negative thoughts because they keep the depression going. In fact, they don't just keep it going, they make it worse."

Second Corinthians 10:4–5 says: "We demolish arguments and every pretension that sets itself up against the knowledge of God, and we take captive every thought to make it obedient to Christ."

With every negative thought that comes into your head, practice that exercise. Picture yourself capturing the negative thought in your hands and demolishing it before you even have a chance to think about it. After you demolish it, picture yourself handing it quickly over to God. Then replace the negative thought with a positive one. Repeat this exercise as often as necessary. Make it a habit to catch those bad thoughts.

"Summing it all up, friends, I'd say you'll do best by filling your minds and meditating on things true, noble, reputable, authentic, compelling, gracious—the best, not the worst; the beautiful, not the ugly; things to praise, not things to curse" (Philippians 4:8 MSG).

Lord Jesus, I give You my negative thoughts right now. Please replace those thoughts with good ones. Help me to focus on the blessings You have given me. Amen.

Eliminate Untrue Beliefs

"I remember feeling very ugly, unlovable, undesirable as a woman, unsuccessful, a total washout as a human being, and a complete failure," admits Marie.

Dr. Archibald Hart suggests that you identify your underlying beliefs about yourself and eliminate the ones that are not true.

"Beneath many of your depressions is a belief," says Dr. Hart. "You may be thinking, *Because I am divorced, I am not a worthwhile person. Because I am divorced, no one's really going to care for me or love me or respect me. Because I'm divorced, I'm a failure, and if I have one failure in my life, then my whole life is a failure.* These are called irrational beliefs. They have no basis in reality, and they need to be challenged because if you don't challenge and deal with them, you will feed your depression by these faulty beliefs."

In the Bible, Satan is referred to as the "father of lies." He will whisper lies to you, hoping that you will begin to believe them. John 8:44 says: "[The devil] was a murderer from the beginning, not holding to the truth, for there is no truth in him. When he lies, he speaks his native language, for he is a liar and the father of lies."

You are a worthwhile, lovable, successful person because God created you in His perfect image. Live your life based on the truth of God's Word.

"So God created man in his own image, in the image of God he created him; male and female he created them" (Genesis 1:27).

Lord, open my ears to hear the wonderful, comforting truth about myself, not Satan's lies. Amen.

Live Within Limitations

Another help in dealing with depression is not to live beyond your physical, emotional, and spiritual limitations.

"It was hard to find limitations," says Bonnie Keen. "I thought that as a person of faith, I couldn't have any limitations. I had to be able to live with anything and everything. Finally, I hit a wall where I realized, *I can't do this.* I remember saying to the Lord, 'I can't live like this anymore. I'm going to have to make choices, and please forgive me if they are the wrong ones.'"

"You can only do so much," says Dr. Jim A. Talley. "Your energy level is down. Your mental capacity is down. Your physical level is down. You have to lower your expectations of what you personally are able to do."

Mike Klumpp shares that men sometimes feel they should be able to handle anything that comes their way: "Men need to realize that they make mistakes like everyone else. They have good days and bad days. They have limitations like everyone else. Being a real man means coming to grips with reality and the responsibilities that come with your reality."

Be willing to set limits in your daily life. Sometimes you need to draw those boundaries right away as new circumstances occur. There are some things you cannot do on your own right now, some things you are physically unable to handle. Living within your own established boundaries will free you to be able to handle other things in your life without becoming overtaxed and overwhelmed.

"Now I take limitations in stride, and with good cheer . . . I just let Christ take over!" (2 Corinthians 12:10 MSG).

Father, teach me to set limits so that I can better handle the things in my life. I give my worries to You. Amen.

Step Over Your Feelings

Sometimes in depression, you need to step over your feelings. When new circumstances arise that cause you to feel bad, you might need to let the new bad feeling go. You don't need to add fuel to every negative feeling that shows itself. Set that feeling aside, and immediately step over the top of it to get beyond it.

Dr. Archibald Hart gives an example of a situation that may arise and cause you to feel bad: "You are divorced and have limited resources. Your child comes to you and says he would like a new jacket. All the other kids have new jackets. You know you can't give your child a new jacket, so you feel guilty. You feel guilty because you have to say no.

"Your child walks away from you. He may be momentarily disappointed, but otherwise he's happy. He's not going to complain about it; he understands the situation. Yet you feel like you are a terrible person. You have to step over that feeling. You can't let that feeling determine what you do. There are times in depression, whether it is guilt or sometimes sadness itself, when you have to say to yourself, 'I'm just going to ignore that feeling.'"

Every new development in your life does not need to add to your negativism or depression. Set limits. Be willing to stay within the limits physically and emotionally.

"Direct my footsteps according to your word; let no sin rule over me" (Psalm 119:133).

Lord, things are different now, and I need to learn from my frustrations, not add to them. Help me in this. Amen.

Relax

"Come to me, all you who are weary and burdened, and I will give you rest. Take my yoke upon you and learn from me, for I am gentle and humble in heart, and you will find rest for your souls. For my yoke is easy and my burden is light" (Matthew 11:28–30).

Here's an important suggestion for dealing with depression: Learn to relax.

"Relaxation is the antidote for so many things, particularly stress," says Dr. Archibald Hart. "Depression is very, very stressful. Recent research has shown that 50 percent of people who are depressed have enlarged adrenal glands, which means that their bodies are responding with a lot of adrenaline as if it were a real emergency. Relaxation can help to lower that stress. If your stress level is lower, you can cope better. If you can cope better, you can handle your depressions better and get over them sooner and bring the healing that God has in mind for you."

Here are some steps to help you relax.

- Approach God first.
- Breathe deeply—in through your nose and out through your mouth.
- Read the Bible out loud, slowly. Focus only on the words you are saying.
- Go back and read the same passage again.
- Imagine your burdens are actual weights on the surface of your body. Gently shake them off.
- Pray that God's Spirit will fill you and surround you with peace and strength.

"The eternal God is your refuge, and underneath are the everlasting arms" (Deuteronomy 33:27).

Eternal Father, teach me to relax today. I will imagine Your strong, loving arms holding me steady so I can rest. Amen.

Get Moving

"You need to recognize that God created you for a purpose," says Dr. Robert Abarno. "Get up out of bed. Start to function. Function is essential to dealing with depression. You can get up out of bed. You can move around. You can make contact. You can talk to your pastor or someone else in the church. You can go to a Christian counselor."

Here is a suggestion from Dr. Archibald Hart: "Set up a contract with someone to whom you can be accountable. Find a friend who will agree to call you at 6:30 in the morning to remind you 'It's time to get going.'

"If you can keep up the exercise, keep your physical activity up, keep your involvement going, you can get over the depression much more effectively. Having a friend whom you can be accountable to can help."

It's time to function again. You can do it. With God's help, you will do just fine.

"Just thinking of my troubles and my lonely wandering makes me miserable. That's all I ever think about, and I am depressed. Then I remember something that fills me with hope. The LORD's kindness never fails! If he had not been merciful, we would have been destroyed. The LORD can always be trusted to show mercy each morning. Deep in my heart I say, 'The LORD is all I need; I can depend on him!'" (Lamentations 3:19–24 CEV).

Lord God, Your kindness never fails. I trust that You will be with me and have mercy on me every morning. I will depend on You from now on. Amen.

What Role Does Jesus Have in Your Healing?

"It's only through Jesus that we truly can be healed of the hurt, and it's only through His Word that we can be enabled to go on," says Priscilla.

Bonnie Keen says, "I didn't know God could go that deep into the darkness. I knew that I could praise Him in the light. I began to praise Him in the dark. In many ways, my depression further cemented the grace of Christ into my heart and the understanding of our human condition and the understanding of how bad pain can beat us up. I felt that Christ kept saying, 'This is why I came. I came for those moments you need to know more than ever how loved you are.'"

Roy explains, "What Satan meant for evil, God will turn to good in your life and in the lives of others around you as you come to understand and know God through His Son, Jesus Christ. Until you experience the grace of Christ, you're not going to give yourself grace, and it is going to be hard to extend grace to other people. Yet it's that grace that brings healing."

Our human nature is based in sin, sorrow, and death. But Christ came to earth to save us from that darkness. He brought abundant life into the world, which is available to all people through Him. God's gift of grace is free to all who desire a personal relationship with Him. He accepts you just as you are. Come to Him with a sincere heart.

"For it is by grace you have been saved, through faith—and this not from yourselves, it is the gift of God" (Ephesians 2:8).

Thank You, Jesus, for Your free gift of grace. You love me more than I can comprehend. Teach me to walk with a full assurance of Your love. Amen.

More Suggestions for Overcoming Depression

Here are some practical suggestions from people who have experienced divorce and from Christian professionals:

Dr. Archibald Hart says, "Support groups help to hold you accountable. They don't feed your self-pity. They force you to face reality. They provide a place where you can share what you're feeling without having to put on a false mask."

Cindy shares, "I started exercising a lot. Taking care of myself really helped."

Joyce says, "I would put on a praise and worship tape. The Lord used that music to soothe the pain."

Rob Eagar says it helped him to get out and see friends, travel, and go to sporting events.

"You need a good diet," says Dr. Archibald Hart. "Eat right. Avoid junk food, sugars, and caffeine; they can play havoc with your emotions."

Cindy says, "I started volunteering in the schools. I got outside of myself, and that really helped. I volunteer for a rape crisis center, teaching children about personal safety."

"Turn to the Lord," advises Dr. Robert Abarno. "Ask the Lord to forgive you. Be honest with the Lord. Spend time in prayer, in Bible study, and worship. Spend time with a prayer partner and with other Christians."

"If you follow this advice, and if God directs you to do so, then you will be able to endure the pressures" (Exodus 18:23 NLT).

Lord God, what shall I do to relieve my depression? Thank You for the advice of people who have been here before. Amen.

Fewer Periods of Depression

"How long must I wrestle with my thoughts and every day have sorrow in my heart? How long will my enemy triumph over me?" (Psalm 13:2).

You probably cried out, at one point, the same question as the psalmist above, feeling that your depression would never end. But as time has been moving along, perhaps now your depression is lessening, and a sense of normalcy is returning to your life.

When Nancy began attending a divorce recovery support group, her new friends noticed that she never smiled and never showed any emotions. Nancy says, "I was just cold. I was dead inside."

As time moved on, Nancy began to realize that she, too, was moving forward through her depression. She says, "I can remember sitting in a meeting one night and finally laughing. Somebody said to me, 'Wow, you have teeth.' I hadn't smiled for so long."

Mike Klumpp offers a suggestion to help you move out of depression one moment at a time: "I had a game I used to play with myself. In the midst of my depression, when I was down and out about my marriage and my situation, I would look for a pretty color. Then I would focus on that color and enjoy it. In every moment, there is something simple that you can enjoy."

"Don't be dejected and sad, for the joy of the LORD is your strength!" (Nehemiah 8:10 NLT).

Faithful Lord, I have been depressed and in sorrow for a long time. Thank You for giving me glimpses of hope and light in my life again. Amen.

Facing Your Loneliness

The Ache of Loneliness

You are home alone, and you long for companionship. You are out with friends, surrounded by people who love you, yet you ache with loneliness. This emotion is deep, and it is difficult for other people to understand. Sometimes people in your church may not understand because they see that you are surrounded by a loving church family. While it is crucial to let yourself be loved by church and family members, the loss of a spouse brings a loneliness that can be healed only through a love relationship with Jesus Christ.

"There were times," says Cheryl, "especially in the evening after I put my children down to bed, when I was home by myself, and I remember sitting on my sofa just wishing that someone was there to put his arms around me and just to hold me and to love me. And I thought, *This is the way it's always going to be.*"

Danny shares: "I was so lonely. The house was so quiet after my wife left with the children. It's amazing how the quietness can be so loud. I didn't want to be in that house."

During the next few weeks, you will learn that there are complex reasons behind loneliness. You will look at some effective ways to deal with your loneliness as well as mistakes to avoid when you're feeling lonely.

"And now how lonely—bereft, abandoned! The once famous city, the once happy city" (Jeremiah 49:25 MSG).

Lord God, it is hard to understand why I feel lonely when I know there are people who love me, but I do. I feel empty and alone. Help me, Jesus. Amen.

When You Feel Isolated

Both physical and emotional isolation contribute to loneliness.

Dr. Les Carter says, "People often think of a lonely person as someone in a dark room staring off into the corner somewhere. Sure enough, that would represent loneliness, but it's much more than that. The easiest way to identify a person who is struggling with loneliness is to listen for that one phrase, 'Nobody seems to understand.' When a person is feeling that emotion of loneliness, there is a feeling of isolation and a sense of separateness in his or her relationships. It's as though there is a huge gap between that person and others, and they can't seem to find a way to cross it."

Marie shares, "I shut myself off from people. I stopped answering my phone. I created my loneliness. It wasn't that I didn't have friends but that I didn't want people around. I didn't know how to be a friend at that moment because I just couldn't handle other human beings; I didn't want them around. I needed them, though—finally figured that out."

Your physical isolation may be by choice, but it is contributing to deeper problems of loneliness. In order to fill the gap you feel between you and other people, you have to get out and interact with them. You will still feel lonely, but that gap will eventually close if you persevere.

"I am like an owl in the desert, like a lonely owl in a far-off wilderness. I lie awake, lonely as a solitary bird on the roof" (Psalm 102:6–7 NLT).

Strong Father, please give me the strength and the will to go out and spend time with other people and to try to bridge the gap. I'm so tired of being alone. Amen.

When You Don't Feel Valued

If you do not feel valued, you will have feelings of loneliness. Knowing you are important to people strengthens you and strengthens the ties you have with them. We encourage you to find your value in Christ first, and He will show you your worth through the godly love of other people.

"It's only when you learn who you are in Christ," says Lauren, "the total acceptance the Lord has of you, the unconditional love He gives to you, and what you are worth to Him, that you fully realize what a valued person you are. You can't get that from anywhere else. You can't get that from your mate."

Read the Bible to learn how much God loves you and what His purpose is for your life.

Bonnie Keen says, "I didn't always feel like He loved me. I didn't always feel like I was somebody who was going to succeed again and have two strong legs to stand on. But the Bible told me who I was. If I kept going back there for my definition of who I was, that could be counted on. It was a choice I made. I didn't feel it emotionally all the time."

Any demeaning thoughts you have had about yourself need to be given to Christ. He will dispose of your harmful thoughts as you embrace the new life He has for you.

"Therefore, if anyone is in Christ, he is a new creation; the old has gone, the new has come!" (2 Corinthians 5:17).

Jesus, my identity, my purpose, and my value are in You. I am a new creation. Help me to live like one. Amen.

When You Feel Rejected

"I had absolutely no idea what loneliness was until I found out my husband was having an affair," says Harriet. "For two months I lived with the knowledge that my husband, the person I had loved and trusted more than anyone in the world, had betrayed me.

"I knew for the first time what loneliness was, true loneliness, and why there's a difference between loneliness and being alone. I could be in a room full of people, and loneliness was there. Loneliness was my constant companion."

Not only do you feel separated from people, you also feel a sense of rejection from them. When you're rejected by someone whose opinion truly matters to you, such as your spouse, you can mistakenly feel that you are a "reject."

"I felt like I had a big 'D' on my forehead," says Sherry. "Everywhere I went, I felt like everybody was thinking, *What a loser. You couldn't make a thirty-one-year marriage work.*"

You are incredibly worthwhile and valuable in God's eyes. He does not judge you or look down on you. He has chosen you to be His special worker, and He'll strengthen you for the task, upholding you every step of the way.

"I took you from the ends of the earth, from its farthest corners I called you. I said, 'You are my servant'; I have chosen you and have not rejected you. So do not fear, for I am with you; do not be dismayed, for I am your God. I will strengthen you and help you; I will uphold you with my righteous right hand" (Isaiah 41:9–10).

"For everything God created is good, and nothing is to be rejected" (1Timothy 4:4).

Lord God, You have chosen me to be Your child. I am a person of strength and worth because of You. Amen.

Spiritual Basis of Loneliness

Mankind was created to be in a right relationship with God, but because we chose to go our own way instead of God's—thus sinning—we can no longer enjoy that right relationship except through Jesus Christ. Our souls long to be in fellowship with our Creator, but our thoughts and feelings often pull us in the opposite direction, to a more self-centered focus.

"Part of the problem of loneliness is a spiritual problem," says Dr. Les Carter. "Every one of us begins life as a sinner, and as a result we are reminded daily that we're not completely linked up with God. One of the major causes of loneliness can stem from not being connected with God the way you want to be."

James says, "One of the greatest tactics from Satan is that he wants you to doubt God, and he'll try to make you think that loneliness means God is not there for you. If he can make you doubt God's ability to take care of you, and you start reacting to the situation in your own strength, then Satan has won the battle. God is the only answer through the whole thing. If you seek to glorify God and not glorify yourself, then you'll win."

All people were created by God and for God. Our loneliness can be filled only when we are in a relationship with Him through Jesus Christ.

"So whether you eat or drink or whatever you do, do it all for the glory of God" (1 Corinthians 10:31).

Holy God, I want to build a relationship with You that will fill my lonely heart. Amen.

Couples-Oriented Society

It can be painfully obvious that this is a couples-oriented society. At restaurants, at the movies, and in the shopping malls, it seems as if everyone is with someone else. Popular songs say you can't live without that special person in your life.

Bonnie Keen says, "Everywhere I went, it looked like there were whole families intact, and I stuck out like a sore thumb."

"I couldn't stand to see happy couples," admits Sherry. "In my Sunday school class were happily married couples, and I loved all of them, but I didn't want to be with them because it hurt, and I was angry."

"We're outsiders," says Bob. "We're the third wheel or the fifth wheel. We're in a couples society, and it's an awkward situation."

The popular song lyrics are wrong. There is only one Person you need for fulfillment. That Person is Jesus Christ.

"I pray that out of his glorious riches he may strengthen you with power through his Spirit in your inner being, so that Christ may dwell in your hearts through faith. And I pray that you, being rooted and established in love, may have power, together with all the saints, to grasp how wide and long and high and deep is the love of Christ, and to know this love that surpasses knowledge—that you may be filled to the measure of all the fullness of God" (Ephesians 3:16–19).

Lord Jesus, fill me with the fullness of God. I want to walk rooted and established in Your love every day. You love me so much. Amen.

Profound Loss

When you go through divorce, you experience a profound sense of loss, and that makes the loneliness deeper.

Harriet says, "What was so bad is that I knew what it felt like to be loved, to be cherished, to not be lonely, to have a full life. All of a sudden it seemed like my life was over. I was convinced that I would never be loved again, that I would die alone. I don't ever want to feel like that again."

Danny shares, "At some of those darkest hours, I would envision Christ on the cross or envision Him going through what led up to the cross—the pain and suffering He endured. When I was able to focus on that, it made my problems seem so much smaller. At my darkest hours I would concentrate on Christ Himself. That helped me tremendously."

Your loss is real and intense, but you will make it through this. Know that Jesus Christ is the One who knows exactly how you feel. He knows how deep your hurts are, and His tears are flowing with yours. Crawl into His strong arms, and let Him love you.

"Joy is gone from our hearts; our dancing has turned to mourning" (Lamentations 5:15).

Lord Jesus, it's hard to imagine that You have felt this kind of pain and that You feel my pain. I feel so alone in this. But I know You are here for me in my darkest times, and I believe in You with all my heart. Amen.

A New Lifestyle

"What helped me get through those lonely days was knowing that God does love me, that He does have a plan for me, and that His plan is for my good," says Selma.

Your daily life is different now. You no longer have the security and comfort of your old routine and of knowing where you belong. The new lifestyle may feel awkward and uncomfortable. This contributes to your loneliness.

Warren Kniskern says, "This is a time to depend upon God like never before. Place your cares and anxieties on Him because He cares for you. He knows the struggles you're going through. Don't lose hope in terms of getting on with your life. There is life after this tragedy."

Your new lifestyle is unfortunately one that you did not choose to be in. But now that you are here, you do have a say as to how you will respond to your new circumstances. Every moment, you are faced with the choice of how you will act and react to the thoughts in your mind and to the situations that occur.

Anyone who has a relationship with Jesus Christ has available to him or her the wisdom and the strength to make right choices through the Holy Spirit.

"Therefore, brothers, we have an obligation—but it is not to the sinful nature, to live according to it. For if you live according to the sinful nature, you will die; but if by the Spirit you put to death the misdeeds of the body, you will live, because those who are led by the Spirit of God are sons of God" (Romans 8:12–14).

Holy Spirit, lead me forward in this new lifestyle. Every day I have a choice. Help me to always choose to respond in ways that please You. Amen.

Family and Friends Pull Back

When a person is going through a divorce, family and friends often don't know what to say or how to interact, so they tend to pull back. This can contribute to your loneliness.

Dr. Les Carter says, "Sometimes families and even churches may be prone to shooting their own wounded. They just don't know what to do with you. They don't know what they should say, so the best thing they know to do is pretend like you don't exist."

James shares, "Friends that I had didn't know how to handle it. Anytime I was around them, I was either crying or upset, so it was tough on them too."

Your friends and family may sincerely desire to help you, but they often do not have the right advice or experience to offer you true comfort. Do not blame them for their inadequacies. You could help them by explaining how they could help you. People feel more comfortable when they know where they stand and what they can do.

During times of hurt and perceived rejection from others, you have a choice to make about those relationships, and we encourage you to choose to build and not break down friendships during this difficult time.

"Though my father and mother forsake me, the LORD will receive me" (Psalm 27:10).

Lord of Love, You never pull away from me no matter what I say or do. Thank You. Amen.

Consequences of Loneliness

Anger and bitterness are consequences of loneliness. The longer you are lonely and the longer you separate yourself emotionally from other people, the greater the chance for negative emotions to build up inside you.

"Life was very empty-feeling, very lonely," says Kim. "I had a sense of being lost, not being a part of something, and it was difficult. I was angry. I was bitter. It was building up inside of me."

Joanne says, "My ex-husband and I had to face each other every day. We worked together. We owned a business together. It was in front of me day after day, and the anger I felt had to be controlled, which I'm not real good at doing."

Take action to remedy your loneliness before the anger, bitterness, and other negative emotions become overwhelming.

Angie feels her loneliness most deeply at the end of the day, and she turns to God through Bible reading and prayer for healing and relief. "I deal with my loneliness by turning to God because He's there," says Angie. "He would never leave me or forsake me. He's my friend. He's my Father."

Another suggestion is to attend a Christ-centered divorce recovery support group, such as DivorceCare®. This group will teach you how to grow closer to God in your pain and will help you learn His purpose for your life. It will also provide you with a network of friends who will help you sort through your emotions and identify your needs.

"A sound mind makes for a robust body, but runaway emotions corrode the bones" (Proverbs 14:30 MSG).

Faithful God, I pray for wisdom to face my loneliness. Please keep my other emotions from building to an unhealthy level. Amen.

Depression and Futility

Loneliness can lead to depression and to the sense that everything is futile, so why bother.

Harriet shares: "I would go to bed and curl up into a ball and burrow down under the covers. I felt like I was just a speck in this deep blackness, almost like when you look up and you see a little star in the dark heavens at night, cold and alone.

"Some people thought I was dying. They told me months later that they thought I had a terminal disease because I rarely spoke and I'd lost so much weight. The loneliness was showing up on my face and in my demeanor. I had once been a confident, fun-filled, always-finding-something-to-laugh-about kind of person. All of a sudden, I felt like a woman who was ninety years old and would be alone forever. I saw no hope."

You, too, may be so lonely and depressed that you are barely going through the motions of living. Remember that God created you for a purpose, and He fully equipped you to fulfill that purpose. Your life has meaning and worth. God made you to be exactly who you are. You are so special to Him.

Make the effort to get out and interact with family and friends. Join a church group or Bible study. Learn God's plan for your new life. Harriet says, "Once I reached the point where I began to let people close to me know what was going on in my life, the loneliness began to dissipate, but it took months."

"For we are God's workmanship, created in Christ Jesus to do good works, which God prepared in advance for us to do" (Ephesians 2:10).

Lord God, I want to have hope. Please give me hope in You. Amen.

Promiscuity

Another consequence of loneliness is promiscuity.

"Whenever you get caught up in promiscuity or get into the party scene, then typically it implies that there is an emptiness, a desire to connect with other individuals," explains Dr. Les Carter. "You may be willing to go whatever route it takes to fill the emptiness. By not dealing well with loneliness, you can have many other consequences."

Greg says, "I was really vulnerable during this time, and whenever a woman paid attention to me, there was that draw and attraction. With all the loneliness I was feeling, any kind of comfort I got from a female made me want to get into a relationship with her or become physical with her. I knew that wasn't where I needed to be." Greg found that the best solution was to focus on developing same-sex friendships and to turn his attention to the Lord and focus on Him.

You do not want to turn to sex or to new relationships with the opposite sex to ease your loneliness. Only God can fill the emptiness you're experiencing. You always have a choice as to how you are going to live each moment of every day. Choose God. Choose to live for Him.

Be careful that you don't react to your feelings or to new situations by seeking any kind of comfort, but that you think first. Prayerfully consider your actions today and how those actions will positively or negatively affect your life tomorrow, next month, or five years from now.

God says, "You will seek me and find me when you seek me with all your heart" (Jeremiah 29:13).

Dear God, I want to put all my heart into a relationship with You. Deliver me from sexual temptation. Amen.

Feeling Out of Fellowship with God

A lonely person can feel out of fellowship with God. In separation and divorce, your love relationship with your former mate has broken, and you may wonder if your relationship with God is still intact.

"Human relationships ideally are meant to be pictures of godly love," says Dr. Les Carter. "When a husband and wife share real, solid love, it's not difficult at that point to know what God's love is like and to feel a sense of richness in the Lord."

Without a loving marriage as a model, you might become confused about where you stand with God.

"I felt so hopeless and alone," says Ginny. "Even though I knew God was with me, I couldn't feel Him."

God is with you, and He will always be with you and will love you with a perfect love. Cheryl says, "I remember there came a time in my life when I realized that God was always going to be there for me and that I might be lonely at times, but I was never going to be alone. Once I realized that, I was able to go forward and not worry about being alone anymore."

The Bible says: "For none of us lives to himself alone and none of us dies to himself alone. If we live, we live to the Lord; and if we die, we die to the Lord. So, whether we live or die, we belong to the Lord" (Romans 14:7–8).

Lord and Savior, You are always by my side. You always uphold me and keep me steady. Thank You for Your promise to never leave me. Amen.

Guilt

"Loneliness rarely occurs when everything is going just right," says Dr. Les Carter. "When you go through experiences of loneliness, invariably you're going to begin looking inward, thinking, *Did I do something to set this up? Should I have acted differently? Is there something wrong with me?* Questions like that can crop up, and the result of this self-doubt can be guilt."

Recognize your feelings of guilt as by-products of loneliness. Bring those harmful feelings and questions to God. He will take your burden. Trust Him in this.

"When I was first divorced," says Elsa Kok, "I was feeling broken, worthless, and disappointed in myself. People would say, 'Elsa, God loves you.' And I would say, 'Whatever.' I didn't buy it. Not at all.

"Moving away from that attitude is a process. Be assured that God does not despise broken people. He knows you're broken. He knows you're going to make wrong choices. What delights Him is when you come to Him with your hurts and poor choices because He can do something about them.

"When you come to Him, He thinks, *I'm so happy to see you. You are an amazing child of Mine. I have handcrafted you. I have given you gifts you haven't even begun to explore yet. I have a hope and a future for you. You'll be so glad you came to Me. This will be a choice you will never regret.*"

God is never ashamed of you. He loves you and wants to relieve you of your heavy load.

"Praise be to the Lord, to God our Savior, who daily bears our burdens" (Psalm 68:19).

Father God, I can't believe You find me so delightful! But I love it that You do. Please take my questions, my worries, and my guilty feelings. Amen.

Lack of Self-Esteem

Loneliness can lead to a lack of self-esteem. When you lose the feeling of value that you received from your marriage, you might begin to second-guess your worth as a person. Don't let feelings of worthlessness take root. They are complete lies. You are so valuable as a person.

Rob Eagar shares what he learned about loneliness and low self-worth. He says, "Probably the best advice I received was that my self-esteem is not based on how other people view me. If someone rejects me, sure the pain is real and it hurts, but my true self-esteem is based on how God views me. God sees me as a lovable, wonderful person who is so valuable to Him that I was worth dying for. That is why His Son Jesus Christ came to earth and died on the cross. I can still get up and walk out and hold my head high because if the God of the Universe loves me and says I am valuable, then His opinion is all that really matters."

Yes, God's opinion is the only one that truly matters in the whole scheme of life.

"You are precious and honored in my sight, and . . . I love you . . . Do not be afraid, for I am with you" (Isaiah 43:4–5).

Holy God, when You look at me, You are filled with love for me and thoughts of how precious I am. I am truly worthwhile. Thank You. Amen.

Rebound Relationships

One of the most serious consequences of the loneliness that comes from separation or divorce is the tendency to enter new, opposite-sex relationships too quickly. These relationships, often called rebound relationships, can cause a tremendous amount of pain in your life.

"The illusion that getting another person will make you happy is a very devastating illusion because it wasn't true the first time, and there's no reason for it to be true a second time," says Gary Richmond.

Lee shares, "I was extremely vulnerable, and I was not as in control of my emotions as I thought because the new relationship was so comfortable. It really was an escape. I realized later that there was so much more healing to do. When someone comes along and is attracted to you and you're attracted to that person, you have to be aware that this is not the time for that."

Dr. Les Carter says, "Many times folks ask, 'Is there a particular period of time that I should wait before I get into other relationships?' Time isn't really the major factor. Rather, it's knowing yourself and your motivations, and knowing who you are and why you want a new relationship."

"I have learned to be content whatever the circumstances. I know what it is to be in need, and I know what it is to have plenty. I have learned the secret of being content in any and every situation, whether well fed or hungry, whether living in plenty or in want. I can do everything through him who gives me strength" (Philippians 4:11–13).

Lord Jesus, teach me to be content in my singleness.
Amen.

Learn to Be Single

You may feel a deep need for a mate, a partner, a companion to ease your loneliness. Be patient; now is not the time. First, you must learn to be single.

"You don't solve loneliness by getting married," says Dr. Myles Munroe. "Some of the loneliest people in the world are married people. Nothing is worse than being lonely in a marriage because you're trapped."

Dr. Munroe says God designed people to be single. He explains, "People walk around with a tremendous misconception of what it means to be single. Singleness, in its basic definition, means to be separate, unique, and whole. To be single means you are separate from everyone else, and you are unique in yourself—which means you recognize there's no one like you, and you have worth within yourself. To be single also means you are whole; you don't depend on other people to make you somebody. Until a person is completely single in these three areas, his or her relationships will always be a problem."

Have you come to the point where you know you are separate, unique, and whole as a person? After you consider each of these three areas in your life, think about the longings and worries you have and the emotions you sometimes struggle with. Learn to recognize areas of your life that need work, and avoid new relationships with the opposite sex until you are completely single. God has a purpose for you in your singleness—don't miss it!

"For everything, absolutely everything, above and below, visible and invisible, . . . everything got started in him and finds its purpose in him" (Colossians 1:16 MSG).

Holy God, You have created me for a purpose that only I can fulfill. I am unique, special, worthwhile, and whole in You. Amen.

Single vs. Alone

Dr. Myles Munroe says not only do people misunderstand what it means to be single, but they also misunderstand what it means to be alone. These words are not synonymous. Let's look at what being alone means.

"In Genesis 2:18 God says to this man, 'It's not good for man to be alone,'" states Dr. Munroe. "God never said it's not good for man to be single. You must understand that singleness is not a problem to God. As a matter of fact, God encourages singleness. He wants you to become unique, separate, and whole.

"'Alone' is what God saw as the problem. The word literally means isolated. God was saying He doesn't want a person to be isolated in him or herself.

"Loneliness is a terrible thing; it's a disease; it's a product of a poor self-concept. It's a product of people who don't believe that they are worth being loved or that they are important, so they feel isolated from the crowd. That is a sickness. God says He doesn't like that. He doesn't want that to happen to anybody. Aloneness is the source of that."

God does not want you to be alone, but He does want you to be single—separate, unique, and whole. Take a moment to think about where you fit in Dr. Munroe's definitions of *single* versus *alone*.

"Look at me and help me! I'm all alone and in big trouble" (Psalm 25:16 MSG).

Almighty God, teach me to be single, but never to be alone. Amen.

Develop a Relationship with God

"My struggles brought me closer to God," says B.J. "He was able to take my anger away when I gave it to Him. He was able to take the depression away. He even took the loneliness away eventually. Grow closer to God, and as you start to dwell on Him and the things of God, you forget all the things that hurt, and He will take your loneliness away."

God wants to meet you right where you are now. He is never surprised or appalled by anything you have done. He wants to ease your lonely heart today.

Dr. Robert Abarno says, "He's always available to you. He says, 'I will never leave you or forsake you.' But you have to make the decision to have a relationship with God. Nobody else can do it for you. You must say, 'I want to be saved. I repent of my sins. I ask You to forgive me of my sins and cleanse me from all unrighteousness. I accept Jesus Christ as my Lord and Savior.' That's a positive action that can result from immense pain."

Beginning or renewing a relationship with the living God is a sure cure for loneliness.

"Whoever drinks the water I give him will never thirst. Indeed, the water I give him will become in him a spring of water welling up to eternal life" (John 4:14).

We encourage you to take that positive action today, and pray the prayer that Dr. Abarno suggests:

Lord God, I want to be saved. I repent of my sins. Please forgive my sins, and cleanse me from unrighteousness. I accept Jesus as my Lord and Savior. Amen.

Link with Others

An important step in your healing from loneliness is to link up with other people who are trying to develop a deeper relationship with God. These are the people who will help you move forward in faith and in life.

"Scripture encourages us to fellowship with one another," says Sabrina D. Black. "It says to encourage one another as long as today is today. As you are spending time with people who are concerned about the things of God, they're going to encourage you in your walk with God. If you are pursuing godliness, then they're going to challenge you when your behavior is anything other than biblical. People who are concerned about godliness will be able to look at Scripture and say, 'This is a clear application. This is a clear violation.'"

Dr. Les Carter says, "I've known people who have attempted to get things right with God, and they attempt to link up with other Christians, but they don't take the next step. They don't tell anybody what's going on inside. Another component of getting beyond loneliness is to open your windows. Let people see who you are. Let folks know how you can be ministered to and, in the process, be willing to hear who they are."

In order to grow in your new relationships, you must be sure to be open with your friends, let them know how they can help you, and be willing to listen and respond to their problems as well. God wants to bless you with close, Christian friends. Ask Him today!

"As iron sharpens iron, a friend sharpens a friend" (Proverbs 27:17 NLT).

Faithful God, I want to grow closer to You. Lead me to friends who have that same desire. I know they're out there! Amen.

Same-Sex Friendships

"My female friends are absolute treasures," says Elsa Kok. "God brought some women into my life who were a lot like me. One woman I met knew a lot about God's Word, and I wanted to connect with her, so I said, 'Can I come over for coffee, and I'll bring bagels?' We connected every Thursday morning for three years, and we still meet on the phone at five-thirty every Thursday morning.

"Friendships don't just happen. You have to take the initiative. You have to work at developing the relationship, but those relationships have taught me what real relationships are about. Those friendships have equipped me in ways I could never have been equipped without them. They've taught me communication, how to work through conflict, how to support and encourage, and how to serve. It is worth the effort."

Cindy shares, "I made new friends through the DivorceCare® support group. My friends and I would have a potluck or rent a movie. It was important for me to have female friends. We had an agreement that if anyone was lonely and feeling bad, even if it was three in the morning, none of us would mind any of us calling each other."

As Cindy mentioned, a Christian divorce support recovery group is a great way to meet new friends who understand what you are going through and who need new friends too. Even if your first impression is to avoid that type of group, please give it a chance. Same-sex friendships are an excellent cure for loneliness.

"A friend is always loyal, and a brother is born to help in time of need" (Proverbs 17:17 NLT).

Healing Lord, give me the courage to attend a divorce support group and to take the initiative to make new friends. Amen.

Giving and Receiving Emotional Support

Emotionally, you have something to give. Other people in divorce situations are hurting, and they need to hear that they are not the only ones who feel devastated and helpless. Part of your emotional recovery is to realize that it is by giving away comfort—honest, deep, pain-filled comfort—that you in turn will truly be comforted.

Phil shares his experience: "One thing my friend and I would do to further that male bonding was to have lunch or dinner with each other. We were both divorced, and we both had children. We were both hurting and needed to be healed. I would call him when something went wrong. He would call me when something went wrong. We struggled through his court dates together, and I was there for him. To this day I can pick up the phone and call, and he will do the same with me."

This type of friend will be a wonderful help and a source of emotional support for you. In the Bible, David and Jonathan enjoyed a friendship blessed by God.

"David got up from the south side of the stone and bowed down before Jonathan three times, with his face to the ground. Then they kissed each other and wept together—but David wept the most. Jonathan said to David, 'Go in peace, for we have sworn friendship with each other in the name of the LORD, saying, 'The LORD is witness between you and me, and between your descendants and my descendants forever'" (1 Samuel 20:41–42).

Father, bless me with the bond of true friendship, like David and Jonathan's. Amen.

Develop Realistic Expectations

To help you deal with your loneliness, you need to develop realistic expectations about relationships.

Dr. Les Carter explains: "Make certain that you have proper expectations regarding the things that can and cannot come from relationships. Many times people who have been through a divorce think to themselves that they want to have that ultimate relationship so they can prove to themselves and to the rest of the world they really are somebody.

"Be realistic in recognizing that there's no perfection, and you're not going to reach that ultimate ideal in your relationships. Then, when you have difficulties, it doesn't mean you've reached the ultimate bottom either."

Take time to think about what you have learned from past and current relationships and how you can apply it to future relationships. You will not learn if you are too focused on yourself and your problems, rather than on forward movement, growth, and application. Remember, your goal is not to have perfect relationships, but to learn how to grow together through hard times.

God is a sure foundation for any relationship. Ask God to guide you in your present and future relationships.

"The LORD will guide you always; he will satisfy your needs in a sunscorched land and will strengthen your frame. You will be like a wellwatered garden, like a spring whose waters never fail" (Isaiah 58:11).

Thank You, Lord, for providing for all my needs. I want to reset my expectations about relationships and learn how to build them up in You. Amen.

What Does
the Owner's Manual Say?

The Bible: What Is It?

"Your word is a lamp to my feet and a light for my path" (Psalm 119:105).

The Bible could be considered the "owner's manual" for life. This manual will help guide you through all of life, especially through tough situations like divorce. It is through the Bible that you will find God's help and guidance for your particular circumstances. The Bible is also where you will find healing and hope.

There are many other books on healing from divorce and other emotional tragedies in life. As good as some of these books are, the best resource to help you heal is the Bible. Over the next several days, you will discover what the Bible says about divorce.

Perhaps you are on the receiving end of a divorce; you did not want the divorce to occur, and you wonder what God thinks of your situation. Maybe you instigated the divorce, and you now wonder if you made the best choices. As you study the Bible and learn God's view of marriage and divorce, keep one thing in the forefront of your mind: God is a God of love and *not* condemnation. His love and forgiveness are infinite, and His Word is full of encouragement and hope for you personally.

"For everything that was written in the past was written to teach us, so that through endurance and the encouragement of the Scriptures we might have hope" (Romans 15:4).

Dear Lord, I want to learn more about You in Your Word, the Bible. I pray that the Bible will be my owner's manual for life. Amen.

Biblical Marriage

To better understand what the Bible says about divorce, we should first review what the Bible says about marriage. The Bible describes marriage as a union between two individuals who become "one flesh."

Dr. Craig Keener explains, "The phrase 'one flesh,' or being part of another person's flesh or bone, is often used in the Old Testament with reference to family relationships; therefore, when a husband and a wife become one flesh, in one sense it means that they become part of one another's family. Yet the Bible portrays the marriage relationship as an even deeper level of intimacy. It's a physical union where you actually share part of your own being with another person."

Lou Priolo says, "When two people become married, they become one person. When that marriage is separated by divorce, there are significant consequences because the one-flesh relationship is severed. That is a difficult thing to adjust to, and it requires all of God's resources to be brought to bear so that you can learn how to live as a person who is no longer one flesh with someone."

In marriage, two people become one. In divorce, that one flesh is torn apart. But be assured that as painful as the divorce is, with God, the healing will be that much more complete.

"For this reason a man will leave his father and mother and be united to his wife, and they will become one flesh" (Genesis 2:24).

Holy God, the tearing apart of my marriage is agonizing. I'm so glad You have the resources to help me survive from day to day. I could never do this on my own. Amen.

A Covenant Commitment

The Bible describes marriage as a serious covenant commitment between two people. A covenant is a solid and binding agreement. When two people say, "I do," you can almost hear God affirming, "I do also," because marriage is totally His idea. In fact, Jesus explained marriage as two people being joined together by God (Matthew 19:6).

"The Bible says that if I make a commitment, it is a commitment for life," says Dr. Spiros Zodhiates. "Marriage is not a feeling. Marriage is a commitment. It's a contract; it's a covenant. I cannot get out of my covenant simply because I changed my mind." The idea that marriage is a *feeling* is prevalent in our society. When one partner feels different about the other, he or she often chooses to follow those feelings and be unfaithful or seek a separation or divorce.

In an ideal world (i.e., the Garden of Eden), marriage is between one man and one woman for a lifetime, and it is a sacred covenant. However, we live in a fallen world, and people choose to disobey God. Breaking the covenant of marriage is a sin, and God hates it (Malachi 2:16), but God will never love you any less. His love is unconditional, and He wants to forgive you and heal you.

"God made mankind upright, but men have gone in search of many schemes" (Ecclesiastes 7:29).

Lord God, I believe that marriage is a commitment, and I wish I weren't in this situation. Thank You that You have never stopped loving me. Amen.

Note: In this section, we are speaking of situations where one or both individuals in a relationship decide to split up based upon their feelings or lack of feelings; we are not addressing situations involving abuse.

A Lifelong Commitment

What is the time frame of the marriage covenant? Lifelong. The Bible says, "A woman is bound to her husband as long as he lives" (1 Corinthians 7:39).

"I had always thought marriage was something that was a lifetime goal and a lifetime commitment," says Don. "Then all of a sudden, as a result of circumstances beyond my control, it was taken apart and torn."

God designed marriage to be a lifelong commitment. When two people get married, they plan to remain together for the rest of their lives. When people divorce, it is often because both people took matters into their own hands and made decisions based on factors not in God's will. Other times, like in Don's situation above, circumstances beyond a person's control occur, and one mate chooses to do something not in God's will. To step out of God's will brings hurt and pain every time.

If your spouse has stepped out of God's will and is abusive or otherwise dangerous, you must remove yourself from harm's way and find a safe place for you and your children to live. Seeking safety does not mean that you have to get a divorce or that you have given up on your relationship; it simply is a response to immediate danger.

Remember, as you read God's Word, He will use it to guide you in the steps you should take in response to your circumstances. He loves you and wants to restore and heal you.

"But you, O God, are both tender and kind, not easily angered, immense in love, and you never, never quit" (Psalm 86:15 MSG).

Heavenly Father, I made a commitment before You to remain in the marriage for the rest of my life, and now look what has happened. This is not what I had hoped for and dreamed of. Please show me what to do next. Amen.

Divorce Breaks the Union

"There is a union in marriage that divorce breaks. It rips hearts apart, and blood spills out everywhere," says Roy.

God binds two people together in marriage. The definition of *bind* here does not mean that He ties two people in a way that imprisons them; rather, He causes the two individual spirits to combine with each other to form a cohesiveness, such as what happens in a chemical reaction. If God has bound people together in this amazing way, do people have the right or the ability to try to undo it? We humans must seek to understand the supernatural, godly forces of marriage and to understand God's character before we try to take matters into our own hands regarding our relationships.

Perhaps you are wondering why we are discussing God's ideal for marriage when your own marriage has ended. It is important for you to learn as much as you can about God's will for all kinds of relationships so that you can continue to grow and mature in Him. This knowledge will also help you in future situations, such as when you counsel friends who are considering divorce or starting new relationships, or if the possibility of reconciliation or remarriage ever arises for you or someone you know. As you draw closer to Christ and draw others to His healing and wholeness, you will continue to heal more fully than you could imagine.

"Can you fathom the mysteries of God? Can you probe the limits of the Almighty? They are higher than the heavens—what can you do? They are deeper than the depths of the grave—what can you know?" (Job 11:7–8).

Creator God, I want to learn more and more about Your ideal for loving relationships. I know this will help me grow and heal. Amen.

God's View

"'I hate divorce,' says the LORD God of Israel" (Malachi 2:16).

The Scripture above is completely clear and not open to different interpretations. God does not mince words when sharing His attitude about divorce. All those who have been hurt by divorce can identify with God's response.

"I can see why God hates divorce because it tears apart the children," says Bonnie Keen. "It tears apart all the people who sat around you at the altar, who believed in your marriage and who stood with you and with the covenant you made. But I know that God does love the people who go through divorce, and I'm convinced that He will move you through that process if you let Him."

He hates divorce, but He loves you, no matter what the circumstances of your divorce.

Nell Ann shares, "God is so faithful. He hates divorce, but He loves the person going through it. He will greatly bless you when you seek His desire for your life. If you draw close to Him, He will truly draw close to you, and He will not leave you or forsake you. You can make it through this. It seems so dark, I know, but you can do it."

God makes the following promise to you:

"He will call upon me, and I will answer him; I will be with him in trouble, I will deliver him and honor him. With long life will I satisfy him and show him my salvation" (Psalm 91:15–16).

Faithful God, You love me no matter what. I'm glad You hate divorce because I hate it too. I pray that You will walk with me through this process. Amen.

Allowed by God?

As much as God hates divorce, He does allow it in some circumstances. We will discuss these circumstances over the next few days.

First, let's look at Jesus' response to a question from the Pharisees about divorce: "'Why then,' they asked, 'did Moses command that a man give his wife a certificate of divorce and send her away?' Jesus replied, 'Moses permitted you to divorce your wives because your hearts were hard. But it was not this way from the beginning'" (Matthew 19:7–8).

Dr. Craig Keener says that God permitted divorce in Old Testament times. He says, "In the Old Testament we find out in Malachi that God says He hates divorce. In Genesis we find out that it was never God's original purpose. It was His purpose that a husband and wife should be one flesh. As our Lord Jesus says, What God has joined together we have no business putting asunder [Matthew 19:6]."

Scholars state that the divorce permitted in the Old Testament was a formal process to acknowledge divorce-like, sinful behavior that had already occurred "because [their] hearts were hard." It was designed to provide legal protection to the person who was being divorced.

There are situations where divorce is allowed, but just because it is permissible does not mean it is the best thing to do. Choose wisely.

"So they are no longer two, but one. Therefore what God has joined together, let man not separate" (Matthew 19:6).

Righteous God, I want to do what You think is best. Amen.

Divorce in the Bible

The Bible describes two specific instances in which a person can initiate a divorce. If you are interested in remarrying someday, it is important to know what the Bible says about the circumstances in which divorce is allowed; then you will know if you have the freedom to remarry. We will discuss one allowance today and the other in tomorrow's devotion.

God allows divorce in the instance of sexual immorality or adultery. If your spouse is or was unfaithful, you have the right to divorce. You are not commanded to do this, but it is an option for you.

"Marriage is a covenant," says Dr. Craig Keener, "and a covenant involves an agreement between two parties before God. If one of those two parties is breaking the agreement, which sex outside of marriage certainly does, then that person has violated the marriage covenant, thereby annulling, so to speak, the marriage covenant."

Dr. Tony Evans says, "God never wants a divorce. He always rules against a divorce, but God recognizes that people are hard-hearted and they won't do right. So He had to bring some protection. In Matthew chapter nineteen, He says, 'except for immorality.'" For you to choose divorce because your spouse was unfaithful is not God's ideal, but He does allow it.

"I tell you that anyone who divorces his wife, except for marital unfaithfulness, and marries another woman commits adultery" (Matthew 19:9).

Dear God, I'm heartbroken and confused, and I just want to do what pleases You. Please give me godly wisdom and assurance in the decisions I make today. Amen.

Departure of a Nonbeliever

Another circumstance where divorce is permitted is found in 1 Corinthians 7:15: "If the unbeliever leaves, let him do so. A believing man or woman is not bound in such circumstances."

This verse means that if you are a follower of Jesus Christ and your husband or wife is not, and he or she leaves you, you are not required to remain together in marriage.

"The party who is left behind can't be held responsible for the breakup of the marriage if that person has done everything in his or her power to keep the marriage together," says Dr. Craig Keener.

Unfaithfulness and the departure of a nonbelieving spouse are two reasons specified in the Bible that allow you to divorce your spouse. Even though divorce is permitted for these reasons, it is not required. In fact, it is better to try to restore the marriage.

Dr. Tony Evans says, "Even when legitimate cases for divorce exist, believers must place reconciliation above their rights. Let's say your mate did commit adultery, but sincerely wants to be forgiven. Even though you have the right to divorce, because your mate was immoral, you always have the responsibility to love. The responsibility of love comes before the right of divorce. If a person wants to be forgiven, you seek forgiveness rather than the right because that's exactly what God did for you." If you are the victim of abuse, staying in a dangerous relationship is not the best way to be a conduit of God's love.

"God has called us to live in peace" (1 Corinthians 7:15).

Lord Jesus, help me to be obedient to You in this circumstance. You have called me first to love. Give me the strength to do so and not to be concerned with my rights. Amen.

Nonbiblical Divorce

You often hear couples say they are getting a divorce because "We just don't love each other anymore" or "We're mutually incompatible." These reasons are not allowed in the Bible. The Bible says if you make a commitment, it is a commitment for life.

"There is no divorce for irreconcilable differences," says Dr. Tony Evans.

For those people who feel they have fallen out of love or are no longer compatible, there is healing and hope for them. Divorce is the wrong decision. If both partners will agree to work on the marriage, grow together in Christ, and receive counseling, that marriage can become intimate and exciting again because it is in God's plan.

Listen to what the Bible has to say about followers of Jesus Christ who decide to end a marriage for this reason:

To the married I give this command (not I, but the Lord): A wife must not separate from her husband. But if she does, she must remain unmarried or else be reconciled to her husband. And a husband must not divorce his wife. To the rest I say this (I, not the Lord): If any brother has a wife who is not a believer and she is willing to live with him, he must not divorce her. And if a woman has a husband who is not a believer and he is willing to live with her, she must not divorce him. For the unbelieving husband has been sanctified through his wife, and the unbelieving wife has been sanctified through her believing husband. Otherwise your children would be unclean, but as it is, they are holy. (1 Corinthians 7:10–14)

Teach me, Lord, to understand and obey Your commands. I want to live life Your way, not mine. Amen.

Not Responsible

Dr. Craig Keener says we should do everything possible to save the marriage, but ultimately we are not responsible for the actions of another person.

He explains, "If the marriage is taken away from you against your will, after you've done everything you can in love to preserve the marriage, God doesn't hold you accountable for that any more than He would hold a rape victim accountable for rape or a murder victim accountable for murder."

In Psalm 55 David cried out to God. He was in distress because a friend of his, someone he trusted and loved, had turned against him, becoming vicious and hateful. David's relationship with his friend had been severed because of the friend's sinful actions toward him. In response, David brought his anguish to God, giving God his burdens and trusting God to sustain him.

Perhaps some aspects of the relationship between David and his friend are similar to what you have faced with your former spouse.

David says, "If an enemy were insulting me, I could endure it; if a foe were raising himself against me, I could hide from him. But it is . . . my companion, my close friend, with whom I once enjoyed sweet fellowship . . .

"War is in his heart; his words are more soothing than oil, yet they are drawn swords. Cast your cares on the LORD and he will sustain you; he will never let the righteous fall" (Psalm 55:12–14, 21–22).

Lord God, I have tried everything to make this marriage work. I have sought Your guidance, help, and counsel. I have been faithful to Your Word, but my spouse refuses to change his [her] ways. Help me to understand that I am not responsible for the actions of my spouse. Amen.

What About Other Situations?

We may not have addressed your particular situation. You may ask, what if my mate is engaged in criminal activity? Is physical, emotional, verbal, or sexual abuse grounds for divorce? What about substance abuse? What about satanic activities?

Please do not confuse personal safety with a discussion of biblical grounds for divorce. If you or your children are in danger, take immediate steps to protect your family. A decision of whether or not divorce is appropriate should not be made in emergency circumstances.

The Bible does not specifically describe grounds for divorce beyond the two we have already examined. It does, however, offer guidelines for decision making in all circumstances. As you faithfully follow these steps, the Lord's direction for your life will become clearer.

1. Prayer:
   Ask God for direction. "For the eyes of the Lord are on the righteous and his ears are attentive to their prayer" (1 Peter 3:12).

2. Bible study:
   What biblical principles apply to your circumstances? "The unfolding of your words gives light; it gives understanding to the simple" (Psalm 119:130).

3. Wise counsel:
   Seek direction from your church leaders. These mature Christians can help you interpret Scripture, pray with you, and offer godly counsel. "Plans fail for lack of counsel, but with many advisers they succeed" (Proverbs 15:22).

4. Guidance from the Holy Spirit:
   That quiet voice in your head may be God's voice, urging you to take action. "But the Counselor, the Holy Spirit, whom the Father will send in my name, will teach you all things and will remind you of everything I have said to you" (John 14:26).

Oh, God, my situation is so scary and confusing. Show me what to do! Amen.

Seek Wise, Godly Counsel

As you try to decide what is right to do in your situation, we'd like to offer a set of guidelines to help you. The first suggestion is to seek wise, godly counsel.

"I feel very fortunate to have had godly counsel. I think it protected me because I was pretty much emotionally spent and didn't have anything to contribute," says Jerry.

Dr. Tim Clinton says, "Get in touch with your pastor, who knows God's Word and will share truths of Scripture. Reach out to a professional Christian counselor. He or she can offer great assistance to you through this time of trouble or sorrow in your life. Don't let it go too long because if it goes unchecked, you'll find yourself in a bad predicament. There is always hope."

The Bible says you can have hope and success as a result of seeking advice from wise counselors. A wise counselor could be a church leader or mature Christian friend, or it could be a professional Christian counselor. All of these people can help point you in the right direction and bring you to a place of certainty and hope. By seeking wise counsel, you are (1) recognizing and admitting that you need help, (2) allowing yourself to express your emotions in a safe environment, (3) becoming accountable to another person, and (4) taking positive action that will help you grow and move forward in healing.

"Where there is no counsel, purposes are frustrated, but with many counselors they are accomplished" (Proverbs 15:22 AMP).

Wise Counselor, thank You for church leaders and counselors and friends who are able to help me through my situation. Guide me to persevere as I seek Christian help. Amen.

Attempt to Heal the Marriage

Another suggestion as you evaluate your situation is to attempt to heal the marriage. If your spouse was unfaithful or your unbelieving spouse left the marriage, you may have the biblical right to divorce, but you are not required to divorce. God's first desire is that married people remain together. Before you make the quick decision to end the marriage, attempt to heal the marriage first.

"If I dismiss my wife because she has been unfaithful to me," says Dr. Spiros Zodhiates, "I act from the right that God has given me. I don't have to. I can forgive that person. Above everything else there is forgiveness."

Margo and Alonzo's marriage to each other had gotten so bad that the court ordered them to be separated. If they were ever seen in each other's presence, they could be put in jail. Margo began attending a divorce recovery group at church, and she sought God in His Word and in prayer. As she began to grow spiritually, she prayed, "God, give us another chance." Margo and Alonzo did get back together. The path was extremely difficult, but, as Margo says, "It's a day-by-day thing. I haven't totally adjusted to it, but I've found God. I trust Him."

God offers each person a fresh start in life regardless of past sins. We can follow His example by forgiving others who have hurt us, and we can accept His forgiveness as we seek to make amends in our relationships.

"God put the world square with himself through the Messiah, giving the world a fresh start by offering forgiveness of sins" (2 Corinthians 5:19 MSG).

Forgiving Savior, so many things seem impossible to me,
but nothing is too difficult for You. Amen.

Prayer

Have you been listening to God lately, or has your voice dominated the conversations? Prayer is a necessary part of daily decision making during divorce.

Sabrina D. Black says, "Prayer is a person going before the Lord being vulnerable, being open not only to talk to God but to listen to God. There is significance in a 'listening prayer,' where you don't just go to God with your wish list, saying, 'Lord, set me free from this. Help me to flee temptation.'

"Those things are important, but it is also important to ask, 'Lord, what is it that You desire from me? How would You have me live my life?' Then, after you have asked, sit still in the presence of God and allow Him to speak to you. This is an essential part of daily prayer."

Listening to God is something you can do throughout your day, not just during a set prayer time. God speaks to people in many ways: through His Word, other people, prayer, and even life's circumstances. As you interact with people today, is God trying to tell you something? As you drive in your car, is God speaking quietly to your heart? Ask the Holy Spirit to help you listen as you pray; this is not something that is accomplished through self-will. Praise Him and worship Him. Come to Him with a thankful heart. Let the Spirit work in you as you pray.

"Listen, listen to me, and eat what is good, and your soul will delight in the richest of fare. Give ear and come to me; hear me, that your soul may live" (Isaiah 55:2–3).

Lord God, I'm listening. Open my ears all day because what You have to say is more important than the thoughts racing around in my mind. Amen.

Ask the Holy Spirit's Help

You can never see the big picture in any given situation. Only God sees your circumstances from all perspectives and contexts. As a result you often pray for the wrong things. You tend to pray for what seems best to you.

One unique aspect of the Christian walk is that God has given you His Holy Spirit to help you make right decisions and to guide your prayers. The Bible says that "the Spirit helps us in our weakness. We do not know what we ought to pray for, but the Spirit himself intercedes for us with groans that words cannot express" (Romans 8:26).

"It wasn't until my relationship with Christ grew stronger that I could stand firm and give my former spouse over to the Lord," says Ginny. "I wasn't responsible for him anymore, and I wasn't his mother. I didn't have to take care of him. That was very hard not to do. I still felt I had to fix him and help him, but that wasn't my job when we were married, and it's not my job now."

You might be avoiding the real problem in your life. The Holy Spirit can help reveal to you the root cause of your problems. Ask the Holy Spirit to direct your prayers.

"You want something but don't get it . . . You quarrel and fight. You do not have, because you do not ask God. When you ask, you do not receive, because you ask with wrong motives" (James 4:2–3).

Holy Spirit, please show me the true cause of my problems. What do I really need to pray about? Guide me today in prayer and in truth. Amen.

Confrontation

Jesus gives guidelines in Matthew 18 on how to confront someone who has wronged you. The goal of these steps is to restore the relationship with that person. Keep in mind that while God does desire that you seek to restore relationships, He does not ask you to continue to accept wrong behavior.

> Step One: "If your brother sins against you, go and show him his fault, just between the two of you. If he listens to you, you have won your brother over" (v. 15).
>
> Step Two: "If he will not listen, take one or two others along, so that 'every matter may be established by the testimony of two or three witnesses'" (v. 16).
>
> Step Three: "If he refuses to listen to them, tell it to the church; and if he refuses to listen even to the church, treat him as you would a pagan or a tax collector" (v. 17).

The first step is to be done in private. The second step involves bringing along one or two spiritually mature friends, relatives, or a counselor. In the third step, you bring the matter to your church leaders and ask them to confront your spouse according to biblical guidelines.

Each of the above steps should be done with a spirit of forgiveness and patience. Give the Holy Spirit time to soften a person's heart so that he or she might respond correctly.

After Jesus gave the instructions above, Peter asked Him how many times he should forgive a person who has wronged him.

"'Lord, how many times shall I forgive my brother when he sins against me? Up to seven times?' Jesus answered, 'I tell you, not seven times, but seventy-seven times'" (Matthew 18:21–22).

Dear Jesus, confrontation is a scary thing. May my motivations be pure. Amen.

Do You Need to Seek Forgiveness?

In divorce, both parties make mistakes. Even if you did not instigate the divorce, you need to seek forgiveness for things you did when you were married and during the divorce process.

"Regardless of what he did to me, the way I responded to him was my responsibility," says Selma. "When I was able to assume responsibility for myself, I was able to forgive him for what he did, and I was able to heal."

In the Bible, Paul wrote a letter to the Corinthian church about their wrongs. When they read the letter and realized their wrong behaviors, they chose to repent. They took responsibility for their wrongdoings. They experienced godly sorrow, which leads to repentance, salvation, and no regret. Read this section of Paul's letter and consider how it applies to your situation.

> I am happy . . . because your sorrow led you to repentance. For you became sorrowful as God intended and so were not harmed in any way by us. Godly sorrow brings repentance that leads to salvation and leaves no regret, but worldly sorrow brings death. See what this godly sorrow has produced in you: what earnestness, what eagerness to clear yourselves, what indignation, what alarm, what longing, what concern, what readiness to see justice done. At every point you have proved yourselves to be innocent in this matter. So even though I wrote to you, it was not on account of the one who did the wrong or of the injured party, but rather that before God you could see for yourselves how devoted . . . you are. (2 Corinthians 7:9–12)

> *Savior God, forgive me for my sins. Help me to recognize what I have done wrong so I can repent, turning from my wrong behaviors and choosing good ones instead. Amen.*

You're Still Valuable to God

Regardless of the reasons behind your separation or divorce, no matter what you have done wrong or where you have failed, you can fully restore your relationship with God and be used by Him.

"If you think that being divorced disqualifies you from being used by God, then you have to cancel a million different people today who are being used greatly by God," says Dr. Myles Munroe. "You're saying that divorce is stronger than the blood of Jesus, the forgiveness of God, and the grace of God. That's ridiculous. Divorce is an incident. It's not a lifestyle.

"God forgives. God forgets. What God forgets, you shouldn't try to remember. God will use you no matter what you've done. If I were to ask you the question, 'Is divorce worse than murder?' obviously you would say, 'No way.' If divorce is not worse than murder, then why did God use Moses? Moses was a murderer and a convict."

Also in the Bible, Paul was responsible for the deaths of many people, and God chose him to be one of the greatest preachers ever. God wants to use you for great works that honor Him. Choose to surrender your life to Jesus, and you will be amazed at what you can accomplish through Him.

"Immediately he [Paul] began preaching about Jesus in the synagogues, saying, 'He is indeed the Son of God!' All who heard him were amazed. 'Isn't this the same man who persecuted Jesus' followers with such devastation in Jerusalem?' they asked . . . [His] preaching became more and more powerful, and the Jews in Damascus couldn't refute his proofs that Jesus was indeed the Messiah" (Acts 9:20–22 NLT).

Dear God, I want to do great things for other people and ultimately for Your kingdom. Amen.

Biblical Guidelines for Remarriage

Statistics show that most people who are divorced will want to remarry someday. If you want to remarry as God allows it, you must understand and follow the Bible's guidelines. In the following explanation by Dr. Craig Keener, the *innocent* party is the one who does not want the marriage to end and who attempts to hold the marriage together.

Dr. Keener explains: "If a divorce is on valid grounds, the innocent party is automatically free to remarry. Paul makes that explicit, especially in 1 Corinthians 7:15 where he says that if the unbelieving spouse departs, the believer is not under bondage. That phrase 'not under bondage' means he or she is free to remarry."

Be careful though. Just because you are free to remarry does not mean you are ready to do so. Dr. Dennis Rainey in *Staying Close* examines God's purposes for marriage. If you are considering remarriage, first decide if your goals for this new relationship line up with God's. God's purposes for marriage are "to mirror God's image, to multiply a godly heritage, to manage God's realm, to mutually complete one another, and to model Christ's relationship to the church"; Dr. Rainey continues, "What these five purposes bring to a marriage are a sense of direction, internal stability, and the stamp of God's design."[3]

Does your new relationship reflect these five godly purposes?

"'For this reason a man will leave his father and mother and be united to his wife, and the two will become one flesh.' This is a profound mystery—but I am talking about Christ and the church. However, each one of you also must love his wife as he loves himself, and the wife must respect her husband" (Ephesians 5:31–33).

Lord, I want to do things Your way this time. Amen.

---

3. *Staying Close: Stopping the Natural Drift Toward Isolation in Marriage* by Dennis and Barbara Rainey. (Thomas Nelson, 1989), p. 110.

Jesus as Your Guide

The Bible provides instruction for all situations in life. One of the best ways to read and study the Bible is to have a guide, and the best Guide you can have is Jesus. Having a personal relationship with Jesus Christ is referred to as salvation in Christ.

"Salvation is a gift," says Dee Brestin. "You need to ask Jesus for it. He has died and paid the price, and unless you ask Him to be your Savior and Lord, then you do not have a relationship with Him.

"Before I came to Christ, I thought, *How boring to read the Bible. How silly to spend your life sitting in church.* After I came to Christ, I thought the Bible was fascinating, and I loved God's people. A change took place in me because God's Spirit came and lived in me when I asked Jesus into my life.

"If you have any doubt, why not be sure today and ask Jesus to be your Savior and Lord. All you have to do is admit your need for forgiveness and your need for Him."

You don't need to know the author of a book to read it and understand or enjoy it. But the Bible is unique. You need to know the Author—God—before you can really receive what He is saying in the Scriptures.

We encourage you to make sure you have a personal relationship with Jesus Christ. It's the key to your healing and the key to understanding what the Bible has to teach on divorce, separation, and other issues in life.

"For God so loved the world that he gave his one and only Son, that whoever believes in him shall not perish but have eternal life" (John 3:16).

Lord Jesus, I need You in my life. Amen.

New Relationships

New Relationships

Should you pursue a new relationship? What if you get involved in a new relationship prematurely? How can you avoid making wrong choices? We will explore the answers to these questions over the next several days.

Perhaps you are already in a new relationship or are interested in pursuing one. Maybe you feel you never want to be in another relationship again. This range of feelings is normal; however, statistics show that approximately 75 percent of people who have been through divorce will someday remarry, and the majority of those second marriages will end in divorce.

Juana shares how she chose to wait and not jump ahead of God's plan for her life. She says, "My life was still in turmoil, and I did not know the answers, but I knew the One who knew the answers. I was willing to wait for whatever God had for me. I waited actively to see what God was going to do with my life. A couple from church mentored and discipled me for fifteen months, and I began to grow in my faith and to learn the Bible. I would come home from work and read my Bible, and I would love it. It was a special time."

In making all decisions of life, the first place to start is by praying and finding out what the Bible says about that particular situation. Your goal should be to see your circumstances from God's perspective and not your own limited view.

"I have set the LORD always before me. Because he is at my right hand, I will not be shaken" (Psalm 16:8).

Lord, no matter where I am in terms of a new relationship, help me realize that putting You first in every decision of my life is the only way to lasting success. Amen.

Too Soon

One reason second marriages fail is because people are propelled into new relationships before they are ready. Sometimes friends and family will push you into a new relationship, thinking it will help you. A new relationship can feel great, but feelings do not guarantee a solid relationship down the road. Do not listen to friends who, though well-meaning, push you to move on before you are completely healed.

You must grieve your losses and know you are whole before you consider a new relationship. If you decide to get on with your life without dealing with the issues at hand, these issues will rise up again at a later time. When they do, the hurt and the pain will be even stronger.

H. Norman Wright shares what happened to a man he knew who remarried before becoming fully healed: "About four years after the remarriage, all of a sudden this man's buried feelings came out because his new partner began to exhibit some behaviors similar to his ex-spouse's. That triggered all of those feelings that had never been dealt with, and the second marriage dissolved. It was a huge mess."

Healing comes from the Lord. Wholeness comes from the Lord.

"If you listen carefully to the voice of the LORD your God and do what is right in his eyes, if you pay attention to his commands and keep all his decrees, I will not bring on you any of the diseases I brought on the Egyptians, for I am the LORD, who heals you" (Exodus 15:26).

Lord, I only need to "get on with" my relationship with You. Help me know what to say to friends who mean well but have the wrong advice. Amen.

The Effect of Children

Another reason remarriages fail is the stress that children can add to the relationship.

"Children are the leading cause of second marriages coming to divorce," says Gary Richmond. "They see the stepparent as the enemy, and they strongly defend the missing parent in the home."

The loyalty of a child to a natural parent is strong. You may wonder how your children could still love your former spouse who betrayed, abused, or abandoned you and your children. You might think that your children would welcome a new stepparent who is kind and loving. Be careful not to make assumptions. They might accept a new person in the home and they might not. Children are a stressor to new relationships and remarriages.

Trying to change your children's feelings or loyalties can be harmful. That is not where you should focus your energies. Instead, teach them about and model the love of God. Let them observe you tenderly caring and praying for them and for the family every day. Bring them regularly to church. Read God's Word daily and share with them what you are learning. True, godly love is the only kind of love that brings healing and peace in a home. If you were ever to remarry, your new spouse should have these same values.

"Fix these words of mine in your hearts and minds; tie them as symbols on your hands and bind them on your foreheads. Teach them to your children, talking about them when you sit at home and when you walk along the road, when you lie down and when you get up" (Deuteronomy 11:18–19).

Lord God, I realize that I must not rush into a new relationship but should focus instead on being a model of godly love to those around me. Amen.

Illusion: You Have Learned from Past Mistakes

Many people enter into new relationships with the illusion that the new relationship will be different, better, because they have learned from their mistakes.

"The only thing you've learned from your mistakes is that you've made mistakes," says Gary Richmond. "You have to learn new methods of behavior in order to overcome the problems you set up for yourself in the first relationship."

Roy says, "Most of the time people go from one relationship to the next with the same broken heart, the same scars, and the same unhealed wounds. The answer to the pain you feel is not another relationship. You've got to take your time and become a healed individual through the grace of God."

Don't repeat the mistakes of the past. Build a solid foundation for your future. God has provided you with the Bible, which is an instruction manual for life. He has also provided strong Christian teachers, counselors, church leaders, and biblically based books to help you establish roots and grow strong in your faith.

"I will show you what it's like when someone comes to me, listens to my teaching, and then obeys me. It is like a person who builds a house on a strong foundation laid upon the underlying rock. When the floodwaters rise and break against the house, it stands firm because it is well built. But anyone who listens and doesn't obey is like a person who builds a house without a foundation. When the floods sweep down against that house, it will crumble into a heap of ruins" (Luke 6:47–49 NLT).

Strong Lord, I want to learn more and build my life on a solid foundation. Help me not to make decisions based on past experiences, but on what I know is godly truth. Amen.

Illusion: Another Person Can Make You Happy

"You are ready to start dating again only when you don't feel like you have to have someone in order to be happy," says Marc.

Never depend on someone else for your happiness. Another person cannot make you happy, and it is not another person's responsibility to do so. If you are considering a new relationship, wait. If you are currently in a relationship, ask the other person to wait before taking the relationship further. There is not a set amount of time to wait. How long you wait depends on how long you were married before, how well you deal with conflicts, and on your personal rate of healing.

Gary Richmond says, "It takes one year of healing for every four years of marriage. Some people have control over that in terms of working it through, and different people heal at different rates, so it's a general statistic. But I've found over time that it's a wise statistic. One of the great tendencies of humanity is for us to say, 'It'll be different for me. This doesn't apply to me.' It really does."

Perhaps you, too, feel that your situation is different, that your new relationship is based on more than feelings or neediness. If that thought has come to your mind, prayerfully consider your past losses, your rate and method of grieving, your spiritual maturity, and your ability to find complete joy in being single. True happiness is found in a relationship with Jesus Christ.

"Though you have not seen him, you love him; and even though you do not see him now, you believe in him and are filled with an inexpressible and glorious joy" (1 Peter 1:8).

Lord Jesus, I believe in You and in the joyful, abundant life You promise to those who love You. Amen.

Whose Love Do You Want?

Rob Eagar says: "When you demand something from God, such as a new relationship, you are blocking God's love from benefiting you in that area of your life. In other words, you are saying, 'Lord, I don't want Your love. I want the love of a man or of a woman instead.' God won't force Himself upon you. He'll say, 'I love you; I'm here for you, but I can't give you My love until you are willing to receive it.'

"Whatever you depend upon for your happiness will always end up controlling you; therefore, if you feel you have to get married in order to be happy, then the approval of the opposite sex will control your self-esteem. How other people view you will dominate the way you view yourself."

If you sincerely desire God's love more than the love of another person, then you might be ready to consider a new relationship. If you think you are ready, then be sure the relationship is His idea and not yours. Remember, do not make decisions based on feelings. Use wisdom, God's Word, prayer, and Christian counsel to make all decisions, large and small. Let your self-esteem be grounded in Christ. If you desire a relationship with God above all else, your heart will truly be fulfilled.

"'For your Maker is your husband—the LORD Almighty is his name—the Holy One of Israel is your Redeemer; he is called the God of all the earth. The LORD will call you back as if you were a wife deserted and distressed in spirit—a wife who married young, only to be rejected,' says your God" (Isaiah 54:5–6).

Almighty God, I want Your love above all else, and I am willing to do anything to be certain of that love. Amen.

Consequences of Moving Too Quickly

"I got speeding tickets every time I got engaged. Two speeding tickets in the same month. It was like the Holy Spirit saying, 'Slow down.' I think God has such a sense of humor," says Bonnie Keen.

If you don't slow down and wait before starting a new relationship, you won't heal.

"I got into another relationship right away," says Angie. "I was elated for a while. I thought, *I am out of here and on to better things.* Thankfully the Lord saved me from that and opened up my eyes to what I was doing. I almost married him. I ended up breaking up with him, and after that the pain was worse than my divorce. It was like going through another divorce. During that period I was so broken, so depressed, and so hurting. God used that experience to take me on my journey of healing."

Let God use your painful circumstances for your healing and growth. You can be a strong, secure person when your identity is in Christ. Slow down and let this happen before you even remotely consider a new relationship. God can heal your deepest pain and meet your deepest needs.

"Slow down. Take a deep breath. What's the hurry? Why wear yourself out? Just what are you after anyway?" (Jeremiah 2:25 MSG).

Holy Father, You have promised in the Bible to supply all my needs (Philippians 4:19). You are God my Healer. I will wait on You. Amen.

Energy Balance: Where Are You?

Earlier we discussed how divorce affects your energy distribution. Let's consider how an imbalance in your energy can negatively affect your decision to begin a new relationship.

At the beginning of the separation or divorce process, emotional demands take up 85 percent of your energy, leaving only 15 percent for mental, physical, and spiritual needs. It takes as long as five years to return to a more even distribution of your energy. Unfortunately, most people enter new relationships and remarry in an unbalanced state, while they are still affected by the emotional impact of divorce and not fully capable of applying mental and spiritual wisdom to the relationship.

Rob Eagar says, "If you come out of a relationship and then immediately jump into another one, your heart does not get a chance to fully heal; therefore, you are walking along wounded emotionally. You are vulnerable, then, to starting this new relationship without a whole heart, and you're going to try to suck your need for acceptance and significance out of this person all the more. You're not really in the relationship for the other person. You're in it for yourself."

Give God the opportunity to take care of you and to reveal His glory and power to you. He knows what you want, and He knows what you need. He loves you and will take care of you if you will let Him.

"Your Father knows what you need before you ask him" (Matthew 6:8).

Holy God, I will depend on You for all my needs. You know what I need more than I do. Help me not to worry, but to trust in You as I seek to regain a proper balance in life again. Amen.

Living in the Past

"There is a tendency for people who have been through the terrible, wrenching event of divorce to live in the past," says Gary Richmond. "Also, when they begin new relationships, they talk about that past with the new person. If the new person cares in conversation about it, a great illusion develops that both parties in the new relationship are becoming more intimate in sharing their feelings than they've ever been before, even with a former mate. They need to be careful to know that they haven't achieved great intimacy just by sharing their problems."

Intimacy with another person is more likely to be developed when you share your dreams for the future. This does not mean fantasies of having a new relationship, but the hopes and plans for your future that you will strive for with or without that other person. These are the dreams and goals God has called you to fulfill.

Juana shares an experience she had during her separation: "I can remember kneeling before God in that quiet, little apartment. I didn't know what the future held, but I could see God's goodness, and I could see that God had this goodness waiting for me in the future. I remember having confidence that my future with God was so bright, and now I am living it."

"The suffering won't last forever. It won't be long before this generous God who has great plans for us in Christ—eternal and glorious plans they are!—will have you put together and on your feet for good" (1 Peter 5:10 MSG).

Loving God, You have amazing plans for me. What would You like me to do for You? Amen.

Looking for Nurture and Rescue

The tendency to look for nurture and rescue in a new relationship is strong, especially because it feels good and right after all the pain you have been experiencing.

"I met my second husband six months after my separation from my first husband," shares Jeannette. "I immediately got emotionally involved because I had this deep, soul-level pain that was just excruciating, and no matter what I did, it wouldn't go away. So I got into this relationship, and slowly it started taking away the pain, and I forgot about the pain. Shortly after that, I got married and knew I had made a mistake, but I had invested too much and didn't want a second failed marriage. I continued in the marriage and tried to save it the best that I could, but you can only do so much and pretend so long. It just fell apart."

You never want to be needy when getting involved in a new relationship. Learn how to be single and how to be whole and fulfilled first. Also, learn about relationships and what makes relationships successful in God's eyes. Several excellent Christian books exist on relationships, communication, emotional healing, and spiritual growth. Also, talk to your church leaders about seminars or conferences you can attend to increase your knowledge. Delve into God's Word and learn more about the wisdom He has for you.

If your heart is crying out to be nurtured and rescued from the pain and despair, let God be your comforter.

"As a mother comforts her child, so will I comfort you; and you will be comforted over Jerusalem" (Isaiah 66:13).

Holy God, may the only neediness I have be for You. Teach me to be single, and teach me what Your Word says about successful relationships. Amen.

Filling the Gaps

Sometimes people mistakenly think they need a new relationship for their healing to be complete. This is never true. True healing involves God, time, and personal and spiritual growth. What is confusing, though, is that a new relationship can cause you to *feel* like you are healing, when you are not.

"The relationship was filling in gaps that needed to be healed, not just filled in. My healing was being delayed, and once the relationship broke off, the hole was even bigger than it was when my wife left," says Marc.

When the painful gaps from your first marriage are being filled with something other than Christ, you can falsely think you are healing. The open wounds and bitter losses from your first marriage and from the divorce process need to be filled with God's healing power.

Here are some ways to begin filling the gaps God's way. You can read the Bible and study specific passages in depth, spend time with Christian friends, pray, do volunteer work, start a new hobby, spend time listening to God, get involved in a Christ-centered support group, attend counseling, read, and enjoy family and friends. This is not to suggest a whirlwind of activity, but relaxed, focused moments spent building relationships with God, family, and same-sex friends.

"By faith in the name of Jesus, this man whom you see and know was made strong. It is Jesus' name and the faith that comes through him that has given this complete healing to him, as you can all see" (Acts 3:16).

Jesus, healing comes through You. Thank You for that promise. Instead of seeking a new relationship, I will focus my energies on maturing in You. Amen.

Spiritual Security

"Everybody's looking for emotional support in another relationship with the opposite sex," says Dr. Jim A. Talley, "and that's the wrong place to look. The emotional support you need comes from your spiritual life being stable first, and that's a right relationship with God."

Examine your heart by reflecting on your recent actions and attitudes. What do they reveal about you? Are you completely secure in your relationship with God, or do you want another person to make you feel secure? Pray and ask God to help you be honest as you consider these matters. Then refrain from getting involved with a new person until you can say with confidence, "God is enough. He's all I need."

Gary Richmond tells how in the Bible Jeremiah's assignment from God was to deliver only bad news: "Jeremiah had the worst assignment in the world. He was told that he could only tell the people bad things. He finally cried out in the book of Lamentations, 'God is my sufficiency even though nobody likes me for what I'm saying.'

"God is enough, and that's an important place to come to so that you're coming out of a position of strength into the potential of a new relationship and not out of neediness. It's sad that people are crawling in hope toward a new relationship in order to be validated by another person."

In the midst of despair and great difficulty Jeremiah said, "Deep in my heart I say, 'The LORD is all I need; I can depend on him!' The LORD is kind to everyone who trusts and obeys him. It is good to wait patiently for the LORD to save us'" (Lamentations 3:24–26 CEV).

Lord God, I will wait quietly on You. You are all I need.
Amen.

How You Respond to Problems

How you respond to problems is one indicator of how much you have stabilized since the divorce. Significant spiritual and emotional stability are necessary before even considering a new relationship.

"When a problem hits you and really hits you hard, do you have a panicked feeling or do you have a problem-solving attitude that will carry you through?" asks Gary Richmond.

When Jim and Lauren met, Jim had been divorced for three years, she for just days. Their courtship was quick. They married ten months after her divorce. But the excitement of the new relationship quickly faded, and the reality of day-to-day living set in.

Lauren says, "It was hard because even though our spiritual walk had strengthened, we had not dealt with all the insecurities from our past experiences. We didn't want to be hurt again. We didn't want to feel rejected. We wanted to guard our emotions. We were both struggling for control the whole time. The fights get pretty bad when two people are trying to be in control. The other thing was that we were both insecure because of our first marriages. We had not gotten to the point where we felt safe and secure within ourselves."

When the problems came, Jim and Lauren were not prepared to deal with them properly because they had not healed fully from their previous marriages. They did not have security and wholeness as single individuals. When two individuals who are not secure in themselves come together in a relationship, the results can be catastrophic.

"For I am the LORD, your God, who takes hold of your right hand and says to you, Do not fear; I will help you" (Isaiah 41:13).

Lord God, I come to You for security, help, and a problem-solving attitude. Amen.

Identifying Your Weaknesses

Everyone has weaknesses. A person who recognizes his or her weaknesses and is willing to work on them is wise.

"You have to heal from your past relationship," says Lauren. "You have to give yourself time to realize what it is you're healing from. You might not know you're insecure or that your self-esteem is so low that you'll appreciate any type of attention. You haven't had time to figure out what went wrong. You have to grow."

Your weaknesses are reminders of God's strength and sufficiency. When you face hardships or are frustrated by your inadequacies, take a good look at the God you serve. He is bigger than your problems. He will empower you with a much greater strength than you can ever generate on your own. Let God fulfill your needs because He is the only One who can. Here is how Paul viewed a burden he was carrying:

At first I didn't think of it as a gift, and begged God to remove it. Three times I did that, and then he told me, My grace is enough; it's all you need. My strength comes into its own in your weakness.

Once I heard that, I was glad to let it happen. I quit focusing on the handicap and began appreciating the gift. It was a case of Christ's strength moving in on my weakness. Now I take limitations in stride, and with good cheer, these limitations that cut me down to size—abuse, accidents, opposition, bad breaks. I just let Christ take over! And so the weaker I get, the stronger I become. (2 Corinthians 12:8–10 MSG)

Strong Father, reveal my weaknesses to me so I can work on them with Your help. I want to be strong in You. Amen.

Thankful for the Hard Times

Think about how you deal with adversity and how you now view past trials. Are you thankful for the hard times? A sign of healing is when a person is thankful for the bad times as well as the good and when a person recognizes that he or she is a better person because of the trials. Now is not the time to be worried about remarriage, but to persevere in becoming the person God has created you to be.

"I don't know if it's God's intent for me to remarry," says Harriet. "But that, along with every corner of my life, is His now, and I don't have to worry about it anymore. He has taken a broken shell of a woman. He has taken this vessel that was emptied of all its contents, and He is turning me into His work, a masterpiece that's His making. I don't even know how to be thankful for that, but I know He'll help me to."

In the Bible verse below, God's instructions on how to face adversity are radical—but so is His healing. Don't settle for anything less than what God wants for you!

"Consider it pure joy, my brothers, whenever you face trials of many kinds, because you know that the testing of your faith develops perseverance. Perseverance must finish its work so that you may be mature and complete, not lacking anything" (James 1:2–4).

Dear God, my trials were, and still are, awful. Show me how to be thankful for the hard times. Give me the strength to persevere and to come out a winner. Amen.

Is Dating Appropriate?

If marital reconciliation with your former mate is possible, dating is inappropriate.

Gary Richmond says, "I have seen time after time where people found themselves involved in a relationship following a separation only to discover that finally their mate wanted to reconcile the marriage. They were then caught with the dilemma of falling out of love with the person they had become attracted to, before they could start the painful process of repairing the damage that had been done in the first relationship. It makes it twice as hard when you let people enter into your life. It adds more problems."

A person who feels the need to date for the purpose of experiencing personal healing should not be dating. A person who is fully healed and whole through Jesus Christ should face the question of dating with wisdom, looking at it from all possible angles, as well as considering where the relationship would be headed in the future.

God's first choice is that you reconcile with your former spouse if possible. Keep that in the forefront of your mind as you make decisions about dating.

"GOD, not you, made marriage. His Spirit inhabits even the smallest details of marriage . . . So guard the spirit of marriage within you. Don't cheat on your spouse. 'I hate divorce,' says the GOD of Israel" (Malachi 2:15–16 MSG).

Holy God, give me the wisdom to make the right decisions about dating and about reconciliation. Strengthen me today. I am so tired of trying to do what is right. Help me to remember that You don't want me to try, but to trust. Amen.

Dating: What Is It?

It is important to examine the kind of opposite-sex friendships you have. You might be dating and not realize it.

Gary Richmond says, "We are by nature two things: romantic and sexual creatures. If we find ourselves being validated, softly spoken to and shown kindness to, we have very little control over drifting into romantic and loving feelings. The best way to avoid that is to avoid being in a situation that calls for romance and wait until it's the appropriate time. In God's time, He makes all things beautiful. In our time, we can really foul it up and make it more difficult to untangle."

Dr. Jim A. Talley defines dating as two people who spend time alone together exchanging emotional energy. Does this definition apply to any of your relationships?

Keep your opposite-sex friendships in the right setting. If you find that in your mind you continually drift down the path of attraction and romance with a certain person, you may need to remove yourself from that friendship. If you are not free to date right now because you are still married or because you are not fully healed, keep yourself away from situations that might tempt you.

Make an effort to build up same-sex friendships instead, or renew relationships with family members. Not only is it important to remove yourself from tempting situations, it is also important to replace those situations with God-pleasing activities or behavior.

"Watch and pray so that you will not fall into temptation. The spirit is willing, but the body is weak" (Matthew 26:41).

Dear Lord, I'm nervous about praying this, but I know I must: Please give me the strength and the courage to end any opposite-sex relationships I have that could potentially hinder my healing and growth. Amen.

The Great Dating Crusade

Rob Eagar, speaker and author of *Dating with Pure Passion*, embarked on what he calls the "Great Dating Crusade" a year after his wife had left him. His goal at that time was to find fulfillment through a new relationship.

He says, "My heart still held this mind-set that if I could find the right woman, then I could find my own happily ever after. That was the basis for my Great Dating Crusade. It led me into a series of roller-coaster experiences where I would meet a new woman and we would hit it off, but no matter how wonderful the new relationship started off, nothing ever worked out. All the relationships crashed and burned."

Rob began to question God at that point, asking, "Where is the love? My heart still feels empty inside." He realized that God wanted him to understand that he was trying to fill his heart with something that could not truly satisfy his needs. Rob desired to be loved, accepted, and celebrated just the way he was, imperfections and all. He realized that Jesus Christ is the only Person who could love him to that deep degree, the only One who could love him unconditionally.

"Mortals make elaborate plans, but GOD has the last word. Humans are satisfied with whatever looks good; GOD probes for what is good. Put GOD in charge of your work, then what you've planned will take place" (Proverbs 16:1–3 MSG).

Lord Jesus, You have loved me with an everlasting love. I give all my hopes and plans, faults and imperfections to You. Amen.

A Quiz

In this multiple-choice quiz, choose one of the following: (a) married or (b) single.

1. What are you the day before you get married?

2. What are you the day before you have your final divorce decree in hand?

3. What are you the day after you have your final divorce decree in hand?

The answers are *b*, *a*, and *b*. The first answer is easy. The second answer is tricky because you may feel single at that point, even though you are not. The third answer is also difficult because you may still feel married because you have been in that state for so long.

"If you are still married, you are not available to date," says Sabrina D. Black. "Even though you feel emotionally divorced from the person, you are still married by law and by God's standards.

"When you start to bring other people into the mix, then you start to make comparisons, which is not fair because this is not a person who has a history with you. This person has come in and seems like icing on the cake."

In the divorce process, taking shortcuts does not lead you to the correct destination, but to twisting, deceiving side roads. If you want to be successful in future relationships, you must follow God's instructions and timing. Think carefully about whether dating is a safe, wise idea.

"Don't look for shortcuts to God. The market is flooded with sure-fire, easygoing formulas for a successful life that can be practiced in your spare time. Don't fall for that stuff, even though crowds of people do. The way to life—to God!—is vigorous and requires total attention" (Matthew 7:13–14 MSG).

Lord God, I want to make decisions that are pleasing to You, and not just do what everyone else is doing. Amen.

Not Just a Piece of Paper

If your divorce is not final, you should not begin a new relationship with a member of the opposite sex.

Dr. Jim A. Talley says, "There are thousands of people who are jumping into another relationship or moving in with somebody. The rationale is, 'Well, I can't afford to finalize my divorce now. It's only a piece of paper.' It's only a piece of paper? If you're driving down the road and the registration of the car you're in belongs to somebody else and you get stopped, it's only a piece of paper. But you go to jail for driving a stolen car. You should not go into another relationship until you have your final divorce decree in hand."

"The first date I went on," admits Marc, "frankly, was a disaster. I was in the separation mode at the time. I wasn't completely divorced, so I felt like I was cheating on my wife even though she was already doing that. I really felt funny. I wasn't ready for dating, and I shouldn't have been at that particular time in my life."

Choose to do what is right regardless of what your former spouse is doing, what others are doing, or what others are pressuring you to do. If you are pursuing a new relationship on your own, choose to do what is right because this is your life you are handling. A wrong decision about a new relationship can lead to even greater harm than the first relationship brought you.

"There is a way that seems right to a man, but in the end it leads to death" (Proverbs 14:12).

Dear God, if I am in too deep already, help me to get out. Amen.

You Are Complete with God

"It's unfair and unrealistic to expect that there is a man or a woman out there who can please you forever or fulfill your heart," says Rob Eagar.

Whether you are married or single, you will be complete only in a relationship with God through His Son, Jesus. Examine your spiritual life to see if you are complete through Christ, or if you feel that another person would help to make you whole.

"My heart will never be fulfilled until I realize that I am complete and that the only Person who truly loves me unconditionally is Jesus Christ Himself," continues Rob.

Humans are imperfect. We are flawed, and we do not have the ability to fulfill another person. But Jesus Christ is perfect. Because of His love, you can be in a right relationship with God, and you can flourish in that relationship. God has a higher purpose for you than to find a mate. Trust Him.

Cathy shares, "Marriage is supposed to be the strongest relational bond here on earth, but I realize now that I put my marriage before Christ. I clung to my husband and depended on him too much. I should have that kind of dependence only on Christ. When everything was taken away, it was like God said, 'Okay, Cathy, you're alone; you're stripped. Now let Me show you who you really are. Let Me show you how much I love you. Let Me show you the person I created you to be.'"

"But I am like an olive tree flourishing in the house of God; I trust in God's unfailing love for ever and ever" (Psalm 52:8).

Faithful God, Your love is trustworthy and amazing.
Whether I remarry or remain single for the rest of my days,
You are all I need to be complete. Amen.

Urgent Need to Find a Mate

"When you've been separated and divorced and you want to connect again, you're almost starving for it," admits Marie.

Sometimes your search for a new relationship or a new mate can take almost a frantic pace. At times like this, you need to slow down and stop. Think for a moment about why you desire this new relationship or mate. Wanting a new relationship right away is damaging on many levels, so be sure that you understand your motivations. You might discover that you are not ready for a relationship at all.

The Bible says that our actions are a reflection of our faith. People around you should be able to see your faith through the actions you take and the decisions you make. What are your actions saying about you?

"I'm always aware that there are children watching me throughout this divorce situation," says Bonnie Keen. "They are watching what I do with my grief, what I do with my anger, what I do with my ex-spouse, and what I do with my body. What do I want them to see?"

As you make decisions about where your life is headed and what your life's foundation is, realize that these decisions do not affect you alone. People around you are watching and learning.

"You see that his faith and his actions were working together, and his faith was made complete by what he did" (James 2:22).

Lord God, may my actions be a demonstration of all You have called me to be. Amen.

Remarriage Mistakes

Jeannette realized she had remarried too soon after her divorce. She shares, "I moved into the relationship so quickly that it was difficult to step out of it. My friends, family, and son were involved, and I didn't want to fail them. So I failed myself and then wound up failing all of them nine years later."

Lauren says, "When you're in a dating relationship, you can't see the problems. Marriage is different from a dating relationship. Jim and I had ten months of bliss. We had not one fight, but it's a completely different thing interacting with somebody twenty-four seven. That's where the problems come in. We weren't equipped to deal with them. It was a negative thing for a long, long time."

Honestly assess your readiness for a new relationship by answering the following questions:

1. Do you need someone else to be happy?
2. Do you live in the present?
3. Do you have a balanced energy distribution?
4. Have you learned to be single?
5. Do you have a problem-solving attitude?
6. Are you aware of your strengths and weaknesses?
7. Are you thankful for trials?
8. Are you spiritually secure and complete with God?

Trust fully in the love and promises of God. He knows what is best for you.

"So we know and rely on the love God has for us. God is love. Whoever lives in love lives in God, and God in him . . . There is no fear in love" (1 John 4:16, 18).

Jesus, You are all I need. Remind me daily to slow down and fix my eyes on You, not on what I think is best for me to do. Guide me to honor You in each decision I make about my new relationship. Amen.

New Relationships God's Way

Once your healing is complete and you are following God's will for your life, you may be ready for a new relationship. A relationship built God's way and in God's time is wonderful.

Bonnie Keen says, "Before my new husband and I started seeing each other, I had a peace with Christ. I said to God, 'I'm going to trust who You are and not who I am, and in Your plans to restore me and not my own.' There came a peace over me.

"I thought, *If I never marry again, that will be all right.* I didn't need a man. I needed God. I needed Christ's grace and the realness of who He is. It's incredible how God has restored me. I never imagined God would restore to me a sense of peace, a sense of love and joy in a sacred marriage, and the ability to walk in grace with my ex and his wife and their children.

"What the enemy wanted to do in the upheaval, the trash, and the mess of my life, God has taken and turned it around because He's a redeemer."

Perhaps someday you will remarry. And if you are walking in the peace and grace of the Lord, you will be blessed anew by the wonder of it all.

"The law of the LORD is perfect, reviving the soul. The statutes of the LORD are trustworthy, making wise the simple" (Psalm 19:7).

"They will rebuild the ancient ruins and restore the places long devastated; they will renew the ruined cities that have been devastated for generations" (Isaiah 61:4).

Lord, if I follow Your path for my life, I will walk in peace. In You, my life will be restored and full, with or without a new mate. Amen.

Financial Survival

Don't Put Off Making Financial Decisions

The financial impact of divorce is beyond what you probably imagined. You cannot put off making decisions about your income and your budget.

Elsa Kok shares her situation: "I understand the place of being financially in a hole. I ended up with all of the debt from the marriage. My credit was absolutely destroyed. Building financial security was a process. I had to get counsel. I had to go to someone and say, 'I need help. I can't pay these bills.' Somebody helped me lay out how I could budget my money; that was not something that came naturally to me."

Take a realistic view of your income; develop a budget immediately. Before you balk at having to create a budget, consider a new definition for the word *budget.* Think of it as "the freedom to live within your means."

Rose Sweet says, "I used to hate the word *budget,* and now I love it because I realize it is a set of boundaries that helps keep me safe from worry. If you don't know how much money is in your checking account, if you don't know what your bills are, and if you are always trying to borrow money, you are in fear and have underlying tension all the time. If you are living within a budget and not overspending, you can enjoy life without that fear."

Over the next few days we will discuss how to create a budget, and we'll offer insights and instruction concerning divorce and finances.

"Get wisdom—it's worth more than money; choose insight over income every time" (Proverbs 16:16 MSG).

Father, I need to make important financial decisions, and I need to establish a budget. Give me the wisdom and the discipline to do this and the courage to ask for help. Amen.

Financial Pressures

"I got a second job," says Marie. "I needed to have a second job because I was digging myself in really deep just to stay even. I was borrowing money from anybody who would lend it to me. It was frightening."

Financial pressures during divorce can be enormous. Financial needs keep coming, and whenever you get one area under control, another comes up. There is often not enough money to meet all the needs.

Cynthia Yates shares her story: "I was trying to hold up under the weight of all the debt my husband and I had accrued. It turned out that my husband had not paid a bill in a very long time. We had been separated for a while, and before I knew it, creditors were calling left and right, and they were threatening me. I was working two, three jobs, menial jobs. After I worked my two jobs during the day, I made arrangements to be able to sweep the floor of a produce warehouse in exchange for free fruit and vegetables for my son and me."

Change your focus from despair to goal setting. We will help you learn to develop a survival plan and stabilize yourself financially. There is hope for every financial situation, no matter how impossible your circumstances may appear.

"Hope that is seen is no hope at all. Who hopes for what he already has?" (Romans 8:24).

Lord God, I can't see an end to this seeming cycle of debt and money problems. But if Your Word says there's hope for me, then I'm going to look beyond my worries to see what You have in store for me. Amen.

Prepare a Crisis Budget Immediately

You may be experiencing a drastic cut in income. It is important to know how to prepare and maintain a budget that fits your new lifestyle.

"I needed to learn how to pay bills and live on a budget," says Cathy. "I had never done this before. I sat down with my father. He helped me lay it out on paper. He said, 'You need to quit subscribing to these magazines; you need to cut back here; you need to give this up.' I needed to change all these things to work my life around this new financial amount."

Making decisions for a crisis budget can be difficult, but you must not put it off. Realize that you will have to do without some things you are accustomed to.

Cynthia Yates says, "You've got to become proactive. This is a situation where unless you start to do something now, it's going to get worse one second from now."

What will you do with the financial amount God has given you?

Jesus tells a parable about three men who were each entrusted by their master with certain amounts of money. The first man "went at once and put his money to work and gained five more [talents of money] . . .

"After a long time the master of those servants returned and settled accounts with them . . . 'Master,' said [the first man], 'you entrusted me with five talents. See, I have gained five more.'

"His master replied, 'Well done, good and faithful servant! You have been faithful with a few things; I will put you in charge of many things. Come and share your master's happiness!'" (Matthew 25:16, 19–21).

Lord Jesus, teach me how to be faithful and wise with the money I have. Amen.

Your Crisis Budget

Follow these instructions to create a basic monthly budget:

1. Write down your monthly gross income from your employment, and add to this number any additional monthly income. Subtract taxes and your tithe. This is the total amount of money you have available each month.

2. Make a chart with four columns labeled "Expense Categories," "Monthly Expenses," "Amount Spent," and "Amount Left Over."

3. Create eleven or more rows under the columns. (The number of rows will depend on the number of expense categories you have.)

4. Under "Expense Categories," write the name of each category or item you spend money on each month; for example, housing, food, car, insurance, debts, entertainment, clothing, savings, medical/dental, miscellaneous, and child care.

5. Under "Monthly Expenses," record the amount needed for each category in a typical month. Use past bills/receipts to help figure these numbers. You can adjust them later if you need more or less. *Your goal is to have your total monthly expenses equal your available income.*

6. Under "Amount Spent," record throughout the month the amount you spend in each category and what you spent it on. This column will help you track your problem areas.

7. At the month's end, under "Amount Left Over," record any surplus or deficit in each category.

You can find online budget calculators and other financial planning tools at Crown Financial Ministries' Web site, www.crown.org/tools.

God promises to provide all you need. He is the giver of all good things, so create and maintain your budget with prayer and thanksgiving for the good things God has provided.

"Give thanks to the LORD, for he is good; his love endures forever" (1 Chronicles 16:34).

Thank You, Lord. Give me wisdom and perseverance as I put this budget into effect. Amen.

Trouble Sticking to a Budget?

Some people have trouble sticking to a budget. It is important that you not overspend in any of your categories because it will be difficult to make that money up later.

If you struggle with this, Larry Burkett's suggestion is to get an envelope for each expense category on your budget. Then, write the expense name and the amount budgeted on each envelope.

When you get paid, put the budgeted amount in each envelope. That amount is all you have for the month to spend on that expense; therefore, when you go to the supermarket, bring your "Food" envelope and shop carefully. When the envelope is empty, you are done spending in that category until next month. Do not borrow from other envelopes.

Perhaps you are not a planner, but it is a good quality to cultivate. God is pleased with a sensible plan, and He will help you stick to it. In the Bible in 1 Chronicles 28, God shows Himself to be a careful planner. He revealed to David a detailed plan for David's son, Solomon, to follow to build the temple. Solomon, like you, may have been overwhelmed by the many details of the plan, but David reminded him that God would be by Solomon's side every step of the way.

"David continued to address Solomon: 'Take charge! Take heart! Don't be anxious or get discouraged. GOD, my God, is with you in this; he won't walk off and leave you in the lurch. He's at your side until every last detail is completed'" (1 Chronicles 28:20 MSG).

Lord God, please be at my side, and give me the strength to stick with my budget. Amen.

Tithe

Your tithe is the amount you give to God. Giving a portion of your income to God shows your thankfulness for His provision and your faith in Him to supply your needs.

"'Bring the whole tithe into the storehouse, that there may be food in my house. Test me in this,' says the LORD Almighty, 'and see if I will not throw open the floodgates of heaven and pour out so much blessing that you will not have room enough for it'" (Malachi 3:10).

"I believe the Lord doesn't demand a tithe. I believe He asks for a tithe," said Larry Burkett. "I also believe that a tithe is the clearest outside indicator of where we are spiritually. It is really a measure of 'Do I trust God, or do I just say that I trust God?'"

Laura Petherbridge shares, "This is what I told God, 'I'm going to continue giving You this 10 percent, and I'm going to trust You for the rest.' Then the blessings from God began coming. Within two weeks my job went from part-time to full-time with a raise. I had several items that I decided to sell, and I received close to what I paid for them. A friend fixed my car for me, free of charge. A family member rolled up three one-hundred-dollar bills and slipped them into my hand as we said good-bye. One time after another, God kept meeting my needs. There was no logical human explanation to it. God was faithful."

"Now faith is being sure of what we hope for and certain of what we do not see" (Hebrews 11:1).

Heavenly God, I want to give You a portion off the top of my paycheck because I trust You to provide over and above what I can even imagine. Amen.

Housing

The biggest hit on your finances is housing. Your home can be a "budget buster" if you are not careful to consider the percentage of your income being used by the house.

"My husband left me with the house and with large house payments. I didn't even make that much money. I ended up getting another job. I worked two jobs for almost two years, twelve hours a day," says Patsy.

"In a two-year period," says Tim, "I went from what I thought was a perfect life to living in an apartment by myself with two houses now for sale."

Susan had to move from the house she and her husband built together because she could not keep up with the expenses after the divorce. She says, "All of a sudden he was gone, and I couldn't pay this mortgage. I stared foreclosure in the eye, and that's a scary thing."

Figure out what percentage of your income goes into the house. Your home should consume about 40 percent of your net income. That percentage includes payments, utilities, insurance, and telephone bills. If that percentage is not affordable, immediately consider other options.

Above all, keep persevering because God does have a place for you to live that is just right for you. He promises to supply all your needs, so rest easy and trust Him.

"God will generously provide all you need. Then you will always have everything you need and plenty left over to share with others" (2 Corinthians 9:8 NLT).

Faithful Lord, I trust in You to guide me to affordable housing that fits my needs and desires. Amen.

Sharing a Home with a Friend

You might consider sharing a house or apartment with another person of the same sex to save on housing costs.

Cheryl and Cathy were both divorced and both had two young children. They decided that living together in Cathy's home would be beneficial for all. Cathy stayed home during the day and watched the children and took care of the housework, and Cheryl went to work to meet the living expenses.

The period of time they spent living together was not without difficulties, but the arrangement was truly a helpful and special time for both of them. Cheryl says, "I think one of the best things I got out of it was having a friend for life. Through thick and thin, no matter what, I can always call Cathy."

If you decide to share a home with another divorced parent to save on expenses, you will have to set down clear rules and expectations. You will need to discuss things such as groceries, meals, transportation, television use, child-care arrangements, housecleaning, expenses, and other things to help your living situation be more comfortable and beneficial to all. It is important that you communicate with the person you are living with and continue to work together, being respectful of each other's feelings and needs.

"Your friendship was a miracle" (2 Samuel 1:26 MSG).

Lord Jesus, thank You for the blessing of friendship. If living with a friend is the best choice for me now, give me the courage and the wisdom to take steps to arrange it. Amen.

Cars

According to Larry Burkett, an automobile should consume about 15 percent of your net income. That percentage should include payments, insurance, maintenance, gasoline, and roadside help services.

If you need a car, then let your need be known, advised Burkett, "because God may have a car out there already in the hands of someone who would like to give it to a needy person. That person may not know a needy person and will end up selling the car for a fraction of what it's worth."

If you need help with maintenance and making decisions about your vehicle, you could help start a vehicle assistance ministry in your church. An idea is to recruit people knowledgeable about cars to meet at the church once every two months on a Saturday morning. At that time, single parents can bring their vehicles for checkups, maintenance, or advice.

"I know nothing about cars," says Laura Petherbridge. "Like many other women it's an area where I can get stressed because I'm vulnerable. My car is a tool that I need, and when it's broken, I no longer have control over it."

Don't be embarrassed to accept help. Be honest about your needs, and other people will respect your honesty and will help in whatever capacity they are best suited. As time goes on, you will marvel again and again at how faithful God is in providing for your needs.

"You sent abundant rain, O God, to refresh the weary Promised Land. There your people finally settled, and with a bountiful harvest, O God, you provided for your needy people" (Psalm 68:9–10 NLT).

O God, You have sent helpful people and other answers to my needs. I trust that You will continue to provide for me. Amen.

Food

Food is an area where you can discipline yourself to remain within your budget. Some practical ideas are to bring a lunch and drinks to work, take advantage of free or reduced school lunches for your children, and cook meals from scratch.

You are probably tempted to buy prepared foods and pop them in the microwave after a long workday. Unfortunately, the cost of prepared foods is typically much higher than if you were to buy the ingredients separately and prepare the same meal. You get more for your money when you prepare your own food. Plus, if you cook extra portions, you can freeze some for future "quick" meals!

Mike Klumpp shares, "I couldn't go out and buy prepared frozen foods because my grocery budget wouldn't allow it. Right now I'm responsible for eight children, and I still keep a $500 per month grocery budget. If you shop smart and cook from scratch, you'll find it's possible. It's the easy, convenient foods we are accustomed to in our culture that wear away at a grocery budget."

Jesus admonishes you not to worry because He will provide everything you need: "Therefore I tell you, do not worry about your life, what you will eat; or about your body, what you will wear. Life is more than food, and the body more than clothes. Consider the ravens: They do not sow or reap, they have no storeroom or barn; yet God feeds them. And how much more valuable you are than birds! Who of you by worrying can add a single hour to his life?" (Luke 12:22–25).

Jesus, help me find new ways to save money on food, while still eating healthy. It's hard to break away from old habits of eating, but I know I need to change. Amen.

Ideas for Saving on Food Expenses

One suggestion for saving on food expenses is to start a food co-op. A food co-op is a group of families who buy food in bulk together to save money. Some groups take turns shopping monthly for bulk items, and they get together once a month to prepare meals in large quantities. Then they divide the prepared dishes into family-size portions in freezer-friendly containers, and each family takes home enough meals to last a month! This saves money, saves time, and gives you the opportunity to build bonds of friendship.

Mike Klumpp offers another idea to save on grocery bills: "Sunday papers are filled with coupons. If you have grocers battling for control in your area, they'll often offer double and triple coupon deals. If you have a product that costs seventy-five cents, and you have a coupon for fifty cents and the store triples that coupon, you just made a dollar and a quarter."

Cynthia Yates offers this advice for saving on food costs: "Most people could feed their family on what they have in the house right now for probably weeks. It takes a little bit of grit, determination, and creativity."

Perhaps one of the above suggestions will be helpful in your situation. But what is most important is that you approach all your financial decisions with wisdom, including how much to spend on groceries and what to buy.

"Wisdom is a shelter as money is a shelter, but the advantage of knowledge is this: that wisdom preserves the life of its possessor" (Ecclesiastes 7:12).

Savior God, forgive me for the times I spend without thinking. Help me to discover new ways of saving money. Amen.

Medical Expenses

"I would have gone to see a doctor, but I didn't because I wasn't able financially to do it," says Jeannette.

Medical and dental care can be expensive. It is good to be honest about your situation with your doctor or dentist. You might be able to work out a payment plan, discount, or bartering plan with them. If your current medical professional cannot work something out, go to your local church and see if someone can recommend a doctor or dentist who might be able to help.

"I know a lot of Christian dentists and a lot of Christian physicians who would help out in a minute if a single parent came to them and said, 'Listen, I want to be really honest with you. I need the care and my children need the care, but I can't afford your fees. I'm willing to work out some kind of arrangement,'" said Larry Burkett.

It can be intimidating and embarrassing to have to explain your marital and financial situation to strangers, but your honesty and sincere willingness to be responsible will bring results. God is working not only in your life but also in the lives of everyone around you. He is always by your side, giving you the wisdom and strength you need for each moment.

"God has said, 'Never will I leave you; never will I forsake you.' So we say with confidence, 'The Lord is my helper; I will not be afraid. What can man do to me?'" (Hebrews 13:5–6).

Thank You, God, that You are always with me. Give me the courage, the strength, and the right words to say as I seek to make arrangements with my doctor, dentist, and other professionals. I will be honest and dependable in these arrangements. Amen.

Entertainment

"On payday my kids and I would always go out to eat and celebrate. They looked forward to payday," says Jan Northington. "They got to choose the restaurant, and they always chose Bob's Big Boy, so we had fries and burgers every two weeks on payday."

You might not think there's money in your budget for entertainment, but this is a necessary category to allocate funds for. If you exclude this category from your budget, you will probably end up pulling money from another category and using it for occasional entertainment activities.

There are several free and low-cost activities you can participate in. Check your local newspaper, library, or community center for these activities: concerts, outdoor movies, magicians, plays, clubs, school fairs, craft shows, sports events, and more.

"Entertainment is important," says Mike Klumpp, "but you may sometimes think you can pay for it as it comes. The danger is that you overspend. You say, 'Well, I've earned the right to this, so I'm going to take my family out to dinner and the movies tonight.' Then you sit down at the end of the week, you look at your budget, and you're short. If you budget for entertainment, you'll live realistically within your means. You can look forward to it; you can reward yourself with it. And it won't come back later and bite you."

Be thankful to God for the money you have. Use it wisely and enjoy it.

"Yes, we should make the most of what God gives, both the bounty and the capacity to enjoy it, accepting what's given and delighting in the work. It's God's gift!" (Ecclesiastes 5:19 MSG).

Heavenly Father, You provide all my needs—even the need for occasional recreation! Help me decide on a reasonable amount to budget for this category. Amen.

Clothing

"To have nothing in your budget for clothing is unrealistic. I've said many times: 'I've never once counseled a naked person,' so I know you've got a clothing budget whether you admit it or not," said Larry Burkett.

Clothing is an expense category you have more control over than others. Two of the best places to purchase clothing are thrift stores and yard sales. Many thrift stores are clean, organized, and selective about the items they sell. You can find brand-name, quality clothing of all styles and sizes at these stores. You can also find new items on the racks. Yard sales are a good choice as well. One suggestion is to go to yard sales or thrift stores located in or near affluent areas. The condition and quality of the clothing are usually excellent in those areas.

Being able to shop at thrift stores and yard sales is a blessing. This is something to be thankful for, especially in our culture where clothing and appearance are emphasized.

When thinking of God's provision of clothing for you and your family members, be thankful and remember there are other people who are worse off than you financially. In the Bible in the book of Isaiah, God reminds us that He wants us to help others who are less fortunate financially. What can you do to help someone else today?

"What I'm interested in seeing you do is: sharing your food with the hungry, inviting the homeless poor into your homes, putting clothes on the shivering ill-clad, being available to your own families" (Isaiah 58:7 MSG).

Holy Lord, You have blessed me with so much. I want to share these blessings with other people who are in need. Please give me the opportunity to do so. Amen.

Savings

"He who gathers money little by little makes it grow" (Proverbs 13:11).

Each month it is necessary to put a set amount of money into a savings account. Laura Petherbridge says, "This is important because inevitably there will be a crisis—perhaps a shingle blows off your roof or the car breaks down or you fall and break your hip and can't go to work. You may have disability insurance, but that might not kick in for a few months. You must have money tucked away so you can manage for a few months or pay for whatever crisis has happened. Saving is not a luxury or an option; it's a necessity."

When you receive your pay, immediately put money into your savings account. This amount does not need to be large, just let it build over time. Don't allow yourself to pull money from it to pay for other budget items.

"It's when you are literally at your worst that you most need to consider saving," says Cynthia Yates. "Saving does not necessarily mean putting aside 10 percent every single week, but it means putting something away as a little security blanket for yourself because you're going to need it."

Scripture reminds us of the importance of saving money:

"On the first day of every week, each one of you should set aside a sum of money in keeping with his income, saving it up" (1 Corinthians 16:2).

Dear Jesus, it seems impossible to save money when I can barely pay my bills. Help me to consider each budget category and think of ways to lower those expenses. Then, Lord, help me to decide on a reasonable amount of money to save each month, and give me the perseverance to save it. Amen.

Miscellaneous

You also need a category in your budget for miscellaneous expenses. Miscellaneous expenses can include a birthday gift, postage stamps, a cup of coffee on the way to work, a small household appliance to replace one that's broken, a haircut, and anything else that does not fall into another category on your list.

"I recommend the miscellaneous go into an envelope, and whatever you buy as miscellaneous, pay for it out of the envelope and put the change back in. When that envelope is empty, you say, 'I will not buy anything else this month no matter what. I'll do without it,'" said Larry Burkett.

If this category is not monitored, the amount of money you spend can grow quickly. Be creative in making do without certain things, and be wise about prioritizing items in this category; for instance, you could decide to get a haircut next month instead of right now. You could bring to work a thermos of coffee from home. You could pay your bills online to save on postage. For birthday gifts, you could make a homemade birthday card, bake some cookies, recycle a nearly new book or stuffed animal, or make a "coupon book" (coupons can include babysitting, a visit, a cup of tea together, a hug, a trip to the park, or a game of basketball, Frisbee, or cards). Saving money can actually be fun.

"Whoever can be trusted with very little can also be trusted with much" (Luke 16:10).

Lord God, every time a new expense comes up, I must stop and pray. First, to thank You for the money I do have, and second, to ask for wisdom about whether or not that expense is necessary at the current time. Amen.

Make Your Needs Known

Make your financial needs known to other people. Everyone has financial ups and downs. Don't let pride stand in the way of letting someone be a blessing to you.

Cynthia Yates says: "Many churches have volunteers who help people set up budgets and savings plans. There are also nonprofit organizations that will help you set up a payment plan if you're in debt. Even some people from collection agencies say, 'We will work with most people and come up with a plan if they will approach us and communicate with us.' Buy a notepad, write down the people you think you can call, and start calling."

In the first Christian churches, the believers shared their possessions, and no one was ever in need. This is a model for churches today. Find out what ministries are available to help you with needs. God's plan is for people to help one another. Today you may need help from someone, and tomorrow someone may need help from you.

Listen to benefits that were bestowed upon the people in the early church, who were faithful to God's teaching:

"All the believers were one in heart and mind. No one claimed that any of his possessions was his own, but they shared everything they had. With great power the apostles continued to testify to the resurrection of the Lord Jesus, and much grace was upon them all. There were no needy persons among them. For from time to time those who owned lands or houses sold them, brought the money from the sales and put it at the apostles' feet, and it was distributed to anyone as he had need" (Acts 4:32–35).

Faithful Lord, give me the courage to let people know my needs and to let them know how they can help. Amen.

Tell God Your Needs

"You do not have, because you do not ask God" (James 4:2).

Have you told God about your financial situation? Have you asked for His help?

"God says that you don't have because you don't ask, and you don't ask because you don't trust," says Elsa Kok. "He wants to help you. He's knocking on the door of your heart. If you open the door and receive Him, He can come in and make an impact. If you just leave Him out there knocking, then He can't impact your life. You may have cried out, 'Why haven't You helped me, God?' Maybe you haven't invited Him to help."

Tim shares, "I never thought God could help me in my daily struggles, in finances, and in decision making. I thought I had to do all that. I know now that if I pray about it, it'll all work out for the good. God knows what's going to happen in the future, and I don't."

God will supply your needs. Sometimes He provides in ways that are mysterious, and other times He provides through the practical help of other people. Don't leave God out of your financial situation.

"Here I am! I stand at the door and knock. If anyone hears my voice and opens the door, I will come in and eat with him, and he with me" (Revelation 3:20).

Savior God, sometimes I worry about money so much, and I don't even think about giving these burdens to You. I'm sorry! Other times I work and work, and think and plan, trying to make ends meet, and I forget again what a faithful provider You are. Forgive me! Amen.

Pride

Mike Klumpp, after divorce, became a single dad of four children. He talks about the financial difficulties he faced and how he put aside his pride in order to best care for his children: "I took an 80 percent cut in income to be home every evening for my family. At the same time I shouldered the debt my wife and I had amassed for ourselves.

"I just didn't have enough money to pay my creditors. I had to be honest. I had to put down my pride and say, 'I'm in a situation where I can no longer provide for my family the way I once did.' I had to recognize it was more important to see to my family's emotional and spiritual needs. I had to back off from the lifestyle I had grown accustomed to and accept the fact that there were going to be some changes."

Cynthia Yates addresses the person who is too ashamed to accept help from other people or organizations: "Are you going to say to your children, 'Gee, there's no food on the table because mommy or daddy was embarrassed'? The Bible tells us that we should be there for each other. There may be a time when you'll be sitting on the other side and be able to reach out and help somebody too."

Please don't let pride stand in the way of asking for help. Let others share the hard times and not just the good times with you.

"Rejoice with those who rejoice; mourn with those who mourn" (Romans 12:15).

Dear Jesus, someday I'm going to help people who are in the same situation I'm in right now. Give me the courage to put down my pride and be the receiver, not the giver, this time. Amen.

Feelings of Failure

You may hesitate to seek outside help because you feel like a failure. You are *not* a failure. Stop condemning yourself, and stop hiding the truth of your situation. Accepting and being honest about your circumstances is wise and mature.

Cynthia Yates tells about a time when a friend came to her home after the divorce and discovered Cynthia's true situation: "One day a friend came to visit and found me in the corner of my kitchen in a fetal position, drooling out of the corner of my mouth. I was rocking back and forth.

"On the outside I had looked like I was managing, but inside I was so scared.

"You could be talking to somebody who looks perfect on the outside but doesn't have a cracker in the cupboard at home. Is it pride? Is it fear that people will think you failed in life? We all fail."

Being honest with your friends will help ease your burdens. Don't cause your friends to miss out on God's miraculous answers to prayer.

In the Bible, four men carried their paralyzed friend to Jesus to be healed. When they arrived, the crowd was so thick they could not get close to Jesus. They decided to make an opening in the roof above Jesus and lower their friend through the roof.

"When Jesus saw their faith, he said to the paralytic, 'Son, your sins are forgiven . . . I tell you, get up, take your mat and go home.' He got up, took his mat and walked out in full view of them all. This amazed everyone and they praised God, saying, 'We have never seen anything like this!'" (Mark 2:5, 11–12).

Jesus, most of my friends don't know how bad things really are. Give me the self-confidence to be honest. Amen.

Reentering the Workplace

The job world is constantly fluctuating, and new technology is being invented every day. This can be intimidating for a person who has been out of the workforce for more than a year.

Cindy was in her fifties when she divorced and had not worked outside the home in twenty years. She advises: "Look into different classes to learn things that will help you in the workplace. Women's centers have computer and finance seminars. Do what you can do to help yourself add to a resume."

Not only is it possible to survive, but it's possible to thrive in a career.

A good place to start in determining which job is best for you is to get help from a career-counseling ministry. These organizations will help you determine what your aptitude is, what career you are best suited for, and how to get the training in that field.

If you already have a job, but it seems like it is not going anywhere, do not give up hope. Your current job could lead to another job as a result of your hard work, as a result of networking, or just because you are in the right place at the right time. Be encouraged; God's timing and circumstances are always best and are often surprising to us.

"He determined the times set for them and the exact places where they should live. God did this so that men would seek him and perhaps reach out for him and find him, though he is not far from each one of us" (Acts 17:26–27).

Lord God, please help me to make the right decisions regarding my job. I want to be open to learning new things. Give me the courage to take action! Amen.

Buying on Credit

Mike Klumpp considers his maxed-out credit cards a "blessing in disguise." He says, "Credit cards are interesting because they look like financial salvation. One thing that happened in my divorce was that my credit cards were already at their limits. I had to learn to budget without a credit card."

Cynthia Yates says, "Credit is your future money used up. If you can't afford to pay the full price for what you want right now, how can you afford the full price plus interest?

"Credit drives the economy. What's happening now, statistically, is people are using credit cards as short-term, high-interest loans to pay for diapers or food. I had an older woman come up to me and say, 'I'm scared because my husband's retirement check is not enough, and every month I go to the bank and borrow money on our credit card. What should I do?' I went to the people in her church and told them the situation. I was assured she would be helped. I followed up a year later, and the woman was well on her way to financial stability."

Don't get sucked in by credit. Talk to people who are knowledgeable about financial matters, and seek wise counsel. Do this if you have debt or might potentially go into debt. Evaluate your current situation, and make a plan to get rid of your debt and to avoid future debt.

"Of what use is money in the hand of a fool, since he has no desire to get wisdom?" (Proverbs 17:16).

Dear Lord, help me to be wise and not foolish about credit cards. Help me to understand I do have options that don't involve going further into debt. Help me discover what those options are. Amen.

Talk with Your Creditors

If you owe money and cannot make the payments, talk with your creditors. Explain your situation in a calm, straightforward manner. Show that you have done your homework, that you know how much money you have coming in and going out, and that you are carefully budgeting your current income. Reassure the creditors that you are willing to work out a payment plan and be faithful to it.

Mike Klumpp says, "I had to go to some of my creditors and ask for their assistance and tell them I was not going to be able to meet my commitments on time or make payments in full. I had to pay some penalties and interest fees along the way, but by and large, the creditors were understanding and helpful. They'd rather work with you and get paid than risk not getting paid at all."

Have a plan in mind when you call your creditors—a plan as to how much you can afford and how often you can make those payments. Understand that you may have to pay certain penalty fees.

"Is there anyone here who, planning to build a new house, doesn't first sit down and figure the cost so you'll know if you can complete it? . . . Or can you imagine a king going into battle against another king without first deciding whether it is possible with his ten thousand troops to face the twenty thousand troops of the other? And if he decides he can't, won't he send an emissary and work out a truce?" (Luke 14:28, 31–32 MSG).

Lord Jesus, help me to be able to "work out a truce" with my creditors. I want to pay back my debt, and I know it's possible only with Your help and guidance. Amen.

Canceled Debts

In some instances, if you are honest with your creditors, they may surprise you by lowering the amount owed or even canceling the debt.

Ed had nine months left on the lease of a house he wasn't living in. He could not find another person to rent it and take over the payments. He shares, "I said to my landlady, 'I can't pay, and I can't get another loan. My mom's got cancer, and I'm buying her medication. I don't know how to pay you anymore.' About five seconds went by and she said, 'Well, you paid for the three months it's been empty, and you've tried, so we'll just tear the lease up.'

"Three months earlier," says Ed, "there was no way she could tear the lease up because she was still making payments on the house. Just when I couldn't possibly pay, she was able to tear it up. The more I think about it, the more I realize I really am in good hands. God is leading me now."

Perhaps you have had someone who, by the grace of God, canceled one of your debts. The Scripture below illustrates Jesus' forgiveness and grace. Jesus canceled our debts (of sin) by dying on the cross. He saved us from future debts by rising from the dead. He guarantees the future inheritance of everyone who calls on His name.

"Two men owed money to a certain moneylender. One owed him five hundred denarii, and the other fifty. Neither of them had the money to pay him back, so he canceled the debts of both" (Luke 7:41–42).

Lord Jesus, I believe in You. Help me to be honest with my creditors and to be willing to work with them to set up feasible payment plans. Amen.

Using Credit Cards to Satisfy Emotional Hunger

"Many times spending takes the place of feeling," says Cynthia Yates. "People run rampant out there with a little plastic card. They don't stop to consider what their income might be. It's not even a factor. The idea is they need that next fix. They need to go out and buy something. They need to reward themselves."

In our culture, buying things is a way to "feel good" if only for a short time. Sometimes people go out and buy things they can't afford to feel good about having new things, to feel good because they are one step ahead of the neighbors, to feel good about getting back at a spouse who shares the credit card, or to feel good because they know they can buy almost anything they want. That kind of "feel good" isn't worth much at all. It's short-lived, it's shallow, and it never truly satisfies. If you have an empty space inside you, buying things will never fill it.

"Why do you spend your money on junk food, your hard-earned cash on cotton candy?" (Isaiah 55:2 MSG).

God can fill you. He can satisfy your emotional hunger. Hold on to your money and use it wisely, and turn to God when you have the urge to buy something to make you "feel good."

"Jesus replied, 'I am the bread of life. No one who comes to me will ever be hungry again. Those who believe in me will never thirst'" (John 6:35 NLT).

Dear God, help me think of a plan I can follow when the urge to spend comes over me. Perhaps I could recite a Bible verse to myself in the store: "[God's] grace is enough; it's all [I] need" (2 Corinthians 12:9 MSG). Amen.

"I Deserve It"

Many people believe they deserve to spend money on themselves. They think, *I work hard; I deserve to get something special for myself.* This is a common and accepted practice in our society. Yet, there is no biblical basis for spending money on something unnecessary when that money is needed for other things.

Cynthia Yates says, "I believe that a sense of ethical stewardship has been replaced by a feeling of entitlement. People are so accustomed to immediate gratification that they want their needs met and they want them met now: 'I'm entitled to have that boat in the garage. I'm entitled to have a latte on my way to work every day.' Yes, you're entitled, but you're also entitled to be able to sleep well at night because your bills are paid. You're also entitled to face your future because you have a retirement nest egg. Let's rearrange some of the thinking about entitlement."

If you are loyal to God's teachings, the Bible says you will prosper, and your house will be full of great treasure. So, when you begin to have "but-I-deserve-it" thoughts creeping into your head, reject them and think of the treasures you are accruing by choosing God's way.

"The house of the righteous contains great treasure, but the income of the wicked brings them trouble" (Proverbs 15:6).

Provider God, yes, it's nice to have special treats, but help me to choose those special treats wisely and to share them with others. Perhaps a walk in the fresh air, a bouquet of wildflowers, a high school sports competition, or a free movie rental from the library. I'll save my money for the things my family and I really need. Amen.

Your Attitude

A good attitude leads to financial success.

"Attitude is pivotal," says Cynthia Yates. "It is the key to any kind of success that you're going to have with anything in life. Attitude represents the strength of your maturity, and it also represents your worldview. If you can change your attitude, you're going to be able to change the way you approach your financial circumstances and the way you approach your life."

Dr. Dennis Rainey says, "Contentment arises from a spirit of gratefulness and thankfulness. It is a courageous choice to thank God for what you have *and* for what you don't have."[4]

You may need to redefine your attitude to get yourself on the right track toward financial success. The Bible instructs us in the type of attitude believers in Christ are supposed to have. Use the Bible to renew your attitude.

"Now we ask you, brothers, to respect those who work hard among you, who are over you in the Lord and who admonish you . . . Live in peace with each other. And we urge you, brothers, warn those who are idle, encourage the timid, help the weak, be patient with everyone. Make sure that nobody pays back wrong for wrong, but always try to be kind to each other and to everyone else.

"Be joyful always; pray continually; give thanks in all circumstances . . . Hold on to the good. Avoid every kind of evil" (1 Thessalonians 5:16–18, 21–22).

Lord God, it's easy for me to blame my bad attitude about money on circumstances or on other people, but I see that in Your Word You instruct me on how I should behave in all situations. Help me to prayerfully follow Your commands. Amen.

---

4. *Pressure Proof Your Marriage* by Dennis and Barbara Rainey. (Multnomah, 2003), p. 56.

Living Frugally Means . . .

Cynthia Yates knows from experience how important it is to live frugally. She offers a wonderful explanation of what it means to be frugal:

"Frugal is not trimming your wicks and living in a cave. Frugal is not eating gruel. Frugal is not walking around saying 'Woe is me' or being some type of tightfisted grump.

"Frugal is being able to enjoy your surroundings. Frugal is making the most out of what you have. Frugal is rejoicing. The Bible says that in all things rejoice. Frugal is rejoicing in the blessings that He has given you—even if it's a broken-down clunker. It is being so joyful to know Him and to make Him known to others around you. Frugal is smart above all things. It is the wise use and care of things around us, including time and finances."

When you consider your financial situation, you are the one who chooses what attitude to take. And choosing to have a good attitude brings honor to God. Looking at the above descriptions of *frugal*, which words best describe the attitude you take when it comes to budgeting your money?

"The wages of the righteous bring them life, but the income of the wicked brings them punishment" (Proverbs 10:16).

"But godliness with contentment is great gain" (1 Timothy 6:6).

Dear Jesus, wow, living frugally actually sounds enjoyable when Cynthia Yates describes it. Help me to change my attitude about my money struggles and be joyful and thankful instead. Amen.

Jesus Makes a Difference

Can Jesus make a difference in the way you deal with financial crises? Yes!

"I don't worry anymore about where I'm going to live or where the money's going to come from," shares Marie. "It comes when it's supposed to come. It works out when it's supposed to work out. Sometimes there is overtime I can do, and I once had somebody send me fifty dollars anonymously. Little things like that are signs that God is on the throne, and if I let Him stay there, everything else will fall into place."

Sue says, "No matter where I am, He's watching over me. Whenever I had fear or panic attacks about finances, I would quote, 'Be still, and know that I am God' [Psalm 46:10]. It has been a hard struggle, but the Lord has gotten me through it, and I'm finally out on the other end."

Nothing the world offers can compare to the peace and contentment offered by Jesus Christ. His provision for you will be abundant and have everlasting rewards if you turn to Him for help. He has already paid the price for you to receive this rich life; just believe and receive.

"Come, all you who are thirsty, come to the waters; and you who have no money, come, buy and eat! Come, buy wine and milk without money and without cost. Why spend money on what is not bread, and your labor on what does not satisfy? Listen, listen to me, and eat what is good, and your soul will delight in the richest of fare" (Isaiah 55:1–2).

Heavenly Father, I will listen to You and trust You to take care of all my financial needs. Help me to rely on You when I am tempted to rely on myself. Amen.

God Will Provide

Elsa Kok shares how God provided for her during the divorce. She says, "God will take care of your needs. I made under $10,000 a year, and my rent was $500 a month. My daughter was going to a private Christian school, and I was tithing to the church. I should not have made it.

"But when we had a need and brought it to God, and we weren't being frivolous with our money, He provided for our need.

"One morning we woke up and there was an envelope of cash on our table. Another time God provided work, so I took an extra job. Sometimes we'd receive an anonymous check in the mail or groceries on our doorstep. God was our provider.

"At times I would say, 'How am I going to pay this bill?' and my daughter would say, 'Mom, remember last time when we prayed about it and God came through? Let's pray.' To see her beginning to trust God for our financial care was amazing. She'd say, 'You know, Mom, God is the father and the husband in this family. He's not going to let us go under.' We'd get on our knees, and God would provide."

Through this experience Elsa not only grew closer to God and stronger in faith, but she had the opportunity to teach her child to do the same. God is good—get on your knees and believe it!

"He will give you all you need from day to day if you make the Kingdom of God your primary concern. So don't be afraid, little flock. For it gives your Father great happiness to give you the Kingdom" (Luke 12:31–32 NLT).

Lord, You are an amazing God who loves me dearly. Please provide for the needs I have today. Amen.

God Is Faithful

Cynthia Yates shares her lowest point during her divorce. She says, "My son and I were put out in the snow on Christmas Eve. I found myself homeless and penniless with a little child, stranded in a log cabin in the Rocky Mountains in the middle of a snowstorm. I had a diet pop and a can of tuna fish, and I didn't have a can opener. You could say it was the lowest point of my life—until you look at the next day, Christmas Day, when I crawled around on all fours in a broken-down old van my son and I had traveled across the country in, looking for sunflower seeds we might have dropped so I could have something to feed him. That was probably the lowest point in my life.

"I had nothing—and that's the moment when I had more than I ever had in my life because that's when God the Holy Spirit started flooding my heart and filling all those empty spaces.

"We live in a fallen world. Christians distinguish themselves by how they handle the hardship that comes their way. It's a matter of trust, and your trust must be in our Holy God. He will direct your path. I am living proof."

The answers to Cynthia's prayers began coming right away, in ways that Cynthia could never have expected. God is always faithful, and her passionate plea to you today is to trust Him.

"Trust in the LORD with all your heart and lean not on your own understanding; in all your ways acknowledge him, and he will make your paths straight" (Proverbs 3:5–6).

Holy Savior, I believe that You are on the throne and that You can be trusted to guide me through these hard times. Amen.

Being Proactive

God will provide and will work miracles, but your part is to *actively* trust in Him. Make forward movements each day to grow in your faith and to make wise decisions about money, work, children, and all aspects of your life.

"You can't just sit back and let the rest of the world take care of life for you," says Cynthia Yates. "You've got to roll up your sleeves. If you've never stood on your own two feet, now's the time. People will help you. There are resources out there, but you're going to have to take that first step."

God doesn't want you to be irresponsible or to spend money foolishly and think, *I can do this because God will come through. He always provides.*

Yes, God is faithful to provide, but He asks you to be wise about financial decisions and to move in the right direction. He often answers prayers through other people and through circumstances, but you have to be prepared to receive His answers.

Sometimes God will allow you to go down a wrong path and suffer the consequences of your own willfulness, but He does this so that you will turn to Him. You will then be in a position to understand how much more sensible His path is, and you will let Him take the reins of your life.

"If any of you lacks wisdom, he should ask God, who gives generously to all without finding fault, and it will be given to him" (James 1:5).

Heavenly Father, I believe that You will provide my needs, but I also know I must not sit back and do nothing in the meantime. You bless the person who perseveres, and I love to receive Your blessings! Amen.

Caring for Your Children

Effects on Your Children

Divorce affects all children who go through it. Some children seem to heal quickly while others appear to struggle for a lengthy time period. Research shows that those who appear to breeze through the divorce will struggle later on.

"To children, divorce is the death of the once-intact family," says Linda Ranson Jacobs. "Children experiencing a divorce need time to grieve. Grieving is hard work, so expect your children to take breaks in their grieving. Don't be misled and think they are over the divorce. They are only taking time out to be children."

Your children will each handle the news of the divorce in different ways, and they will have different methods of coping during and after the process. Anger, guilt, fear, withdrawal, aggression, denial, regression, self-blame, and depression are common reactions.

Children can survive and become healthy, competent members of society, but it takes hard work on the part of the adults around them. As a single parent it's important to stay connected to God and a church family and to develop family and community support systems for you and your children.

Some churches offer programs specifically for children whose parents are going through separation and divorce. DivorceCare for Kids™, www.DC4K.org, is a fun and powerful program for children ages 5 through 12 to learn to cope with and heal from the confusion, pain, and the many consequences of divorce.

God promises help for single parents.

"A father to the fatherless, a defender of widows, is God in his holy dwelling" (Psalm 68:5).

Holy Father, my children need You as much as I do, and they also need me. Give me the wisdom and the strength to teach my children how to cope and how to recover. Amen.

How Infants and Toddlers React

Children react differently to the news of the divorce and to the divorce process depending on their age. Young children can sense problems through their parents. Infants can tell when a parent is physically but not emotionally present. It can affect their eating and sleeping patterns. Even if one or both parents are emotionally involved and bonded to the children, the children's routines are interrupted as a result of the separation or divorce. Different households, different sounds and smells, and changing bedtimes can affect both infants and toddlers. Toddlers can be affected by the disappearance of furniture and other household items as well as by the constantly vanishing parent. It is important to establish daily routines to help your children feel secure.

Many infants and toddlers will experience ear infections and other illnesses such as upset stomachs, constipation, diarrhea, and colds. For a divorcing parent, a sick and fussy child only adds to an already stressful life. The children, in turn, will feel the stress of the parents, and this will contribute to the ever-increasing insecurities they are already feeling.

Relate to your children with love and tenderness each day. Learn how to have a heart that is gentle and kind toward everyone. If you harden yourself toward your former spouse or toward anyone else involved in the situation, your children will pick up on it and learn from it, despite your intentions to keep it from them.

"A tenderhearted person lives a blessed life; a hardhearted person lives a hard life" (Proverbs 28:14 MSG).

Teach me, Jesus, to live my life modeled after Yours. I want to be kind, compassionate, and loving to everyone, and I want my children to learn from that example. Amen.

How Preschool Children React

Preschool children may appear to take the news well at first. This may be because they don't understand what is actually happening, but as time goes by, they begin to realize the other parent isn't coming home. One of the first responses is fear. They may be clingy and may regress to behaviors such as thumb sucking, tantrums, and toileting accidents.

Linda Ranson Jacobs says, "Parents need to reassure the children they are safe and talk to them often, explaining what is happening and what will be happening. Children don't need sordid details of the adults' problems; they need reassurance that the parent will be there to meet their needs.

"When leaving children in preschool or day-care, make every effort to pick them up at the same time every day. Young children can sense when it's time for the parent to come. If a parent is late, the children will wonder if the parent is going to return. Trust levels can be hard to maintain if parents are not consistent with schedules and promises."

Do not be fearful about the impact the divorce is having on your children. God does not want you to be anxious. Know that God can take horrible, impossible situations (such as divorce) and turn them around for the good of those involved. Take wise, practical steps today to help your preschool-age children through this difficult situation.

"'So then, don't be afraid. I will provide for you and your children.' And he reassured them and spoke kindly to them" (Genesis 50:21).

Teach me, Jesus, to trust in You. I know divorce can be harmful to my children, but I also know I can trust in You and learn how to care for these precious little ones. Lead me forward with confidence. Amen.

How Children Ages 5–8 React

Children ages five through eight can have a great deal of anxiety about their parents' divorce. They don't have the thinking skills or the experiences to understand they will be taken care of and that life will go on. The fear of the unknown is scary for them. They wonder if the other parent will leave too. Children this age need to be reassured they are safe.

When children are on emotional overload, their schoolwork can be affected. They may have trouble focusing and processing information. Often this results in academic and behavioral problems at school:

- Being easily distracted
- Becoming discouraged or frustrated quickly
- Being overly tired or sleeping in class
- Showing aggressive behaviors on the playground
- Acting out with peers
- Saying hurtful or angry words to peers or teachers
- Being oversensitive to comments from peers and teachers
- Having difficulty concentrating
- Having low or failing grades

As a parent, it is important that you talk with your child's schoolteacher and become aware of what is going on in the classroom. If what you hear disheartens you, do not be reactive, but be proactive. Work with the teacher, your child, the school, and after-school providers to best meet the needs of your child during this difficult time.

"The LORD . . . sustains the fatherless" (Psalm 146:9).

Lord God, I didn't realize that my child would be facing these difficulties. Thank You that You will support and sustain us through this. Help me take the time to be in regular contact with the school. Amen.

How Children Ages 9–12 React

Children ages nine through twelve suffer a wide range of effects. One of the most devastating is the development of a poor self-esteem.

"That's the age when they begin to try to define who they are," says Dr. Bob Barnes. "That's the critical age for self-esteem, the age when they wonder how valuable they are, when they start to place blame and they look for somebody to blame this divorce on.

"That's the age when they may step into behaviors that are way beyond them—when the preteen boy thinks he's the man of the house and the preteen girl gets a little distant from Mom and is even sexually precocious.

"That's the age of dreams. They dream the other parent is coming home one day, and they wonder how they can make that happen. That's the age when they say they want to live with the other parent, partly to spark a reaction from the custodial parent and partly to see if the other parent will take them in."

Perhaps your children are exhibiting some of the behaviors Dr. Barnes describes above. Always persevere in love, giving them your time and positive attention. Before you react to things they say and do, think about their possible motivations and underlying fears. Listen to your children. Model for them how to love, how to forgive, and how to rely on God when life becomes overwhelming. God is a constant presence and strength for both you and your children.

"So we say with confidence, 'The Lord is my helper; I will not be afraid. What can man do to me?'" (Hebrews 13:6).

Lord God, if my children and I follow Your paths, we will make it through this process healed and whole. Lead us every step of the way. Amen.

How Teenagers React

"I had three teenagers at the time of my separation and divorce, fourteen, sixteen, and eighteen," shares Cindy. "One was very angry. Another one went into a depression. Another one acted out with her behavior. Everybody handled the divorce and the separation differently."

Teenage children can be profoundly affected by divorce. Some parents think their teenage children are old enough to understand the situation and that they are coping without any major difficulty. Do not be fooled into thinking this. Take time for regular, honest discussions with your children.

Plan these talks to take place at a consistent location, somewhere free from distractions. Your teenager will know immediately if you are not giving him or her your full attention and may resent it. These talks can develop into opportunities where he or she feels safe enough to express fears, hurts, and disappointments that would otherwise be kept inside or come out as a torrent of angry words. Know what is going on inside your child; don't make assumptions based on outward appearance or based on first responses to your questions.

If your teenage children refuse to open up to you, then encourage them to talk with a third party, someone you can trust to give them godly counsel and love. Tell them you hope they will be able to talk with you at some point as well, and continue to provide one-on-one time and to build up the relationship.

"Be strong. Take courage. Don't be intimidated. Don't give them a second thought because GOD, your God, is striding ahead of you. He's right there with you. He won't let you down; he won't leave you" (Deuteronomy 31:6 MSG).

Dear God, it's hard not to be angry or hurt when my children say unkind things to me or refuse to open up to me. I am glad to know that You are striding ahead of me; You are with me; and You'll never let me down. I need You, Lord. Amen.

Helping Your Children After High School

Bob's children were in junior high and high school when his divorce occurred. He lived more than a thousand miles away from them after the divorce but kept in constant communication with them, continued to pray for them, and made sure they were financially provided for.

"The time after high school was an important period in their lives," says Bob. "It was a time when they were separated physically from both houses and parents. They began to establish their own lifestyles and their own value systems, and that is when they came to Christ. They began to try to make some sense out of what happened.

"I can remember walking with my oldest daughter one summer evening, and she just sobbed her heart out as she began to realize what had happened regarding the divorce." His other daughter and his son had similar, heartfelt conversations with him.

"It was late teens, early twenties, when they began to come to grips with what happened," says Bob. "I think it's a matter of timing, and we need to stand pat and be available for our children to work through these issues so they become adjusted and have productive lives."

God loves your children even more than you do! He will not fail them, and He won't fail you.

"GOD, your God, will cut away the thick calluses on your heart and your children's hearts, freeing you to love GOD, your God, with your whole heart and soul and live, really live" (Deuteronomy 30:6 MSG).

Through You, Savior, my children and I can find the freedom to live life abundantly. Lead me forward as I parent my children. Amen.

Differences in the Ways Boys and Girls React

Distinct differences have been observed in the ways boys and girls deal with the divorce of their parents. Keep in mind, though, that every child and family is unique.

Lee talks about how his children have reacted to the divorce: "They've all handled it differently. My son is withdrawn and has not said a whole lot about it. My middle daughter, who's very outgoing, was angry with her mother. My oldest daughter is angry and very vocal."

Dr. Bob Barnes says that "in a father-absent home, a girl might date a little earlier and get more sexually active than other girls. In the father-absent home, the boy might become sullen and rebellious; there is no male role model."

Linda Ranson Jacobs says, "Boys in a fatherless home may try to be extra macho or manly. They may want to enroll in weight lifting and body-building classes. Girls in a home without the mother may tend to be exceptionally feminine and want to dress too grown up for their age. Each gender may try to overcompensate for the absent parent."

Encourage people in your church to be role models for your children. Ask a strong Christian couple, whose children are the same age as your children, to invite your children to spend time with their family. It is good for your children to be exposed to a healthy, two-parent family.

"How precious is Your steadfast love, O God! The children of men take refuge and put their trust under the shadow of Your wings" (Psalm 36:7 AMP).

Dear Lord, help me to be sensitive to the unique reactions of my children—not judging and not assuming, but being open to listen and offer support. Amen.

Children Dream
of Bringing Parents Back Together

"If I had one wish in the whole world, it was to get my parents back together," says Melissa.

Almost all children in divorce desire to bring their parents back together again. This is a natural response. God designed families to stay together. He designed marriages to stay together. The children can sense that it is wrong to be apart, and they want to change that.

Another reason children want their parents to reconcile is due to feelings of blame. They may feel responsible for what has happened, and they feel that getting Dad and Mom back together again will relieve the guilt and make everything right again.

A third reason children push reconciliation is because the divorce has caused them to grow up more quickly than they anticipated. They are burdened by the responsibilities in their lives and just want to be kids again with kid-size worries. Allow your children to be kids. Be careful about overburdening them with adult problems and responsibilities.

Teach your children that they can only go forward from here, and they must look to the future with excitement and hope. The future may not include marital reconciliation, but life can still be relaxing and fun when you and your children learn to move forward toward healing and recovery.

"Know also that wisdom is sweet to your soul; if you find it, there is a future hope for you, and your hope will not be cut off" (Proverbs 24:14).

Savior God, grant me the wisdom to understand the motivations of my children and to raise them up in the hope and healing that come through You. Amen.

Emotional Responses

You and your children will experience some of the same emotions as you process the divorce. Anger, low self-esteem, sadness, and loneliness are just a few feelings that each of you may go through. Be aware that you and your children may experience these emotions at different times and at different levels.

"Children will experience a different set of feelings as well, such as split loyalties to each parent, guilt, and the feeling that everything is their fault," says Linda Ranson Jacobs. "These feelings are natural and to be expected. You can help your children by letting them know their feelings are normal. Teach them how to deal with and overcome these difficult emotions."

"All I could do was be the best dad I could be," says Jerry. "I tried to minister to my children in every way that I could. There were deep hurts and anger that had to be worked through. Since I was the custodial parent, I was the beneficiary of a lot of their feelings. I had to deal with that and kindly take it into consideration because I knew they were venting a lot of their anger toward me because I was the most available."

If you are the custodial parent, you are likely the one who gets the brunt of your children's conflicting emotions. Pay attention to their actions and responses, and always ask questions.

King Artaxerxes in the book of Nehemiah asked, "Why do you look so sad? You're not sick. Something must be bothering you" (Nehemiah 2:2 CEV).

Dear Lord, help me to deal with my own emotions in a healthy manner so that I can teach my children to do the same. I pray that my children will feel free to share their hurts and worries with me. Amen.

Anger

Dr. Archibald Hart says you must first understand the purposes of anger in order to help your children through it. Anger has four purposes: to force your system to protect itself from hurt and fear, to help you overcome obstacles, to put right what has been wronged, and to let you know that something is threatening to you.

Have your children responded in anger because they might feel threatened by a new development in the home? Do you have a child who might be attempting to right a perceived wrong? Are your children covering up hurts and fears?

Dr. Hart and Dr. Les Carter offer advice on how to respond to your children's anger:

1. Understand the purpose of the anger
2. Respond to the anger with tremendous empathy
3. Avoid becoming defensive
4. Give your children permission to talk about it
5. Be willing to use the word *divorce*
6. Let them know that you are struggling with feelings and adjustments too
7. Do not feel you have to solve their problems or give an immediate answer

Adults may not realize that anger can be scary to a child when the child doesn't understand what is happening. Take time to let your children know that being mad is a normal reaction to the breakup of the family. Tell them that while they may be hurting on the inside, it is not okay to hurt others.

"A soft answer turns away wrath, but a harsh word stirs up anger" (Proverbs 15:1 NKJV).

Loving God, I pray that my children will open up to me and share their struggles and their feelings. Help me to know the best way to help them. Amen.

Expressing Anger Appropriately

"Children rarely know how to express their anger in appropriate ways," says Linda Ranson Jacobs. "Most children express their anger through lashing out and using disruptive behaviors. They may scream, kick, hit, cry uncontrollably, throw things, and resort to temper tantrums. Many times their expression of anger only serves to get them in trouble.

"Some children will experience a tremendous amount of energy when they are angry. Give them constructive ideas about what to do with the energy they feel when they are angry. Teach them to vacuum floors, practice soccer, run, wash walls, or play a musical instrument. If a child is screaming and shouting insults, that is not the time to approach the child. Explain to the child that when he or she is calm, you will be more than happy to sit down and discuss things. This may mean putting space between you and your child."

As a parent, you can model appropriate ways to express your anger. Children will learn by watching what you do more than by hearing what you say. Encourage your children to talk about their anger. Give them permission to say, "I am mad." Encourage them to think of ways to deal with their anger the next time it arises.

You may not understand why your children have to experience all of this anger. It says in the Bible you don't have to understand, just rely on God.

"I want you to know me, to trust me, and understand that I alone am God. I have always been God" (Isaiah 43:10 CEV).

God, I do want to rely on You. Help me to model trust in You so my children will see and know that You will take care of their hurts and their hearts. Amen.

Loss of Self-Esteem

Another effect of divorce on children is a loss of self-esteem. A loss of self-esteem is a loss of confidence in one's value. Children feel power-less because their world is falling apart, and they feel incapable of keeping things together.

Parents can help rebuild the loss of self-esteem by giving children back some of their power. Building self-esteem can be accomplished through giving children choices and allowing them to make their own decisions when applicable. This can be as simple as allowing a pre-schooler to choose his or her own clothes, permitting an elementary-age child to select what the family will eat for dinner, and allowing a teen to choose an appropriate bedtime. Start with easy decisions, and gradually increase the importance of the decisions as the child grows and matures.

Linda Ranson Jacobs says, "You may not be able to bring the other parent home, but you can help the children realize they have a choice to love both parents. They have a choice to love and honor God. When children have some control over their lives, they will feel better about themselves. You will feel better about yourself as a parent when you realize your children are becoming independent."

Continue to build up their self-worth by loving them uncondition-ally, helping them understand they can't be perfect at everything, teaching them to accept the disappointments, and teaching them to accept themselves for who they are. In God's eyes, your child is beau-tiful and special and wonderfully made.

"It is clear to us, friends, that God not only loves you very much but also has put his hand on you for something special" (1 Thessalonians 1:4 MSG).

Precious Savior, You love my children so much. Help me to build them up in that love. Amen.

Depression

Children can go through periods of deep depression as they grieve the losses that accompany divorce. The following symptoms of depression are common in children: withdraws from others, prefers isolation, does not want to talk, appears sad, has no energy, has no interest in hobbies or other activities that used to be of interest, cries often, and is sensitive and easily offended.

Dr. Archibald Hart says, "Research has shown that children as long as ten years after the divorce are still depressed. What is at the root of the depression is the loss they have experienced. Not only the loss of a parent, but the loss of dreams, the loss of ideals, the loss of the intact home. God has designed us to respond to loss with depression, which can be damaging to children [if they do not learn how to recognize and cope with it]. Of all the emotional consequences of divorce, that is the one emotion that parents pay the least attention to."

Pay attention to your children and their emotions. Take the time to notice changes in their behavior, and talk with them about it. If they are sad because they miss the other parent, let the children know your feelings will not be hurt if they want to talk about it. Teach them how to grieve their losses, and teach them about the comfort of God.

"God, Who comforts and encourages and refreshes and cheers the depressed and the sinking, comforted and encouraged and refreshed and cheered us" (2 Corinthians 7:6 AMP).

Lord, You are my Comforter and my Encourager. Refresh my spirit today and help me take the time to pray with my children and teach them about You. Amen.

Mistakes Parents Make

Divorce is tough for you as a parent, and you are going to make mistakes along the way. The purpose of discussing common mistakes parents make is to help you avoid them and to alert you to potential problems.

"I'm rebuilding my relationship with my son," says Harriet. "He had to take on a role that was much older than what his twelve years should have had to handle. For almost a year he looked after me. Now I'm trying to get the roles back to the way they're supposed to be. I've tried not to put him in difficult places in this whole ugly business. Most of the time I've succeeded. A lot of the time I've failed.

"I remember one time when I was being critical about the other woman, and I told my son, 'Honey, I don't want you to hate her because I don't want hate to be part of your life.' He looked at me with all the directness of a twelve-year-old, and he said, 'Oh, Mom, yes you do.' The reality of that was so strong it forced me to look deeply at who I was showing up as to my son."

You will make mistakes, and it's okay. Walk forward. Keep trying, and keep walking with God.

"I lift up my eyes to the hills—where does my help come from? My help comes from the LORD, the Maker of heaven and earth. He will not let your foot slip—he who watches over you will not slumber" (Psalm 121:1–3).

Holy God, when I make mistakes, help me to keep moving forward and not condemn myself. Teach me how to be a godly parent to my children. Amen.

Criticizing Your Former Spouse

You may make the mistake of saying negative things about your former spouse in front of your children. There are several reasons you might be tempted to do this, but for their sake, it is best to refrain.

"It can be harmful when parents openly say things against the other parent," says Lynda. "At times in anger or hurt I would express that I was upset. I know that bothered my children and hurt them. I think that's a mistake."

Wayne Hudson explains, "What the parent really wants here is an ally. You want your children on your side. Because of that, you have a tendency to tell them things they shouldn't hear and to expose them to things they should never be aware of. You need to fight the overwhelming urge to do that. Understand that these are just children and they're not emotionally equipped to cope with such stress."

Think about recent instances where you said something critical about your former spouse. What were your motivations? How did your children react? Did you think before you spoke?

If critical words have become a habit for you, do not despair. You can work on developing a new habit, one day at a time. The next time a negative word is about to come out of your mouth, wait. Consider your words, your motivation, and how it might affect your children.

The Lord promises to help us in our weakness.

"Set a guard over my mouth, O LORD; keep watch over the door of my lips" (Psalm 141:3).

Lord God, sometimes I can't seem to hold my tongue when I should. Help me to be a godly example to my children in the words that I say and the attitudes I have. Amen.

Using Children as Spies

Parents of divorce often use their children to find out what is going on in their former spouse's life. You might not even realize you are doing it, or you might think you should do it to protect the children. It is important that you do not use your children as spies.

Dr. Bob Barnes says, "That's not fair to a child, and eventually it will cause more anger. When a parent uses a child as a little snoop, it will cause the child to manipulate to get his or her own way and manipulate even the things that are going on. The child needs to be permitted to be a child."

You may not like the way your former spouse conducts his or her time with the children. You may feel that your former spouse is not being a good influence on the children or is not making wise decisions about food, entertainment, rest time, or discipline. If you have concerns, you must not bring the children into the middle of it. If the children want to talk about their time with their dad or mom, let them know you are open to listening without judgment, but that you understand if they would rather not talk about it.

"Do not exasperate your children; instead, bring them up in the training and instruction of the Lord" (Ephesians 6:4).

Dear Jesus, I only want what is best for my children, and I realize that sometimes I have hurt them unknowingly. Give me the words to say to apologize to my children and to let them just be children. Amen.

Using Children as Messengers

Another mistake parents of divorce often make is to put kids in the middle by using them as messengers. For the most part, children know when they are being used, and they resent being placed in this role. It will only serve to build a barrier between you and your children. Your children need you as a strong parent they can depend on and trust to be there for them. Children don't want to see their parent as weak and incapable of taking care of adult issues.

"I hate being in the middle," says Melissa, whose parents divorced. "Why can't my parents just talk?"

Dr. Archibald Hart says, "Don't use children to communicate messages from you to the other party. Children resent having to carry messages back and forth."

If you have something to say to your former spouse, find a way to relay the message without using your child as a go-between. There are several ways to communicate that do not involve your child: telephoning, e-mailing, writing a letter, or arranging to meet together at a neutral location when the child is not present. All of this can be done without putting your child in a stressful position.

"When I was a child, I talked like a child, I thought like a child, I reasoned like a child. When I became a man, I put childish ways behind me" (1 Corinthians 13:11).

Lord God, sometimes I do get petty or childish in my behavior. Forgive me. I need to be able to communicate with my former spouse for the sake of the children. Guide me in that. Amen.

Restricting Visitation

A parent with custody will often try to restrict visitation to the other spouse. That's a mistake that can hurt your children.

"He will always be their dad; she will always be their mom. There's no divorce taking place there," says Dr. Bob Barnes.

Linda Ranson Jacobs says, "Children will automatically have divided loyalties. They may look like one parent but act like the other. They may exhibit some talents from Mom's side of the family and have interests or hobbies from Dad's side of the family. Children need an opportunity to know both parents. They deserve to be able to explore both family heritages."

When you and your former spouse separated or divorced, it was a process that occurred between the two of you and not your children. They are still the children of both parents—100 percent each. That percentage does not change when the children see only one parent on weekends or holidays.

By restricting visitation, you may be inadvertently forcing your children to choose which parent they will be loyal to, which parent they will side with. Don't burden your children with this. They desperately need to have regular contact with both parents. They have enough anxiety and insecurity as it is.

"Do not irritate and provoke your children to anger [do not exasperate them to resentment], but rear them [tenderly] in the training and discipline and the counsel and admonition of the Lord" (Ephesians 6:4 AMP).

Righteous God, these children are more Yours than they are mine or my spouse's. You love them so much and want what is best for them. Teach me how to be the best parent I can be. Amen.

Making Too Many Changes

Another mistake often made by parents of divorce is to make too many changes in the lives of their children too soon.

"Making changes too fast is a big mistake," states Dr. Archibald Hart. "Children need time to make adjustments, depending to some extent on the age of the child, but particularly children between ages five and fourteen."

Dr. Bob Barnes says, "Many times amidst the anger and the pain, the custodial parent yanks the family's support system in one sudden move and says, 'We're out of here. We're going to move.' The children desperately need that support system. There needs to be a time of trying to calm down before big decisions are made."

Are you planning any changes that might be disruptive to your children? Could they be postponed?

"Another mistake that parents make is not realizing the loss of rituals," says Linda Ranson Jacobs. "Children have rituals that adults don't realize are rituals. A high-five every morning from a parent becomes a point of connection for the child, or a 'ritual.' When the parent leaves, the ritual leaves too. The remaining parent cannot replace the parent, but he or she can develop new rituals. If parents don't develop healthy rituals for the children, the children may develop unhealthy rituals."

"Careful planning puts you ahead in the long run; hurry and scurry puts you further behind" (Proverbs 21:5 MSG).

Savior God, may my decisions be based on careful planning and wisdom. Protect my children's hearts and spirits during this confusing time. Amen.

Forcing Kids to Choose

Children do not need to be put in the position of having to choose which parent to live with, which parent to spend holidays with, or which parent to go out with Saturday night. Having to make those choices can be devastating for a child, and some children will try to please both parents.

"I remember one experience that to this day brings hurt," says Kennie, whose parents divorced. "My sister and I were with my dad, and my dad had called my mom on the phone. He wanted us to do something with him and so did my mom. My dad said to me, 'Well, you choose. Do you want to come do something with me, or do you want to go back with your mom and play Putt-Putt?'

"I didn't know how to read him. I thought, *Does he want me to stay? Does he want me to go? What should I do?* So I said, 'Well, we'll go back.' Then he put on his sunglasses, and as he was driving us back, I could see the tears just coming down his face. That was devastating to feel that pull and have to make choices."

Help your children to know that your love for them is not based on the choices they make or their words or behaviors. Show them that you love them unconditionally.

Unconditional love is what the heavenly Father has for you and your children. His love never fades, no matter what you do or say.

"The LORD appeared to us . . . saying: 'I have loved you with an ever-lasting love; I have drawn you with loving-kindness'" (Jeremiah 31:3).

Heavenly Father, help me to show my children today in so many ways that I love them dearly. Amen.

Making Promises You Can't Keep

Children have many requests and demands concerning things they would like to have, places they would like to go, and what they would like to do. Sometimes parents make the mistake of saying "yes" to their children without thinking it through, perhaps to put the child off or because they feel bad saying "no." Practice saying, "Let me think about that." This will give you time to consider all the possibilities so you can make a wise decision, and it will help your children learn patience. Be sure to show them that their requests are important to you by remembering to give them an answer. "Let me think about it" does not mean "Hopefully you'll forget you asked."

If your child wants something you can't afford, then discuss what alternatives are available. Include your child in the discussion. If he or she wants to go visit someone or go somewhere special, consider all the details before making a decision.

"Your children depend on you to be truthful," says Linda Ranson Jacobs. "They would rather be told the truth than a lie. To children, a broken promise is a lie. Children will remember those broken promises and their trust of you will be diminished."

When your children are older, you'll want them to remember how important they were to you and how you took time to evaluate their requests. You can build a solid foundation for them now to be able to trust others in the future.

"Above all, my brothers, do not swear—not by heaven or by earth or by anything else. Let your 'Yes' be yes, and your 'No,' no, or you will be condemned" (James 5:12).

Dear God, I pray that I am always a person true to my word and that my children will learn from my example. Amen.

Premature New Relationships

Another common mistake a parent can make is to enter into a new relationship too soon—before healing has occurred for both the parent and the children. As an adult you realize that life will go on. You understand that one day you may remarry and have another spouse. Children don't see things this way, and they don't have the option of choosing another parent; their parents will be their parents forever.

Most children harbor the idea that their parents will eventually get back together again. They are not ready for someone else to enter the picture. When they see their parent in a new relationship, it can be scary. They may worry that they are losing a parent again, that they will receive less attention with a new person around, or that things will change again in their already-changed lives.

"When my mom started dating, it bothered me," shares Melissa. "Every time she would get a boyfriend, I would always try to make him not want to be with us. Even if he had been the nicest guy in the world, I would not have liked him. Maybe I just didn't want to lose her since I already had lost my dad."

Do not consider dating until you know that you are healed and content with your single status. When you do begin dating, go slow; do not bring the children into the picture until you know where things are going.

"Wait for the LORD; be strong and take heart and wait for the LORD" (Psalm 27:14).

Dear God, help me to take my time in new relationships and not involve my children unnecessarily. I want to follow Your plan for my new relationships and not rush into anything. Amen.

Custody Battle

A messy custody battle is one of the most damaging aspects of divorce for children. Do everything you can to keep your children from becoming directly involved in the legal proceedings.

If you have any choice in the matter, keep your children as far removed from a court battle as you can. If your state allows mediation, try that route first and keep it between the adults. Children are not ready to make decisions against either parent. If you do not have a choice and your children are subpoenaed, be sure to have a strong support system of people who will pray with you.

Your children will be hurt, anxious, and confused. They need to see you drawing on the Lord's strength and seeking His peace during this time. Children will learn how to handle situations like this by watching you. Be very careful that your behavior is godly and peaceable.

In the Bible, Ephesians 6 explains the importance of putting on the "armor of God" each day so that you will be strong enough to withstand any trials that you face. Read these verses with a prayerful attitude. Make a decision to put on this armor every day, whether you are going to court, trying to keep your children out of court, or just facing another difficult day.

"Put on the full armor of God so that you can take your stand against the devil's schemes" (Ephesians 6:11).

Faithful God, today I will put on Your full armor so that I will be able to stand firm, rooted in Your love and truth. Amen.

Loss of Structure

It is important that your home have rules, boundaries, a basic schedule, and an authority figure for the children at all times. They should be clear about their responsibilities. They should know the rules and the consequences. Communicate with your child-care provider and make sure he or she knows what your expectations are for your children.

A loss of structure at home can be devastating for a child. Children need consistent routines they can count on. When one parent leaves, schedules and routines change. Children feel more secure when they know what is going to happen next. Routines bring a sense of security and safety to the home. Each parent needs to develop a set of rules and routines. Children can then adapt to both homes.

"I had a lot of unsupervised time," says Loren, whose parents divorced. "Do not let your children be unsupervised, especially between the hours of three and six. I got in the most trouble in the afternoon when I got home from school, doing things I didn't have any business doing."

Dr. Bob Barnes says, "If there is no structure, if it's just up for grabs, then everybody is wondering, *Who's in charge here? What's happening here?* The relationships will be strained; there will be anger, and the child who is prone toward withdrawal will really withdraw."

"Discipline your children while you still have the chance; indulging them destroys them" (Proverbs 19:18 MSG).

Father God, sometimes I am too exhausted to bother with rules and routines. I pray that no matter how tired I am, I will follow through in loving discipline with my children and seek to maintain structure in my home. Amen.

Parenting or Providing?

Sometimes in the effort to make ends meet and support your family, you may lose sight of your parenting responsibilities.

Dr. Bob Barnes says: "Establish daily: 'What's the priority, parenting or providing?' You need to decide to sit at your children's bedside and talk with them tonight and do the laundry later—even though you are exhausted. Then, you need to make the decision to choose parenting first again tomorrow night, or there may be nightmares later on when the kids are out of control because there was no nurturing parent; there was just a provider."

Trying to be a supermom or superdad as well as a superworker can be draining and discouraging. Remember how great and mighty God is. He does not expect you to do this on your own strength.

Pray about ways you can change your day to be less stressful and more parenting-friendly. Perhaps you could go to work earlier in order to be home when the children get off the bus. Consider asking the church for teenage volunteers to come once a week for an hour to do housework or yard work. Perhaps you could share responsibilities with another single parent, such as cooking healthy meals, grocery shopping, or running errands.

"God's love, though, is ever and always, eternally present to all who fear him, making everything right for them and their children" (Psalm 103:17 MSG).

Dear God, show me how to arrange my busy mind and my busy schedule so that I always put God-pleasing things first—like snuggling up and laughing with my children! Amen.

Where Can You Find Help?

Right now you may feel you do not have the energy to deal with all of the issues regarding your children. This is a natural feeling. God never intended you to parent your children alone.

With help, you can be successful at single parenting.

Dr. Bob Barnes says it is crucial that single parents get involved in a local church that has the resources to help. Find opportunities in your church to establish relationships with people who will be good role models for your children.

Connect with a healthy, functioning, two-parent family in your church that has a child the same age as your child. Ask that family to help you parent your child. This will allow you to have another person to talk with regarding various school projects, church activities, and other parenting issues that come up.

Cindy shares, "I was fortunate enough that I have a sister-in-law who is a social worker at a women's center. When all of this was happening, she said, 'You need to get help, and you need to make sure that those kids are taken care of first. Focus on the kids. If you focus on the family and your children, everything else is going to be okay.'"

"I was young and now I am old, yet I have never seen the righteous forsaken or their children begging bread. They are always generous and lend freely; their children will be blessed" (Psalm 37:25–26).

Lord God, when I worry and fret, may I lay my fears aside and seek You in prayer and in silence, knowing that You will supply all I need. Amen.

Noncustodial Parents

As a noncustodial parent, you may sometimes be confused about what your role is. Be aware that you still have a strong influence on your children, regardless of how often you see them. Your children are very aware of your actions and decisions regarding their lives. Be involved, and consistently reassure them of your love.

Another important suggestion is that you provide your children with a sense of continuity. It is comforting and reassuring for your children to know when they will see you; to be able to contact you in between through telephone, e-mail, or letters; and to know that you will be contacting them. Always remember that you are still the parent, an authority figure, role model, and disciplinarian, and not a best buddy.

"Sons are a heritage from the LORD, children a reward from him. Like arrows in the hands of a warrior are sons born in one's youth. Blessed is the man whose quiver is full of them" (Psalm 127:3–5).

"My child, don't ignore it when the LORD disciplines you, and don't be discouraged when he corrects you. For the LORD corrects those he loves, just as a father corrects a child in whom he delights" (Proverbs 3:11–12 NLT).

Lord God, help me to be a positive, consistent, loving influence on my children. Thank You that You provide the grace I need to move forward in love and to continue to build these relationships. Amen.

Can Kids Recover from Divorce?

Here's a little encouragement for you: Children can and do heal from the experience of divorce and turn out well.

Laura Petherbridge says, "I often meet parents who think, *If my children don't have both parents, they are going to grow up very dysfunctional.* If the custodial parent is emotionally healthy, spiritually stable, and walks closely with God, the children can grow up to be really wonderful, secure kids."

God loves you and your children so much. He is willing and able to help you and your children every day and every moment of your lives. Turn to God for help, and trust Him to guide you in making the right decisions for your child.

Consider bringing your kids to a DivorceCare for Kids™, DC4K™, a program for children whose parents are experiencing separation or divorce. DC4K™ uses Scripture, arts and crafts, music, DVD dramas, exercise, games, and role-playing to help children of divorce learn coping skills, build their self-esteem, and experience healing from the difficult emotions of divorce. Visit www.DC4K.org to find a program near you.

"He who fears the LORD has a secure fortress, and for his children it will be a refuge" (Proverbs 14:26).

Lord God, my children need a secure fortress and a refuge during this time of confusion and instability. Sometimes I feel so helpless as I watch them grow and make their own decisions. I give my children to You, and I trust in Your promises that my children will grow to be healthy and strong in a relationship with You. Amen.

Long-Term Stability for Your Family

Some children who seem to adjust well to the immediate problems of divorce experience deep problems later in life. Therefore, after you have helped your children achieve a sense of stability in their current life situation, you need to take steps to help them avoid the long-term effects of divorce. There are many things you can do to help minimize and eliminate the effects of divorce on their emotional health, future relationships, and spiritual lives. We will discuss these over the next few days.

It can be disheartening to think that your children will be affected by the divorce even into adulthood, but with God's guidance, your children can learn to live healthy and victorious lives. Entrust your children to Him and be a model of godly love to them every day. Keep in mind that you won't be able to help your children stabilize their lives if you aren't modeling for them what a stabilized life looks like. Take heart, though; if you have a relationship with Jesus and are seeking to serve Him, you are in God's hands, and He will be there for you. Psalm 121:5–8 is a promise from God to you and your children that He will never fail to watch over you and to keep you from harm.

"The LORD watches over you—the LORD is your shade at your right hand; the sun will not harm you by day, nor the moon by night. The LORD will keep you from all harm—he will watch over your life; the LORD will watch over your coming and going both now and forevermore" (Psalm 121:5–8).

Thank You, Lord, that my children can live life to the fullest through Your enabling. Amen.

Training Your Children

"Single parents need to get their hands on resources that will help them learn. There are some things a child needs to know," says Dr. Bob Barnes.

But he warns, "Don't try to do everything at once. You can make yourself feel horribly guilty if you read a book and think, *Man, there are lots of things my child needs to know, and I'm not teaching any of them.* And then you do nothing because you can't do them all. Just do one thing at a time."

Train up your children one step at a time and with clearly defined goals. List some specific things that you would like your children to learn, to accomplish, and to take with them into their adult lives; think of spiritual, emotional, physical, educational, relational, and financial goals. After you have listed these areas to work on, prioritize your list and come up with practical steps to help you and your children achieve each goal. For example, if you would like to help your children grow spiritually, you could decide to read the Bible with your child. Plan these devotions to occur at a regular time each week or month. What is important is that you stick with it once you begin.

"Train up a child in the way he should go, and when he is old he will not depart from it" (Proverbs 22:6 NKJV).

Dear God, help me to take things one at a time, but to continue to persevere in training up my child. Amen.

Being a Good Example

The first step in training your child is to set a good example.

"If you want to teach your child how to handle money," says Dr. Bob Barnes, "you need to set an example in that yourself. If you want to teach your child how to handle sexuality, then as a single parent you can teach that lesson better than anybody else. You need to stay pure."

Your children are watching how you handle problems, how you react to new situations, how you communicate with other people, and how you show love. Your example in their lives is crucial for their development. Ask God to help you recognize where you are having difficulties and to help you change for the better.

Sometimes you will have to humble yourself and apologize to your children or to other people. This is difficult, but so important. God wants adults to become like little children by following their example of humility, love, sincerity, and joy.

"At that time the disciples came to Jesus and asked, 'Who is the greatest in the kingdom of heaven?' He called a little child and had him stand among them. And he said: 'I tell you the truth, unless you change and become like little children, you will never enter the kingdom of heaven. Therefore, whoever humbles himself like this child is the greatest in the kingdom of heaven. And whoever welcomes a little child like this in my name welcomes me'" (Matthew 18:1–5).

Father God, I want to walk in childlike faith and live my life as the obedient child of a Loving Father. Amen.

The Four Es

Dr. Bob Barnes names the four Es of child rearing: example, exposure, experience, and encouragement. Yesterday's devotion relayed the importance of setting a good example. The second step is to expose your children to the responsibilities and the lessons of life.

"Exposure is walking with them through life," says Dr. Barnes, "helping them, for instance, as they figure out how to spend their money. Exposure is reading books to them about their sexuality. So first you set an example, and then you expose them to the things they need to learn."

Another step in training your children is to let them experience things, to learn by doing. Dr. Barnes says, "That means you get out of the way and let your children make their own decisions sometimes. You may be thinking, *Do you mean I should let my child buy that cheap toy that's going to break in a week when I know it's a waste of money?* Yes, there are times when a child needs to learn the lesson that 'Sometimes you may waste your money, and it hurts, doesn't it?'"

The fourth E is to encourage your children. When they're doing a good job, you need to say, "I am very proud of you."

Follow Jesus' example with your children:

"And he took the children in his arms, put his hands on them and blessed them" (Mark 10:16).

Heavenly Lord, I pray for my children today that they grow in love and obedience and that they come to have a saving relationship with You. Amen.

Philosophy of Life

A key job for you as a parent is to help your children develop a philosophy of life.

"Everybody has a philosophy of life," says Dr. Bob Barnes. "A philosophy of life is what you're counting on to get you through in life. So, if you want to help your child develop a philosophy of life, consider carefully what philosophy you are modeling in your home each day. Is it 'If we can just get to the next paycheck, we'll be fine'? Or is it 'All we need is a car that actually runs'? Perhaps your philosophy is 'If I can get married again, then everything will be okay.'

"Your philosophy of life needs to be a faith in Jesus Christ, where you are counting on the Lord whether or not you understand the circumstances. Your children need to see that your philosophy of life is your faith in Christ. They will walk out of your home with some kind of philosophy, and it needs to be God."

If you think that your philosophy of life is your faith in Christ, are you sure that your children see it that way? Be open with your children about your faith and your reliance on God instead of on material things or circumstances. You will want to make a conscious effort to express to your children how Jesus Christ is a solid foundation that they can live their lives on.

"He alone is my rock and my salvation; he is my fortress, I will never be shaken" (Psalm 62:2).

Faithful Lord, I put my trust in You. I know I can count on You no matter how bad things seem to be. I pray that my children, too, will trust in You. Amen.

Helping Your Child's Self-Esteem

Many children whose parents separate or divorce develop a low self-esteem. Low self-esteem can occur in a child for different reasons: (1) the child may believe he or she caused the divorce, (2) the child may struggle with feelings of failure because he or she cannot seem to bring the parents back together, or (3) the child may have feelings of abandonment when a parent remarries. There are several ways you can help your child's self-esteem:

"The parent needs to interact in that child's life. The parent needs to sit on the side of the bed and listen to the child's fears. You prove your love by giving time," says Dr. Bob Barnes. "Give your children chores. Many times single parents do not take the time to teach chores, or they think, *It's easier for me to fold the laundry than to go behind them and fix it.* Children know that, so they'll make a mess of the chore so they don't have to do it again. If you train your children to do chores, then they have the sense of being a valuable, contributing member of the family."

"Watch what God does, and then you do it, like children who learn proper behavior from their parents" (Ephesians 5:1 MSG).

Dear God, my child's self-esteem is low, and sometimes it feels like there's nothing I can do about it. Help me realize that I can. I pray for opportunities to put new ideas into practice that will build up my child. Amen.

Spend Time Together

Be there for your children! You have to be there emotionally as well as physically. Children can sense if you are only giving them your presence; they want and need all of your attention.

"I drew a lot closer to my kids," says Lee. "I really made myself available to them. The first Christmas we had, which was only three months after my wife left, was a wonderful Christmas. The children and I had anticipated dreading it, but we built new memories; we started some new traditions; and we stayed up until three o'clock in the morning.

"I realized how important it was just to be there. I found that with kids you can't sit down and say, 'Let's talk about it' and expect them to immediately open up. You have to give them your presence, and maybe three or four hours into an innocent evening of fun, they will open up with their feelings and concerns. Sometimes it's three in the morning! So you have to change your lifestyle a little bit to be available for them."

Enjoy the time you spend with your children. Choose activities that involve talking and laughing together—play a card game, have an ice-cream sundae party or a make-your-own pizza night, clean the basement together while listening to upbeat music, ask getting-to-know-you questions, such as "What's your favorite . . . ?"

"For our earthly fathers disciplined us for a few years, doing the best they knew how. But God's discipline is always right and good for us because it means we will share in his holiness" (Hebrews 12:10 NLT).

Father God, show me areas of my life I can change that will enable me to slow down and spend more time with my children. Amen.

Visitation

The way you deal with visitation and interact with your former spouse will affect your children. Take care that you communicate in a way that is friendly and without blame for the sake of the children. If you are struggling with visitation issues, here are some suggestions to better handle these difficulties:

"There are no good answers for visitation," says Dr. Bob Barnes. "It's not God's plan. It's not ideal. The best-case scenario is for you to decide that regardless of your ex, you are going to try to cooperate and compromise.

"Your ex may always want you to drop the children off and pick them up and never participates in the transportation. It's not fair, but you are not dealing with the nurturing of your ex anymore. You are dealing with the nurturing of your children. You don't want your children to arrive under strain all the time because you and your ex are furious with each other. The children lose here.

"You have to decide that you are going to go the extra mile. Maybe you've gone the extra mile for eight years now, and you are tired of it. Do it for the Lord's sake and for the children."

If you are angry or frustrated with your former spouse and you show it, then you are teaching your children to be angry and frustrated when things are unfair or don't go their way.

"The righteous *man* walks in his integrity; His children *are* blessed after him" (Proverbs 20:7 NKJV).

Heavenly Father, help me to stop focusing on what's fair and what's not. Every time I grumble about my former spouse's behavior, I am injuring my children. When they look at my words and responses, I want them to see a reflection of You. Amen.

Your Attitude About Visitation

Dr. Bob Barnes says, "You need to not get in those little verbal battles and games that happen between ex-spouses regarding visitation. Do the best you can to cooperate. Whether your ex cooperates with you or not is his or her decision. You need to do the best you can for your children's sake, and you need to not compete with these visitation times. Be happy for your children when they come back happy, and do not make them feel guilty about good things that have happened in their lives. You need to be mature and be glad for your children; even though what your ex is doing just grates on your nerves.

"Strive to do the best you can. Every time you make a mistake, when you raise your voice at your children and when you say something you wish you hadn't said, you need to apologize to your children and to your Lord. The beauty is you're going to be able to start over tomorrow."

Remember that the relationship between you and your former spouse has changed. You are no longer working on a marriage, but you are now two people parenting the same children in separate households. Your focus should be on your own parenting skills and issues.

"Serve wholeheartedly, as if you were serving the Lord, not men" (Ephesians 6:7).

Heavenly Father, help me to create a loving, safe, and comfortable home for these children You have entrusted me to raise. Amen.

Your Former Spouse's Questionable Lifestyle

Some of you have a former spouse who is living an immoral or questionable lifestyle. Should you send your kids into this environment for visitation? That's a difficult question.

While you cannot control what goes on in your former spouse's home, you can control your reaction to the situation and the words you say to your children about it. Sometimes your children are quick to tell you things that happened at the other parent's house that they know you will disapprove of. Do not prompt your children to tell you these things. That places the children in the middle again, and your role is not that of detective or police.

Your children may come home and say, "We saw some R-rated movies that you didn't want us to see." Here is where you check your own response before blurting out disparaging words against the other parent. Dr. Bob Barnes recommends that you say something like, "I'm sorry about that. Your dad and I, or your mom and I, have differing opinions on those kinds of things. I'm sorry that happened. Do you want to talk about the movie itself? Let's do that."

Hopefully your former spouse will be open to calmly discussing your concerns, but if this is not possible, do not despair. Even though you can't be with your children at all times, God can and He is. Read the following Bible verse out loud with conviction.

"I know whom I have believed [God!], and am convinced that he is able to guard what I have entrusted to him for that day" (2 Timothy 1:12).

Lord of all, I entrust my children to You today and every day. Thank You that You will protect my children from harm when I am not there. Amen.

New Relationships
from Your Child's Perspective

New relationships can have a profound effect on your children. You might be looking forward to having a new relationship, but, with few exceptions, your children are not.

Children for the most part don't want to share their parents with someone else. A new relationship can be scary, confusing, and uncomfortable for the children. Your own perspective on a new relationship is nothing like the perspective of your children. Listen to your children's fears and concerns, and reassure your children how special and important they are to you. Always answer questions with thoughtfulness. You might be feeling giddy with the prospect of a new relationship, but your child is likely to be completely serious and concerned.

"Some children encourage their parent to date. They say they want another mother or father," says Linda Ranson Jacobs. "Your children see how lonely and unhappy you are, and they think that if you found another partner, you would be happy. The children may put their own needs aside out of love for you." Carefully consider your children's possible motives for saying they want you to date. More than likely your children deep down really don't want you to date.

"See that you do not look down on one of these little ones. For I tell you that their angels in heaven always see the face of my Father in heaven" (Matthew 18:10).

Lord Jesus, I love my children so dearly. What precious gifts You have given me. May the words I speak to my children be filled with love, encouragement, and wisdom. Amen.

Before You Enter a New Relationship

"I made a mistake after my separation and the first part of my divorce," admits Cindy. "I started dating a very nice man. Then I realized, *Wait a second*—as flags were going up—*this is the same kind of guy I just divorced.*

"Fortunately, he said to me 'You're not ready to date yet,' for he, too, had been divorced. At first I thought, *What do you mean? I know when I'm ready to date and when I'm not.* But he was right. I wasn't ready."

Cindy, with her three teenage children watching, made the decision that she needed to experience complete healing before she began to date again. She realized that she needed to be okay on her own, and she knew she could move forward only with God at the helm of her life.

Before you enter a new relationship, you *and* your children need to be healed. Teach your children that God can be the One to meet all of your needs, and He will provide the healing you so desperately need.

"With all your heart you must trust the LORD and not your own judgment. Always let him lead you, and he will clear the road for you to follow. Don't ever think that you are wise enough, but respect the LORD and stay away from evil. This will make you healthy, and you will feel strong" (Proverbs 3:5–8 CEV).

Strong Father, You are my hero. Lead my life. Strengthen my resolve. Help me to be a good example to my watching children. Amen.

When Should You Involve Your Kids?

"Do not immediately introduce the children to the person you are dating," advises Gary Richmond. "Tell the children that you are dating and if anything comes of the dating, you will keep them apprised so they don't have the constant fear of the unknown. They will be secure in the fact that if they do not hear any more, that nothing serious is happening."

When you bring together the person you are dating and your children, a relationship will begin to form between them. Perhaps the person you date likes to talk with your children, plan surprises for them, bring gifts, or play their favorite games with them. If the new relationship ends, then the children will have to deal with feelings of abandonment again. That is not fair to them.

Dr. Bob Barnes says in a dating relationship you "have the privilege of teaching the children how to date, how to stay pure, and how to not rush into anything."

Every moment of your life is a teaching opportunity for your children.

"Only be careful, and watch yourselves closely so that you do not forget the things your eyes have seen or let them slip from your heart as long as you live. Teach them to your children and to their children after them" (Deuteronomy 4:9).

Faithful God, when I am uncertain, encourage me to make good decisions, ones that You would approve of. Teach me more about what Your Word says. Amen.

Showing Affection in Your New Relationship

How do your children feel when you show affection to the person you are involved with?

"It's very disturbing to children. That should be something that's shown to them more if the relationship is turning into a marriage than in the dating situation," says Gary Richmond. "Children think this is inappropriate behavior. They don't feel comfortable seeing their parent be affectionate with a stranger or someone outside of the family. It isn't natural to them.

"In many cases in dating relationships, the couples are more demonstrative as dating couples than they were as married people, so the children have never witnessed this before, which is frightening to them."

Jan Northington says, "It's important to allow your kids the freedom to express their feelings in a safe way and in a safe place. That is so hard. When you are in the midst of your own emotions, you want to jump in and make your point. That's the time you have to step back and allow your children their own feelings and help them put their feelings into words and be honest."

Ask your children how they feel about you dating. Ask them if anything makes them feel uncomfortable or worried regarding your new relationship. Ask them how they feel about the affection they see between you and the person you are dating. Answer your children's questions with age-appropriate answers. Consider coming up with a compromise so that both the children and the adults can feel comfortable with the amount of affection shown.

"Children take pride in their parents" (Proverbs 17:6 MSG).

Dear Lord, I pray that my children will grow up to be proud of the way I raised them, the example I provided for them, and the things I exposed them to. Continue to guide me in godly wisdom. Amen.

Single Sexuality

The Desire for Sex

The desire to have sex is natural, and when you were married, you were free to satisfy that desire. Your longing for sexual intimacy won't go away just because you are separated or divorced. In the coming days, we will help you gain an understanding of the sexual issues that are or will be confronting you at this stage in your life.

Rose Sweet says, "Sexuality after divorce is one of the toughest things to deal with. You've been sexually involved in your marriage. It's normal. It's natural. It's healthy. Now you don't have it. What do you do with those feelings?"

Elsa Kok says, "Your natural inclination, if you've been in a married relationship, is if you kiss and that kiss is passionate, that right away leads to sexual contact. You have to set strict boundaries when it comes to dating and relating to the opposite sex."

"It is God's will that you should be sanctified: that you should avoid sexual immorality; that each of you should learn to control his own body in a way that is holy and honorable, not in passionate lust like the heathen, who do not know God . . . For God did not call us to be impure, but to live a holy life" (1 Thessalonians 4:3–5, 7).

Holy God, I want to honor You and remain pure. To tell You the truth, though, sometimes I'm just too tired to be strong in this area, and sex sure feels good. But I choose to turn to You for help and strength. I know that what You will give me is far beyond the rush illicit sex will give me. Lord, Your gifts are deep, lasting, and strong enough to build a life's foundation on. Amen.

Sex Is Pleasurable

Sex is pleasurable on many levels, and sometimes the desire for sexual affirmation is overwhelming. Sex not only feels good physically, it also satisfies emotional and spiritual needs—when practiced within the bonds of marriage. Unfortunately, because of the satisfying nature of sex within marriage, your body and mind can fool you into thinking that it will be satisfying outside of marriage as well.

When a person of the opposite sex shows interest in you, you feel affirmed and attractive; you feel a spark that you thought was out for good, and you want more of it.

Laura Petherbridge says, "Many times when you first start dating again, it's been so long since anybody has treated you this nicely, or made you feel special, that it's easy to drop your guard."

There is a better way to fulfill these desires. Jesus Christ can meet your every need. He can satisfy the hunger within you. God has called you to rise above your feelings and be filled with Him.

"I pray that your hearts will be flooded with light so that you can understand the wonderful future he has promised to those he called. I want you to realize what a rich and glorious inheritance he has given to his people. I pray that you will begin to understand the incredible greatness of his power for us who believe him" (Ephesians 1:18–19 NLT).

Dear Jesus, I am so loved and valuable to You. I pray that my heart is flooded with Your light and that I can face the future with Your power. I believe You have chosen me to have an amazing future. Amen.

Society Embraces Sexual Freedom

Our culture approves of and encourages sexual expression and sex outside of marriage. Daily we are bombarded by sexual images and with the message that sex outside of marriage is good.

"Sex is all around us, but that's no excuse," says Dick Purnell. "Just because everybody jumps off the bridge and dies doesn't mean you have to do the same thing."

Kay Arthur says, "Sex has become everything in our society today. Because there's no fear of God before our eyes, we flaunt our sexuality. We sleep around. We live with people. We don't get married. We think of sex as the cure-all."

Take a moment to consider what you believe about every aspect of a sexual relationship—from showing interest, to flirtation, to holding hands, to kissing—everything that leads up to and surrounds the act of sexual intercourse. Define your beliefs ahead of time so that you can stand firm on your convictions. If you are unsure about the rightness or wrongness of a particular thing, you will likely convince yourself that it is right when the feelings and emotions start coming in. Search the Bible and pray to God to help you make the right choices about what you believe concerning every aspect of sex *before* you find yourself in those situations.

"People may be pure in their own eyes, but the LORD examines their motives" (Proverbs 16:2 NLT).

Lord, it certainly makes the temptation greater when I see sexual images all over, but I know that I can choose to be different. Help me to have wise and strong convictions about every aspect of the sexual experience. May I learn from You. Amen.

God's Perspective

God designed sexual pleasure to be expressed and enjoyed within the bonds of marriage.

Rob Eagar says, "Satan wants you to think the best sex is forbidden sex. God says the best sex is in any committed marriage relationship because in that environment you're free to be yourself and another person is celebrating you for who you are. Plus, the commitment is there, so as you give your body and soul over to another person, you're confident that that person is in it for the long haul too. Hot sex happens when you are bonding yourself on all levels, and God says that can only be found in a marriage relationship."

When you are interested in a member of the opposite sex, you must remember that your body is God's temple. Christ dwells within you if you have asked Him to do so. This man or woman you are interested in should honor you and your body in the same way he or she would honor the Lord Himself. Are you receiving that kind of honor? Are you showing yourself that same reverence?

"In sexual sin we violate the sacredness of our own bodies, these bodies that were made for God-given and God-modeled love, for 'becoming one' with another. Or didn't you realize that your body is a sacred place, the place of the Holy Spirit? Don't you see that you can't live however you please, squandering what God paid such a high price for? . . . So let people see God in and through your body" (1 Corinthians 6:18–20 MSG).

Father, my body is a sacred place. Please forgive me for past sins against my own body. I turn away from those sins and embrace the purity of a life with You instead. Amen.

Breaking the "One Flesh" Bond

Sexual intercourse—and the words, touches, and thoughts that go with it—is God-created and God-approved within the bonds of marriage. Sex is so amazing that when a couple comes together, they supernaturally bond. Even after intercourse is over, the couple is still bonded because sex cannot occur without that supernatural bonding occurring as well. Genesis 2:24 says the couple becomes "one flesh."

"If sex were just physical," says Paula Rinehart, "any of us could walk away and feel nothing from it. But there's a real bond that's made. When people go through the breaking of multiple sexual bonds, they are losing a little bit of themselves over and over. Often when I relate to a woman who's had a number of men in her life, I feel like I'm relating to someone for whom the lights are on, but I can't get into her personality. She's simply been through the breaking of too many bonds."

Maybe you have engaged in sex outside of marriage or are worried you have lost an irretrievable part of yourself from your prior marriage. Dr. Linda Mintle offers this reassurance: "Sometimes people who have divorced wonder if a part of them has been forever lost. No, in God's economy, that part of you can be recovered through prayer and through asking God to restore that loss to you."

God can redeem you from any situation and sin. He can free you and restore wholeness to you. Just ask Him.

"I have swept away your offenses like a cloud, your sins like the morning mist. Return to me, for I have redeemed you" (Isaiah 44:22).

Redeemer God, You alone have the power to rescue me from my own pit of sinfulness and despair. You can mend my broken bonds and make me whole in Christ. Amen.

God's Limits Are for Your Protection

God is not trying to punish you or make things more difficult for you by limiting sex to marriage. He is protecting you. You are already vulnerable emotionally because of the separation or divorce. A sexual relationship can cloud your judgment, setting you up to be hurt. Also, deliberately disobeying God will block joy and peace in your life.

Physically, there are many consequences to having sex outside of marriage: sexually transmitted diseases, pregnancy, and being forced to do something against your will.

Rose Sweet explains the spiritual importance of sex: "Some might think God is being unreasonable to limit sex to marriage, but that's because we're ignorant. Most of us haven't really tried to understand the fullness of what sex is. Sex is a renewal of the marriage bond. It's a renewal of a covenant—just as God was with His people in the Old Testament and as Christ is now with the church. In other words, it's saying, 'I take you forever, completely, and in every way, and I will never bring any harm to you.' You can never have that in a casual or in an emotionally committed but non-married sexual relationship."

Choose to stay within God's limits for your sexual experiences. If you are not sure what God's limits are, search God's Word for principles that apply to those situations. One suggestion is to read Ephesians 4–6 together.

"This is love for God: to obey his commands. And his commands are not burdensome, for everyone born of God overcomes the world . . . Who is it that overcomes the world? Only he who believes that Jesus is the Son of God" (1 John 5:3–5).

Lord Jesus, I can overcome all situations and be victorious because of You. Lead on! Amen.

Rationalizing That Sex Is Okay

Have you made the decision to abstain from sex outside of marriage? If so, be prepared ahead of time for rationalizations that may creep into your head. Satan is real, and he whispers lies in your ear to try to convince you to go against what you believe.

If you aren't seeking God's constant protection, you may begin to believe the lies and do things you weren't planning on doing because "it's not *that* bad" or "it's not like I'm doing such and such."

When faced with decisions, don't take what seems to be the easiest path or the one that will make you happy the quickest; it might lead to even worse difficulties than you've already had.

You are a strong individual when Christ is in your life, and God has sent His Holy Spirit to enable you to make the right decision when faced with temptation. He is also there to help you make decisions that will keep you from being in those situations in the first place.

"Finally, be strong in the Lord and in his mighty power. Put on the full armor of God so that you can take your stand against the devil's schemes . . . Stand firm then, with the belt of truth buckled around your waist, with the breastplate of righteousness in place" (Ephesians 6:10–11, 14).

Almighty God, I choose to abstain from sex outside of marriage from this point forward, but You know I can't resist the temptation on my own. Suit me with Your armor and prepare me to stand firm. Amen.

"It's the Other Person's Fault, Not Mine"

Some people, after having sex, will rationalize their actions by blaming the other person. Maybe not to the extent of saying, "It's *all* his or her fault," but more subtly in the mind.

If you have engaged in sex outside of marriage, perhaps you have had thoughts such as these:

- *I truly would not have done that if the decision had been wholly mine to make.*

- *I felt like I had no choice at that point.*

- *He (or she) wore me down insisting that we should, and I got tired of worrying about it.*

Number one: the decision is wholly yours. Number two: you always have a choice. Number three: the stress you feel when the other person insists you have sex will be much greater if you give in. Plus, if the other person thinks sex is an option right now, then you need to think carefully if this is the kind of person you need or want in your life.

"Blessed is the man who perseveres under trial, because when he has stood the test, he will receive the crown of life that God has promised to those who love him. When tempted, no one should say, 'God is tempting me.' For God . . . does [not] tempt anyone; but each one is tempted when, by his own evil desire, he is dragged away and enticed. Then, after desire has conceived, it gives birth to sin; and sin, when it is full-grown, gives birth to death" (James 1:12–15).

Holy Savior, teach me to make wise decisions each day and not to shift the blame to someone else when things don't go as I planned. Amen.

"I'm Entitled to It"

Our society has the mentality that we are entitled to feel good, to have nice things, and to go after whatever it is that we want. Society says if you work hard, you deserve it.

Paula Rinehart comes across this same mentality as she counsels people in divorce. She often hears, "Given what I've been through, of course I need the validation and the healing of a sexual relationship outside of marriage."

You may think that you deserve to have sex and that God's limits should not apply in your situation. But you may not be thinking of the potential pain and destruction you are opening yourself up to by engaging in sex outside of God's plan. You may not be thinking of the harmful consequences to others around you.

Being saved by Christ is not based on a person's work or achievements, and it is not something anyone deserves. As a matter of fact, the Bible says because we are sinners by birth (not inherently good), we deserve punishment. But Jesus came and died on a cross to pay the penalty for our sins, and then He rose again and is alive in heaven today. You can choose to accept His free gift of love and life, not because you deserve it, but because He loves you so incredibly much.

"What marvelous love the Father has extended to us! Just look at it—we're called children of God! That's who we really are. But that's also why the world doesn't recognize us or take us seriously, because it has no idea who he is or what he's up to" (1 John 3:1 MSG).

Father, what I need is You, not sex. Thank You for loving me. Amen.

"I'm Only Going This Far and No Further"

Setting boundaries ahead of time for your relationships is a crucial step. You need to be prepared not to budge once you've set those limits. When you are *not* in a relationship, it's easy to say, "These are the boundaries for sure." But when you meet someone who is wonderful, you are tempted to go just a little bit further.

You may think, *Well, a good-night kiss never hurt anyone.* Then, before you know it, that good-night kiss gets more passionate, and you continue to push the boundaries, setting new ones slightly further out.

Elsa Kok says, "You have to set a firm line, and you have to agree on that line and not continue to press the boundaries to keep it more exciting. The amazing thing is when you set those boundaries and keep them, you're forced to get creative in how you express your care for someone. It opens communication that you may never have thought of before because now you are forced to say things and not just express them physically. It actually builds the romance and enhances the relationship because you are doing things a different way."

Take care not to rationalize your actions. Instead, seek a better way of doing things.

"Can a man scoop fire into his lap without his clothes being burned? Can a man walk on hot coals without his feet being scorched?" (Proverbs 6:27–28).

Jesus, it says in Philippians 4:13 that I can do all things through Your strength. Strengthen me to stand firm in my beliefs. Amen.

"I'm Not Hurting Anyone"

Can you truly say that no one will get hurt if you have sex outside of marriage?

"First of all," says Dick Purnell, "you don't really know another person's heart. It says in Jeremiah 17:9 that 'the heart is deceitful and desperately wicked.' How can you know if you have hurt another person? You don't even know your own heart. The only One who knows your heart is God.

"You are also hurting yourself because you've lost self-control; you don't really know what love is all about; and you've gotten yourself into a situation you don't know how to get out of. You are setting a pattern for others who are watching you. Many times children will look at adults and say, 'If that's the way they act, that gives me an excuse to act the same way.'"

Sex outside of marriage is harmful. Please be careful of deceiving yourself that it is not.

"The heart *is* deceitful above all *things*, and desperately wicked; who can know it? I, the LORD, search the heart, *I* test the mind, even to give every man according to his ways, according to the fruit of his doings" (Jeremiah 17:9–10 NKJV).

Dear God, sometimes my thinking gets skewed because I can't see the whole picture. Help me to back up and look at my situation from Your perspective and from the perspective of those around me. Amen.

"But This Relationship Is Different"

Yes, this relationship may be special and unlike anything you've ever experienced. But this is not a good reason to have sex with that person. As a matter of fact, it's an excellent reason *not* to have sex with him or her.

If your new relationship is orchestrated by God, then you have many wonders to look forward to in the future if God calls you to be married. If you have sex with this person before marriage, your relationship will not be as good as it would have been had you followed God's original plan.

Elsa Kok says, "In a dating relationship some people justify moving further sexually because they are in love; they have strong convictions towards Christ; and they're going to get married anyway. They rationalize that they don't have to follow the rules like other people do. They say, 'We're just loving each other.'

"God's guideline is set for you because He is protective of your heart and He loves you. He is not robbing you of joy. He wants to protect the relationship, and He wants to protect your heart."

Show your love for Christ and for the other person by staying within God's protective limits.

"If you love me, you will obey what I command . . . Whoever has my commands and obeys them, he is the one who loves me. He who loves me will be loved by my Father, and I too will love him and show myself to him" (John 14:15, 21).

Savior God, You have blessed me with a new relationship. May this relationship truly be different with You as the foundation. Amen.

"We Are Already Married in God's Eyes"

We have said this before. Either you are married or you aren't married. There's no in-between state.

Dick Purnell says, "The only way you're married in the eyes of God is to walk down the aisle between God and people and commit your life to the other person in a ceremony. You are showing, with witnesses, that you're serious and you're committed. Having the excuse that 'we're married in the eyes of God' doesn't hold water; it's worse than a sieve with the water going right through it."

In an age where cohabitation is common and accepted, it is difficult for some people to understand that sex and marriage are sacred and holy and worthy of our respect.

God has a perfect design for marriage—for your marriage. If you devote yourself to God and God's plan, you will experience a life that is fulfilling, secure, and joyful. He wants what is best for you. Even when your plan for sex and marriage may *seem* better to you, know that His plan *is* better.

"As obedient children, do not conform to the evil desires you had when you lived in ignorance. But just as he who called you is holy, so be holy in all you do; for it is written: 'Be holy, because I am holy'" (1 Peter 1:14–16).

Righteous God, may Your holiness be reflected in my life. If I've made decisions already that are not right in Your eyes, please forgive me and help me to make things right by choosing Your way now. Amen.

"I Need to Be Reassured
of My Virility/Attraction"

Divorce delivers a strong blow to your feelings of worth and desirability. As a result, you are vulnerable in situations where someone is attracted to you.

Bonnie Keen says, "After divorce there is a tremendous need for touch and for somebody to affirm your sexuality. It's wise to say, 'Okay, I know that I'm vulnerable here.'" Because you have this knowledge of yourself, you can prepare in advance to avoid those situations and find other self-affirming activities to do.

When someone affirms your sexual desirability, you may be tempted to have sex to prove a point to your former spouse. You may think, *You didn't think me desirable, but I'll prove that somebody thinks I'm attractive and fun to be with and that I'm a good sexual partner.*

You do not need to prove anything to anyone. God knows you; He knows your heart; and He places tremendous value on your inner and outer beauty.

Elsa Kok says, "God is saying, 'You don't have to go there. If you feel you aren't irresistible, come to Me. I'll remind you how precious you are. I'll remind you how beautiful you are.' You may want to be irresistible. But trust me, for a relationship, it's okay to be resistible."

"You, dear children, are from God and have overcome them, because the one who is in you is greater than the one who is in the world" (1 John 4:4).

Heavenly God, You think that I am attractive inside and out. Help me to walk in that confidence and to come to You when I need reassurance. Amen.

"God Will Forgive Me Later"

The Bible says God will forgive all your sins if you ask Him with a sincere and repentant heart. Many times people will make the decision to go ahead and sin, or in this case, to go ahead and have sex outside of marriage, since God will forgive them later. These people forget that God looks at the sincerity of a person's heart when He grants forgiveness. He does not forgive just because a person says the words "forgive me." The Bible says that before you seek forgiveness, you must first repent. To repent means to turn away from your sin and move in the opposite direction.

God's gracious gift of forgiveness cannot be used as a license to do whatever you want with the thought that He'll clean you up in the end. Dick Purnell says, "Forgiveness and the power to change are two sides of the exact same coin. When God works in your life, change is what He wants to see—change for the good and for the better, not just, 'Oh well, He'll forgive me.'"

You cannot try to manipulate God's character—expecting Him to forgive when you want to be forgiven, to bring about a change when you want a change, or to answer a prayer a certain way because you feel that's the best answer.

"Repent, then, and turn to God, so that your sins may be wiped out, that times of refreshing may come from the Lord" (Acts 3:19).

Father, forgive me for thinking I can take advantage of Your forgiveness. Forgive me for not coming before You in reverence. I want to change my ways. Amen.

The Consequence of Pain

Having sex outside of marriage results in serious consequences. One consequence is the immense pain that comes at the end of any sexual relationship. Because you supernaturally bond with every person you have sex with, ending that relationship will result in a tearing of the bond even if that bond was created only through a onetime act.

Rose Sweet says, "If you're sexually involved after divorce, there is a huge price to pay because sex is not isolated to the sexual act. God designed sex to be a whole-person experience. Sex was intended to image God's free, full, faithful, and fruitful love. That fourfold love is present only in marriage. When sex does not reflect these four factors, it hurts everyone from the couple to the children to society."

The Bible says you are not even to think about having sex outside of marriage. When these thoughts come into your head, pray immediately or prayerfully repeat a Scripture verse. Then find a healthy, fun way to release that energy.

"The night is nearly over; the day is almost here. So let us put aside the deeds of darkness and put on the armor of light. Let us behave decently, as in the daytime, not in orgies and drunkenness, not in sexual immorality and debauchery, not in dissension and jealousy. Rather, clothe yourselves with the Lord Jesus Christ, and do not think about how to gratify the desires of the sinful nature" (Romans 13:12–14).

Lord God, I don't want to build a sexual bond with another person only to have it torn to shreds. I can't build my life's foundation on shreds and pieces. Thank You that You have given me the option of wholeness and health through Jesus Christ. Amen.

The Consequence of Destroyed Trust

"I believe that trust is the crown jewel of a relationship," says Dick Purnell, "and when that's violated, it is very difficult to ever get it back. One of the most important consequences of sex outside of marriage is mistrust. You never know if you can trust the other person; you don't even know if you can trust yourself."

Having sex outside of marriage not only erodes your ability to trust now, but it also affects the trust relationship in a remarriage. Dick Purnell says, "When you get married, the consequence goes right into your marriage because you've lacked self-control. How can you trust the other person to have been pure for you when you weren't pure for him or her?"

By God's grace, you can change your ways, and you can rebuild your capacity for trust and become pure again through Him.

"For the grace of God that brings salvation has appeared to all men. It teaches us to say 'No' to ungodliness and worldly passions, and to live self-controlled, upright and godly lives in this present age, while we wait for the blessed hope—the glorious appearing of our great God and Savior, Jesus Christ, who gave himself for us to redeem us from all wickedness and to purify for himself a people that are his very own, eager to do what is good" (Titus 2:11–14).

Dear God, trust is so important. I want to be able to trust myself and to trust others in a relationship. May I learn about trust from You. Amen.

The Consequence of Diminished Pleasure

Rob Eagar says, "The more you get involved in sex outside of marriage, the more the power of sex is going to diminish because you're not truly experiencing sex in the way it was designed by God. Premarital sex becomes a superficial act that objectifies another person for your selfish pleasure, and you can't have intimacy with an object. That's why sex outside of marriage will eventually become a boring, hollow experience."

This happens because you are trying to fill the emptiness in your life with something other than God. If you don't truly open yourself to God's love, then you won't be able to fill the holes. God can fulfill you, but you must let Him fill you His way, not your way. Surrender yourself fully to Him, and stop any patterns of sexual activity that you've gotten yourself into. He can help you with that as well.

"With the Lord's authority let me say this: Live no longer as the ungodly do, for they are hopelessly confused. Their closed minds are full of darkness; they are far away from the life of God because they have shut their minds and hardened their hearts against him. They don't care anymore about right and wrong, and they have given themselves over to immoral ways. Their lives are filled with all kinds of impurity and greed" (Ephesians 4:17–19 NLT).

Fill me, Lord, with Your righteousness and truth. The pleasure I can receive from a life lived for You will far outweigh any temporary pleasure that sex outside of marriage brings. Amen.

Hurts Those Around You

If you have children or nieces and nephews, know they are watching you and learning from you. Even young adults in your neighborhood and church are looking to you as a role model, whether you want them to or not!

Kay Arthur shares, "I went from one man to another. I wasn't considering my future or the future of my two little boys who were watching me. I didn't know the impact of what would happen one day when my oldest boy came down the stairs and saw me making love to a man. Now, God forgave me, but there were wounds for that little boy, and there were consequences of that sin that carried on."

Teri shares, "When my heart was broken because of divorce, I had sex outside of marriage, and I lost the respect of my children. When your boy looks at you and says, 'Mama, I have lost all respect for you,' that hurts."

The act of sex is not confined to you and another person. It can affect everyone who knows and loves you. Choose to abstain not only for yourself, but for the sake of others.

"If I've let myself be seduced by a woman and conspired to go to bed with her, . . . I'd deserve the worst punishment you could hand out. Adultery is a fire that burns the house down; I wouldn't expect anything I count dear to survive it" (Job 31:9, 11–12 MSG).

Lord, my family and friends are dear to me. I don't want to hurt them through my actions. Thank You that I have the power to change with You in my life. Amen.

Injures Your Physical Health

Having sex outside of marriage is a health risk. Sexually transmitted diseases, even deadly ones, are prevalent in today's culture. STDs can cause sores, rashes, infertility, cancer, liver failure, neurological problems, and death. According to the American Social Health Association, "The estimated total number of people living in the US with an incurable STD is over 65 million. Every year, there are approximately 15 million new cases of STDs, a few of which are curable . . . At least one in four Americans will contract an STD at some point in their lives."[5]

Just because a person seems clean, nice, and respectable, does not mean that person does not have a sexually transmitted disease. If that person admits he or she had an STD at one point but it is gone now, this may or may not be true. STDs can lie dormant for years. Also, symptoms of many of these diseases may not be obvious.

Laura Petherbridge says, "When you sleep with someone, you are sleeping with every person that person has slept with. That's not a very pretty picture. It takes away all the romance and all the fun. You're putting yourself in danger physically."

May this verse be a prayer for you: "May God himself, the God of peace, sanctify you through and through. May your whole spirit, soul and body be kept blameless at the coming of our Lord Jesus Christ" (1 Thessalonians 5:23).

Father, forgive me for my sins, lead me not into temptation, and purify my body. Amen.

---

5. American Social Health Association. "Facts and Answers About STDs: STD Statistics." http://www.ashastd.org/stdfaqs/statistics.html.

Risks Pregnancy

When you have sex outside of marriage, the possibility that a child will be conceived is always a factor, even when birth control is used. That's a profound and long-lasting consequence.

"What happens if you get pregnant with this person you're dating?" asks Laura Petherbridge. "You're grieving the death of your marriage, and now you're pregnant with someone else's child. Could it get more complicated than that?"

With all the consequences of sex outside of marriage, people still struggle with it and still do it. This temptation is difficult to resist for so many reasons. God is not asking you to try your hardest to resist the temptation. He is asking you to come to Him. He wants you to sit at His feet and learn from Him. He will show you how to tap into His mighty power, which will enable you to be victorious over your struggles.

"Our only power and success come from God" (2 Corinthians 3:5 NLT).

"For though we live in the world, we do not wage war as the world does. The weapons we fight with are not the weapons of the world. On the contrary, they have divine power to demolish strongholds. We demolish arguments and every pretension that sets itself up against the knowledge of God, and we take captive every thought to make it obedient to Christ" (2 Corinthians 10:3–5).

Almighty God, be my power and strength to resist temptation and to be obedient to Christ in all things. Amen.

Clouds Your Judgment

"If you don't have sex when you're dating, you will know that person cares about you for who you are and not for what you can give him or her," says Elsa Kok. "It purifies the relationship and takes it to 'Does this person love my character? Does he or she love what's in my heart? What my hopes and dreams are?'

"That totally gets sidelined if you start sleeping together because then you're just consumed in that, and you don't deal with issues as well. A struggle may come up, but then you kiss passionately, and the next thing you know, you're sleeping together, and the struggle is set to the side. You don't know if the person's going to stay through conflict once you get married because you're not addressing the conflict when you're dating. It clouds everything to sleep together."

Rob Eagar says, "Touching someone sexually makes your heart desire to bond with that person. What happens is your emotions and feelings get cranked up to such an intense level that you tend to overlook more important aspects of the relationship, such as character, spiritual depth, or maturity. Once you get involved sexually, it can cloud your thinking, and you look at the relationship too much from an emotional standpoint rather than a factual standpoint concerning a person's integrity and commitment to loving you."

"Watch and pray so that you will not fall into temptation. The spirit is willing, but the body is weak" (Mark 14:38).

Dear Lord, when it comes to sex, sometimes I don't think very clearly. Live Your power through me to resist sexual activity so that my judgment will not be clouded. Clear my vision, and help me to see with Your eyes. Amen.

Hurts Your Relationship with God

Having sex outside of marriage hurts your relationship with God. Since God is the source of life, peace, hope, comfort, security, and power, cutting yourself off from God will bring serious consequences.

Dick Purnell says, "The big downer when you get involved in sexual immorality is the loss of intimacy with God. When you are not connected to the vine of Jesus Christ, the eventuality is you're going to dry out and shrivel up the second you open the door to all the other fleshly desires that are in your soul—the carousing, the violence, the anger, the frustration. All this will start flooding your life, and you'll feel powerless with the onslaught."

If you feel that you've moved far away from God, it's never too late to turn back to Him. He will welcome you into His arms in a heartbeat. He wants the best for you.

"God wants you to live a pure life. Keep yourselves from sexual promiscuity. Learn to appreciate and give dignity to your body, not abusing it, as is so common among those who know nothing of God . . . God hasn't invited us into a disorderly, unkempt life but into something holy and beautiful—as beautiful on the inside as the outside. If you disregard this advice, you're not offending your neighbors; you're rejecting God, who is making you a gift of his Holy Spirit" (1 Thessalonians 4:3–5, 7–8 MSG).

Lord God, the last thing I need right now is something that will cause me to dry out and shrivel up. I've had enough of that. Help me to turn from my wrongs and draw strength from You. Amen.

Have a Plan

Staying sexually pure takes work, but the end results are worth it. If you've made a decision to abstain from sex outside of marriage, your first action should be to establish a plan to resist sexual temptation. This plan can include (1) keeping yourself away from sexually charged situations, (2) finding other outlets for your energy, (3) establishing boundaries for your relationships, and (4) strengthening yourself spiritually through prayer and Bible study.

Sabrina D. Black says, "You need to learn how to pray yourself through sexual stimulus and realize that when you are feeling sexually aroused, you may need physical activity. What are some things you can do to keep yourself moving or to distract yourself from thinking about the sexual stimulus too much?

"Be careful about the types of movies and TV programs you watch and the books you read. Those things can stimulate you, and you don't want to create any type of arousal. Pray, read the Word, trust God to keep you, and make wise choices instead."

Even if you have tried to have a plan and failed at it, do not lose heart. Today is a new day. Believe that you can resist any temptation through Christ and act on that belief.

"I tell you the truth, if you have faith as small as a mustard seed, you can say to this mountain, 'Move from here to there' and it will move. Nothing will be impossible for you" (Matthew 17:20).

Well, Lord, mustard seeds are tiny, and my faith is often that tiny too. Thank You that all I need is a little bit and I can move mountains. Amen.

Establish Boundaries

"It is important that you establish guidelines right up front," says Sabrina D. Black. "You do not want to compromise your beliefs. You need to let the person you are dating know that sex is not an option for you. Sex is reserved for marriage, and until you are married, there will be no sex, and there will be no foreplay that leads to sex. There will be no fondling; there will be no touching. You can't afford to allow yourself to go too far."

Bonnie Keen says, "When I went out with my [now] husband on our first date, he was a gentleman. I said to him, 'I want you to know that I'm not going to sleep with you. I don't know what you're thinking, but I'm not sleeping with anyone until I'm married again.' He honored every physical boundary every step of the way because he wanted to honor God, and I am so grateful. It made me love him even more. You have to set your own boundaries, and you have to be with somebody who will help you keep them."

You may think that it would be impossible to find a person who is this honorable. Perhaps past experiences have caused you to become somewhat biased about the opposite sex. Godly, upright people do exist, and you can be one of them!

"Just because something is technically legal doesn't mean that it's spiritually appropriate. If I went around doing whatever I thought I could get by with, I'd be a slave to my whims" (1 Corinthians 6:12 MSG).

Holy Savior, I want to honor You with my thoughts, actions, and decisions. I, too, want to be honored by the other person in any new relationships. Amen.

"Flee Sexual Immorality"

Rose Sweet says, "If the pressure keeps coming and coming and you're getting weaker and weaker—quit standing in front of the bakery window. Remove yourself. It's as simple as that.

"You sit and struggle, asking, 'What should I do? I'm trying to enforce these boundaries.' Get up and walk away. Get out of the car. Go home. Don't go out with that person anymore. If all your friends are pressuring you, get new friends. Now, of course, this involves severing relationships. But move on and let God replace what you let go of."

Many people fall into a sexual relationship because they are "people pleasers." They don't want to cause tension or stir up a conflict in a relationship by constantly being the one who says, "No." As a result, they do something they seriously regret, harming everyone involved. Sticking to your boundaries and upholding your beliefs may cause others to look down on you, to say hurtful words, or to try to make you feel guilty or wrong. You need to get beyond what others think and trust God.

"Flee from sexual immorality. All other sins a man commits are outside his body, but he who sins sexually sins against his own body. Do you not know that your body is a temple of the Holy Spirit, who is in you, whom you have received from God? You are not your own; you were bought at a price. Therefore honor God with your body" (1 Corinthians 6:18–20).

Father, give me the courage to say no and to flee from any situation in which I feel pressured or uncomfortable. Amen.

Dangers of Pornography

Laura Petherbridge says, "Pornography can appear to be a good alternative to having a sexual relationship with a person, but it does the opposite. It totally distorts what the human sexual relationship should be. It destroys the need for human connection, the God-given intimacy between a husband and a wife.

"God gave us sex as a wonderful thing in a marriage. When we twist that into something that is self-serving and self-focused and definitely not God-focused, it strips away all of the beauty and the romance.

"In the future when you remarry, your mind will have been twisted into thinking that sex is something totally opposite to what God created it to be. When you use pornography in place of a relationship, you are setting yourself up for failure in marriage. You're destroying the future marriage. Pornography sets a standard that no human being can ever live up to, and this destroys the marriage. It is much more treacherous than most people think."

Jesus explains in Matthew 5 that *thinking* about sex outside of marriage is just as wrong as doing it. This is a radical idea for many people who think that as long as they are not actually having sex, they have done nothing wrong.

"You have heard that it was said, 'Do not commit adultery.' But I tell you that anyone who looks at a woman lustfully has already committed adultery with her in his heart" (Matthew 5:27–28).

Savior God, there is no place for pornography in a life lived for You. Strengthen me to stay far away from this temptation. Amen.

Stay Connected to Jesus

"I am the vine; you are the branches. If a man remains in me and I in him, he will bear much fruit; apart from me you can do nothing" (John 15:5).

If a branch is not connected to the tree, it has no life source. It has no roots. It can't be productive. Your biblical responsibility is to remain connected to the vine. By remaining connected to Jesus, God will give you the power and strength to be able to accomplish more than you could imagine.

Dick Purnell says, "You need a power outside of yourself that is beyond the human realm. When the Lord Jesus Christ says, 'I am the vine, and you are the branches,' it means that there is a division of function. He is the vine—He brings the power, the joy, the stability, and the peace of mind. The branch simply connects to the vine. As long as the branch is connected to the vine, it is drawing a whole new power, a whole new joy, a whole new peace of mind from the vine."

If you aren't connected with Jesus as the spiritual vine in your life, we encourage you to surrender your current life to Him and let Him be your source of new life. Inviting Jesus into your life is the most important thing you can do as you heal from your divorce.

"I am the true vine, and my Father is the gardener" (John 15:1).

Holy Jesus, I want to be connected to You in all areas of my life. I pray that through this connection, my life will be full of good "fruit." Amen.

It's Not Too Late

You may be at a point where you have been or are now sexually active. We want to encourage you that it is not too late. You can restore your purity and, in the process, grow closer to God.

"God is the author of purity," says Elsa Kok. "He can create purity where there is none. So if I come to God and say, 'Never again will I go into the arms of a man unless I am married,' I am confident I am pure—even if I don't have a history of purity. And should I marry, I'm going to marry with a clean conscience and a clean body. God does restore purity. It is never, ever too late.

"The value of waiting in purity is tremendous. I had a friend who got remarried after fifteen years. She had also been sexually active when she was younger. She made a decision for purity and remained pure for the marriage. She said, 'Oh, Elsa, it was so worth the wait.'"

If you are a believer in Christ, then you live by a different set of rules—God's rules, which are governed by grace.

"Offer yourselves to God, as those who have been brought from death to life; and offer the parts of your body to him as instruments of righteousness. For sin shall not be your master, because you are not under law, but under grace" (Romans 6:13–14).

Lord God, I want to be pure. Forgive me for my sins, and help me to start a fresh, new path of righteousness. Thank You! Amen.

Forgiveness

Choosing Forgiveness

If you choose *not* to forgive your former spouse, what are you going to do with the resentment you carry and the grievances you have? What are your plans for them?

Harold Graham says, "You take these grievances and hug them to yourself as if they are your most prized possessions, when really they are the very thing that's taking the life out of you, taking your health, taking your fellowship with God, taking your ability to minister, and taking your ability to love."

Forgiveness is hard. Impossible, you may say. Over the next several days, you will learn how to forgive and why it is important.

Laura Petherbridge says, "Many of us feel that we don't have the ability to forgive, and I would say that's absolutely true. If you're looking within yourself to be able to come up with a way to forgive, you're not going to get far. Within your own strength, you do not have the ability to truly forgive. I know of only one way to obtain the capability to forgive someone who has inflicted a wound as severe as divorce. That is to humbly bow before Jesus Christ and say, 'I don't know how to do this. I need You to teach me and to show me what true forgiveness looks like. I am willing to learn.'"

Approach God with honesty about your feelings and a willingness to grow.

"If you forgive someone's sins, they're gone for good. If you don't forgive sins, what are you going to do with them?" (John 20:23 MSG).

Dear God, I can list several reasons why I should not forgive my former spouse, and I feel that my reasons are justified. But, Lord, I guess I don't really know what forgiveness means. Please teach me more. Amen.

The Importance of Forgiveness

"Forgiveness is never easy. Your emotions will never ever, ever, ever want to forgive," says Harold Graham.

Easy? No. Necessary for your healing? Absolutely.

Muriel shares, "The key for me in getting on with my life was to be forgiven by God, to forgive myself, and to forgive my ex for his part in the breakup of the marriage."

Our model of forgiveness is God. Sometimes we forget just how much He has forgiven us. We often don't realize how sinful we are compared to a holy, perfect, and righteous God. Isaiah 64:6 says that all our righteous deeds, the things we pat ourselves on the back for, are "like filthy rags." Imagine what our bad behavior looks like! Yet God still forgives us.

Kay Arthur says, "How can I, who have been forgiven for what I have done against a holy and perfect and righteous God, how can I, who have been forgiven so very, very much, refuse to forgive another when I've received forgiveness from God?"

It is difficult to comprehend how much God has forgiven us for. Spend time in prayer today quietly reflecting on God and on what He has done for you.

"For if you forgive men when they sin against you, your heavenly Father will also forgive you. But if you do not forgive men their sins, your Father will not forgive your sins" (Matthew 6:14–15).

Forgive me, Father, for thinking that my former spouse does not deserve to be forgiven but that I do. Help me to follow Your example of forgiveness. Amen.

Forgive Everyone Involved

Forgiveness can seem utterly impossible. The hurt and rejection cut too deep. The pain is aggravated when it's not only your spouse who has wounded or abandoned you, but also your former spouse's parents or siblings, friends you had shared as a couple, or others who have chosen to "take sides."

You may justify your unforgiveness with many seemingly good reasons: "I can't forgive the lies and deception"; "I can't forgive what he or she did to the children"; "I can't forgive the shame that person put me through"; or "I can't forgive them for trying to turn my children against me."

"Many people," says Sabrina D. Black, "are sitting somewhere nursing their wounds and saying, 'It's not right. It's not fair; they should come back and make this up to me.' Those people keep getting hit. If they would get up, even though it's not right or fair, and get themselves into recovery, they will go on with their lives."

God commands us to forgive. Because He commands us, then it is possible for us to forgive, no matter what the circumstances. He doesn't promise that it will be easy, but He promises that it can be done.

"It'll take a miracle for me to forgive my husband and his mistress—well, our Lord is in the business of miracles," says Harriet.

"Then Peter came to Him [Jesus] and said, 'Lord, how often shall my brother sin against me, and I forgive him? Up to seven times?' Jesus said to him, 'I do not say to you, up to seven times, but up to seventy times seven'" (Matthew 18:21–22 NKJV).

Lord, help me to forgive. Amen.

The Consequences of Unforgiveness

There are some serious consequences if you choose not to forgive, and these consequences will significantly affect your future. Harold Graham says when you do not forgive, you become an "angry, cynical, always-assuming-the-worst type of person." He says, "Unless you make that decision to forgive, all that emotional turmoil is going to make you a very unpleasant, lonely person for the rest of your life."

Dr. Myles Munroe talks about how unforgiveness eats away at a person's life. He says, "Unforgiveness destroys your life. You become crippled. You become bitter. You become strapped by hatred and anger. You develop ulcers, and you develop growths and cysts and high blood pressure. All of these things are products of unforgiveness. That's why a lot of people who are still bitter because of broken relationships end up getting sick physically. They have mental problems. They develop an emotional instability. Unforgiveness is a culprit that brings death."

Yes, but forgiveness brings freedom and life. The first thing you need to do, before you take any action or make any kind of plan, is to make the decision to forgive.

"For You, O Lord, are good, and ready to forgive [our trespasses, sending them away, letting them go completely and forever]; and You are abundant in mercy and loving-kindness to all those who call upon You" (Psalm 86:5 AMP).

Forgiving Lord, I cannot do this by myself. Please help me make the decision to forgive. I don't want to become like the people described above. Amen.

The Danger of Not Forgiving

"Bitterness is a poison that can destroy you, and it never destroys the person it's aimed at. A way to get through bitterness is to forgive," says Christine.

Dr. Les Carter says, "I recall one woman who came to me ten years after her divorce. She was talking about her son's marriage and her daughter's graduation. Her ex was going to be at both. She had never resolved the fact that he had rejected her. She kept going over in her mind, *How could he have done this to me? Can't he see that he just ripped apart a family?* Her children would say, 'Mom, we know the facts. We know he did it. We can't go back and rewrite history.' She would always come back with those infamous words, 'Yes, but . . .'

"That is a woman who is so stuck in the past that it's as though she is willing to hold on to that divorce, to hold on to that anger, as being the defining element in her personality."

If you do not forgive the person who has hurt you, you are making it impossible to receive God's forgiveness for yourself. You do not want to cut yourself off from God's forgiveness. You need that forgiveness for your own freedom and healing and to release God's power in your life.

"In prayer there is a connection between what God does and what you do. You can't get forgiveness from God, for instance, without also forgiving others. If you refuse to do your part, you cut yourself off from God's part" (Matthew 6:14–15 MSG).

Lord Jesus, I do not want unforgiveness, bitterness, and resentment to define my personality. With Your help, I can be free from this. Lead me through every thought and every decision. Amen.

Forgiveness Is Not a Feeling

Many people have a wrong definition of forgiveness. One wrong idea is that you cannot forgive someone until you "feel" like forgiving him or her. Forgiveness is not a feeling. Certainly Jesus did not "feel" like forgiving when He was on the cross. Nevertheless, He said, "Father, forgive them, for they do not know what they are doing" (Luke 23:34).

Doug Easterday says, "If you are waiting for a feeling in order to forgive, you'll have a long wait—forever. You will not feel like forgiving. Your feelings can be your enemy."

Forgiveness is a choice you make. It needs to be separated from your feelings. To truly choose to forgive someone, you will need God's help.

Laura Petherbridge says, "Pray these words: 'Lord, make me willing to move toward forgiveness. I'm not willing yet. But if You'll teach me how, I'm going to trust You and believe You can.' If you reach out to God with sincerity and seek Scriptures that teach about forgiveness, it moves you closer toward a willing heart. Review Christ's sacrificial cost to obtain forgiveness for you, and within a short time you will see forgiveness through His eyes."

You do not need to try to change the feelings you have toward the other person when you forgive, but be willing to let God transform your heart as time goes by.

"Therefore, as God's chosen people, holy and dearly loved, clothe yourselves with compassion, kindness, humility, gentleness and patience. Bear with each other and forgive whatever grievances you may have against one another. Forgive as the Lord forgave you" (Colossians 3:12–13).

Holy God, I do not feel like forgiving, and I am even a bit afraid to choose to be willing to forgive. Please help me sort out my confusion. Amen.

Forgiveness Is Not Pretending You Weren't Hurt

Laura Petherbridge says, "Forgiveness is such a complex issue during divorce because it appears as though you're letting the other person get away with the offense. If you forgive, it feels as though you are saying, 'My wound isn't real. This stab to my heart and the pain of rejection isn't significant.'"

Your wounds are real, and they are important to God. He never wants to see you hurt. You do not need to make excuses for your feelings or pretend to other people that you were not hurt that badly. This behavior does not solve anything. Be honest. You were hurt, and it's lousy. But physical and emotional wounds should not keep you from forgiveness.

"How do you forgive when you've been hurt so badly?" says Jan Northington. "Forgiveness comes in knowing the facts and being willing to let them go. Forgiveness is the only thing that allows you the kind of peace that will turn your mind from injustices in your life toward God."

When you forgive your former spouse, it does not release your former spouse from being responsible for his or her actions. It does release you from orbiting around those hurtful events.

"But I tell you: Love your enemies and pray for those who persecute you" (Matthew 5:44).

Lord Jesus, I hurt so much. Why did this happen to me? Help me to be honest about my pain, but willing to learn how to forgive. Amen.

Forgiveness Is Not Justifying the Other Person's Actions

You do not need to justify your former spouse's behavior in order to forgive. Some people mistakenly think forgiveness only occurs when you finally understand why the other person did a certain thing or acted a certain way. Forgiveness is acknowledging that what the other person did was *not right* and giving it up to God.

Harriet shares, "Oh, how I hated my former husband when I found out he was the one who made the decision to have the affair. It's only now, months later, that I realize I had to feel the anger and hate I felt because I had to acknowledge it was in my life.

"It's through the ministering of the Holy Spirit within me saying, 'Harriet, these things are here; let's look at them together, and then let's give them up to the heavenly Father' that there is power. As I give Him the things that are standing in the way of me living victoriously, I can look at new life.

"The love of my Savior and His daily walk with me have brought me where I am now. And I can say, 'Praise God. You are so good because You have let me be my own person. You've let me walk through this valley, holding me tightly.' Each day I'm stronger and more confident. For the first time in my life, there is real joy in my heart. Joy that's from within."

"Cast your cares on the LORD and he will sustain you; he will never let the righteous fall" (Psalm 55:22).

Lord, what my former spouse did was wrong, and I've been suffering so much as a result. I confess that I have been harboring resentment in my heart. I want to turn my life around now and receive Your comfort and forgiveness. Amen.

Forgiveness Does Not Mean Trust

Forgiveness does not mean you have to trust the other person again. Forgiveness and trust are different entities, and neither one is dependent on the other.

"Trust is giving a person the benefit of the doubt that he or she is not going to behave a certain way in the future," says Harold Graham. "Whereas, forgiveness is simply setting down the load, never to pick it up again. Two totally different things."

Sue says, "One simple but great revelation to me was the fact that learning to forgive did not mean I had to trust again. It seemed like such a basic concept, but there was so much anger that I was not able to see that until I heard other people share it. Once I started praying and meditating on that fact, it had a big part in my healing."

Trust is something that needs to be earned, especially if the other person has broken your trust at some point. Learning to trust another person again can take a long time, and sometimes you will never trust that person because he or she may continue to betray your trust. God, on the other hand, can always be trusted. He will not betray you or let you down, and He can teach you to forgive.

"Those who know your name will trust in you, for you, LORD, have never forsaken those who seek you" (Psalm 9:10).

Heavenly Lord, I do not know if my former spouse will ever earn back my trust. Thank You that You aren't asking me to trust him or her, but instead You are asking me to choose freedom and release in You. Amen.

What If You Do Not Forgive?

If you do not forgive, you may get in the way of the work God is trying to do in the other person's life.

"Early in my divorce process," says Laura Petherbridge, "I was thinking of people I know who have gone through divorce and years later are still very bitter. I prayed, 'God, I don't want to end up a bitter woman, but I don't know how to let it go because the hurt is so deep. Please show me how to resolve this resentment.'

"I learned to pray for the 'other woman,' which probably seems like an impossible thing. It was not by my own strength. Something deep within me knew my own healing would come. I asked God to help me to see her as He views her. I began to see her as a lost person who believed that taking another woman's husband would make her feel better about herself. She was no longer my enemy, but instead an empty woman without God in her life. The bitterness began to melt away."

When you forgive, you allow God to work in the other person's life. Walking in obedience has a net positive effect on you and on people around you. Keep persevering in prayer for those who have hurt you. As Philippians says, "Keep pressing on."

"Forgetting what is behind and straining toward what is ahead, I press on toward the goal to win the prize for which God has called me heavenward in Christ Jesus" (Philippians 3:13–14).

God, You are above all. You love everyone and have such a different perspective from mine. Teach me how to pray for my former spouse and those who have hurt me. Amen.

Forgiveness Is Not Relieving the Other Person of Responsibility

Forgiving someone does not mean you are letting that person off the hook. The wrongs that have been done to you and to your children need to be righted, but it is not your responsibility to bring that about. God is a just and righteous judge. He is the only One who can judge and condemn a person for an unrepentant heart. This is not your job.

Doug Easterday explains what your responsibility is in forgiveness: "Forgiveness is getting your heart right with God. The people who have wronged you are still responsible before God for what they've done. You're not alleviating them of their responsibility. You're simply transferring it to God where it actually belongs. If you require them to answer to you, you have just the same amount of problems they do."

Harold Graham shares how his pastor once explained forgiveness: "When you forgive, it seems like you're taking that person off the hook. But what you're really doing is taking him or her off your hook and allowing God to put that person on His hook. As long as you have that person on your hook, you block God from that person and you also block God from you."

Your job is to be right with God and not seek vengeance or hold on to blame. You must let go of that person's wrongdoing so you can be right with the Lord.

"Do not judge, and you will not be judged. Do not condemn, and you will not be condemned. Forgive, and you will be forgiven" (Luke 6:37).

Holy God, I'm holding on too tightly to things that are only hurting me. Forgive me for blocking Your work and healing in the life of my former spouse and in me. Amen.

Forgiveness Is a Choice

"It's not a matter of how you feel," says Harold Graham. "It's not even a matter of how you think. It's a matter of your will. Your will is the part of you that makes your decisions. Either you will or you won't, or you do or you don't. It is that cut-and-dried. The difficulty is once you make that decision, your emotions will kick in and say, 'Time out, I really don't want to do this.'"

If you can let go and forgive, you will experience great freedom.

Nell Ann says, "He didn't deserve forgiveness. He didn't ask for it, and he didn't want it. I thought, *Why should I forgive him?* Finally, I realized it was not for him. It was for me."

Cindy shares what she learned about forgiveness: "Forgiveness is the hardest thing in the world. I felt like my heart and gut had been ripped out and thrown against the wall and left for dead. When I met with the pastor, I said, 'I can't forgive him. This is too hard for me.' He said, 'Let's look at it like a business deal. Let's say your husband owes you ten thousand dollars. Let's say he can never pay you back this ten thousand dollars. Forgive the debt. Just forgive the debt and move on. It doesn't mean you have to go back and do business with him.'"

Choose to forgive the debt. Your former spouse cannot repay you for all the hurt and pain. Forgive the debt, and accept the freedom that comes with forgiveness.

"But with [God] there is forgiveness" (Psalm 130:4).

Dear God, I cannot forgive through my own strength.
Thank You that there is forgiveness with You. Amen.

Forgiveness Is a Decision You Make

Forgiveness is a decision only you can make.

"Forgiveness is a decision you make," says Doug Easterday. "I can't do it for you. Even the person who offended you can't. God can't do it for you. You're the only one in the history of the world who can make this choice. Therefore, you have something to say about your own destiny if you choose to forgive."

James shares, "I didn't want to stand in God's way anymore. I wanted to do everything I possibly could to heal and not prolong the healing."

"Forgiveness," says Harold Graham, "is literally a decision that you make, and any decision must be followed by an action, or it's the same net effect of not making the decision at all."

Writing in a journal can help you in the process of forgiveness. Make a list of those you need to forgive. Write down what each person did to hurt you and what you wish had happened instead. You might want to write a letter to your former spouse, not to mail, but to use as an exercise of release that leads toward forgiveness. Tell your spouse in the letter how much you were hurt, all the agony, rage, and despair, and then tell your spouse how you are trying to learn to forgive. Tell your spouse you have learned forgiveness is a choice and how forgiveness can be accomplished only through Christ. Write that you have chosen to forgive him or her and that you are moving on in your life.

"The Lord our God is merciful and forgiving, even though we have rebelled against him" (Daniel 9:9).

Holy Spirit, enable me to make this decision. I want to be able to choose forgiveness, to choose it every time the hurt rises up again. Amen.

Forgiveness Is Obeying God

In the Bible, God commands everyone to forgive. Harriet chose to be obedient to God, and she discovered that God miraculously transforms the lives of those who choose to obey.

"The first time I said, 'Lord, I really want You to help me forgive,' what I was saying wasn't registering in my heart. The only reason I did it was because I knew it was something that God wanted me to do.

"Well, our Lord is in the business of miracles, and He is in the business of changing hearts. While I can't say that I've completely let go of the anger, the hatred, the resentment, and the bitterness, with each new day my Father is helping me to get rid of those things in my life. You know what else? I'm finding more and more that when I'm saying, 'Lord, please help me to forgive my husband and his mistress,' I'm not just giving lip service. I'm finding that He who creates changes in people's hearts is hard at work creating a change in my heart.

"A year ago I would have gleefully hired a hit man to take both of them out of the picture. No more. I just want Jesus to find them because I know that the path they're on is one they will never return from. I know the only hope in this world for all of us is through the love of Jesus Christ."

Choose to forgive in obedience to God.

"When you stand praying, if you hold anything against anyone, forgive him, so that your Father in heaven may forgive you your sins" (Mark 11:25).

Lord Jesus, You are my help and my hope. May I choose to forgive because You want me to. Amen.

What If You Don't Obey God?

You may be thinking, *What if I choose not to forgive?*

"If you don't forgive," says Doug Easterday, "what you're saying by the inference of your actions is what that person did to you is more important to you than going on with God. There isn't anything that someone could do to you that would be more important than going on with your personal relationship with Jesus Christ."

If you don't forgive, you create a barrier between God and you. Holding unforgiveness in your heart is a sin. Dr. Myles Munroe says, "If you don't forgive, you cannot even pray. So if you are divorced and you still harbor bitterness in your heart toward that person who was in your relationship previously, then you have literally cut off your relationship with God. You have hindered your prayer life, and there is therefore no way you can actually ask God to heal that person or change that person because He can't even get through to you. Forgiveness is the key to getting on your way to healing because God can heal you only if He can reach you, and He can only get to you if you have forgiven the person who hurt you."

You are blocking yourself from the power of answered prayer when you choose not to forgive.

"If I had cherished sin in my heart, the Lord would not have listened" (Psalm 66:18).

Lord Jesus, help me to realize that nothing is more important than being in a right relationship with You. Amen.

Is Forgiveness a Onetime Event?

"Forgiveness is a process," says Danny. "You can say to someone, 'I forgive you,' and it's just talk. It's not something you feel like doing. It's something you decide to do in order to let it go. No one really wants to forgive when the hurt is so bad. That feels so alien. Who wants to forgive someone who's hurt you so badly? But when you do forgive, you see that God will not only work in your life, but in the other person's."

Forgiveness is a process, not a onetime occurrence. Jesus said to forgive a person who has wronged you seventy-seven times. He was basically saying to stop counting. Each time unforgiveness comes up in your heart, you need to choose once more to forgive.

"It's a daily thing, going before God and saying, 'Okay, Lord, I forgave yesterday. Now I need You to help me do it again today,'" says Laura Petherbridge.

The act of forgiving will be something you will need to choose, apply, and practice. You can make forgiveness a lifelong habit by training your mind to reject those thoughts that would cause you to harbor unforgiveness, resentment, or blame.

"Then Peter came to Jesus and asked, 'Lord, how many times shall I forgive my brother when he sins against me? Up to seven times?' Jesus answered, 'I tell you, not seven times, but seventy-seven times'" (Matthew 18:21–22).

Lord Jesus, may I choose to have a heart of forgiveness again and again and again in obedience to You. Amen.

Taking Responsibility
for Your Actions and Attitudes

Forgiveness is when you refuse to let the other person's actions and attitudes dictate your actions and attitudes.

Selma shares, "It finally hit me that when I had been saying, 'I forgive him for what he did to me,' I was not really forgiving him. Inside, I was thinking, *Yes, I assume some responsibility for all of this, but I wouldn't have done it if he hadn't done whatever he did to me first.* Regardless of what he did to me, the way I responded to him was totally my responsibility, not his."

Forgiveness and taking responsibility involve more than saying the right words. They are both actions. Think about what actions you can take that will show you have forgiven the other person and that will show you are taking responsibility for yourself.

"Live in harmony with one another. Do not be proud . . . Do not repay anyone evil for evil . . . If it is possible, as far as it depends on you, live at peace with everyone . . . 'If your enemy is hungry, feed him; if he is thirsty, give him something to drink. In doing this, you will heap burning coals on his head.' Do not be overcome by evil, but overcome evil with good" (Romans 12:16–18, 20–21).

Dear Jesus, my inclination is to say, "I won't forgive until my former spouse does this, says that, or stops doing what he or she is doing." I understand, though, that if I think that way, I'm letting my former spouse control my actions and attitudes. I pray that my thoughts, words, and responses today are pleasing to You instead. Amen.

What If the Other Person Doesn't Respond?

Sometimes people mistakenly think that forgiveness must be a reciprocal action, that you cannot be fully free unless the other person will accept the forgiveness offered. Even if the other person does not respond to you the way you had hoped, you still become free when you forgive.

"If you've been obedient to God's Word and have forgiven the other person and he or she fails to forgive you, the other person has the problem and has to deal with God. You're free," says Dr. Robert Abarno.

"There is a point where your involvement in the process stops," says Doug Schmidt. "After you have offered forgiveness and the opportunity for repentance, you are released from that that burden. You don't have to keep offering forgiveness, especially if it keeps getting rejected or mocked. There's a point where you say, 'I've done all that I can legitimately do, and now I'm released from my obligation.'"

God honors those who have a sincere heart and who want to forgive and be forgiven. Do not let yourself be discouraged if the other person will have nothing to do with it. Continue to pray for that person, but move on in freedom.

"Brothers, listen! In this man Jesus there is forgiveness for your sins. Everyone who believes in him is freed from all guilt and declared right with God" (Acts 13:38–39 NLT).

Holy Lord, I wish that my former spouse would accept my forgiveness, and I would like it if he or she would seek my forgiveness as well. But even if my former spouse does not respond to me, I will walk today in the assurance of a new life in You. Amen.

Forgiveness Is Always Undeserved

If your former spouse or someone else has hurt you deeply, you might be entertaining thoughts of how that person will realize his or her wrongs, apologize, and try to make things right. You may feel that the other person needs to do this before you will forgive.

Forgiveness, though, means you do not hold the other person accountable to you. In forgiveness, you give the person to God and let God be the One he or she answers to.

Howard says, "I felt that in order to be able to forgive her, she needed to repent first. I wanted her to grovel. I wanted her to say, 'I did you wrong. This was a terrible thing I did to you.'"

Howard continues, "On the cross when God said, 'Forgive them for they know not what they do,' He was offering forgiveness, and no one was repenting. No one was sorry. They were wagging their heads, crying out with slurs. In the midst of it He was able to forgive, even when no one around Him was repenting. It was an amazing thing. I have to be able to do that, and if someone wants to take my forgiveness, it's up to that person."

When Jesus was on the cross, He forgave all the horrid things people were saying and doing to Him. He continued to forgive them even when their spiteful words and actions didn't stop.

"When they had come to the place called Calvary, there they crucified Him . . . Then Jesus said, 'Father, forgive them, for they do not know what they do'" (Luke 23:33–34 NKJV).

Lord Jesus, help me to stop entertaining thoughts of my former spouse groveling at my feet. I want to follow Your example of forgiveness. Amen.

Forgiveness and Reconciliation

Forgiveness and reconciliation are not the same thing. It is important to know the difference so that when you do forgive your former spouse, you do not automatically expect to be reconciled in some way.

"Forgiveness is getting your heart right with God. Reconciliation is getting your heart right with people," says Doug Easterday.

"Forgiveness is letting go of the burden," says Harold Graham, "and reconciliation is renewing or redefining a relationship."

The Bible says that you should live in peace with other people and that you should make every effort to do so. Living peaceably with others starts with forgiveness—holding no grudges, anger, or bitterness against that person. Yes, reconciliation is ideal, but not always possible. People can get hurt by rushing to reconcile after forgiveness has taken place. Sometimes living in peace means leaving the other person alone for a while and not aggravating the situation.

If your former spouse is not showing genuine remorse, says Doug Schmidt, acknowledging wrong behavior, showing a willingness to bear the burden of the damage, and doing everything humanly possible to correct the behavior, then yes, you are still required to forgive. But the next step would be to back off and protect yourself from further damaging behaviors. Do not equate forgiveness with reconciliation.

"Let us therefore make every effort to do what leads to peace and to mutual edification" (Romans 14:19).

"Do two walk together unless they have agreed to do so?" (Amos 3:3).

Lord of hope, I pray that someday I will be reconciled with my former spouse, but I realize that for now my part is to forgive. Amen.

Forgiveness Is Willingness to Move in the Opposite Spirit

Forgiveness is a willingness to move in the opposite spirit. It's easy to be nice to people who are nice to you, but how do you react to people who are mean and hurtful to you? Dr. Dennis Rainey says, "The way to become willing [to forgive] is to trade the insult-for-insult relationship for a *blessing-for-insult* relationship."[6]

Doug Easterday says, "If someone is being unkind, what is the opposite? Be kind to them. If someone is berating you and being negative and demeaning, what's the opposite? Being encouraging, building him or her up, and loving him or her. I believe that as you walk in the opposite spirit, you can expect God to work on your behalf."

God responds the same to all people. Jesus said the Father "causes his sun to rise on the evil and the good, and sends rain on the righteous and the unrighteous" (Matthew 5:45). God's actions are based on who He is, not on how people treat Him or respond to Him. We are called to follow His example. In the Bible, Jesus offers a foundational new view for everyone who believes in Him and chooses to live for Him.

"You have heard that it was said, 'Love your neighbor and hate your enemy.' But I tell you: Love your enemies and pray for those who persecute you . . . If you love those who love you, what reward will you get? . . . And if you greet only your brothers, what are you doing more than others? . . . Be perfect, therefore, as your heavenly Father is perfect" (Matthew 5:43–44, 46–48).

Holy Spirit, I can only do this through Your strength and enabling. I want to walk in the light of Your perfection. Amen.

---

6. *Staying Close: Stopping the Natural Drift Toward Isolation in Marriage* by Dennis and Barbara Rainey. (Thomas Nelson, 1989), p. 262.

Have You Really Forgiven?

You might be wondering how you will know if you have truly forgiven.

"Real forgiveness always brings peace. If you're remembering something and you have no peace, then it hasn't been forgiven," says Rev. Harold Graham.

Test yourself in this. Bring to mind something that your former spouse has said or done that used to cause you great anger or resentment. Do the old feelings rush in, or do you feel peace as you place this memory in the Lord's hands?

Harold Graham offers another good suggestion to help you know if you have forgiven: "You will know you have truly forgiven someone when you're finally free of the baggage that comes along with it. How many times do you say you've forgiven and have the old feelings rise up on the inside of you? To have no improvement of life, no improvement of your Christianity, no improvement of your health, and no improvement in how you feel would be good indications that forgiveness hasn't happened. The reverse would also be true. If your health improves, if your ability to relate to people improves, if your spiritual walk deepens, if your ministry suddenly becomes effective, if your worship suddenly becomes real, that would be a good indication that forgiveness has truly happened."

God's peace and healing are supernatural. They are deeper than anything a human could produce through hard work or willpower. God's way brings you blessed freedom and a release of your burdens.

"Peace I leave with you; my peace I give you. I do not give to you as the world gives" (John 14:27).

Savior and Lord, I pray for peace and for improvement in my life. I pray for a deeper spiritual walk and for worship that is real. You are my source of all things good. Amen.

Forgive Yourself

You become your own greatest enemy when you do not forgive yourself.

"Sometimes it's hard to forgive yourself after divorce because you don't want to admit you did anything wrong," says Rose Sweet, "and because the other person is usually pointing the finger at you or other people are putting you down for your failure in the marriage. That's giving God-like power to all those people who are putting you down. Just stop. Go to God and say, 'Lord, show me what I've done wrong. Help me seek forgiveness, and help me let go of everyone else's opinion of me.'"

"The most difficult person to forgive may be yourself," says Doug Easterday, "because you were there when you made mistakes, and you remember your attitude and the inappropriate things you have done, said, or even thought. But forgiving yourself is such an important arena. It means that you choose to walk in the higher realm."

Forgiveness is a process that will take time, and it is also a choice. Choose to forgive yourself just as God forgives you, even when you don't feel you deserve it. One awesome characteristic of God is that you don't have to measure up to certain standards to deserve His love. You don't have to follow certain rules or act in a particular way. He loves you no matter what you have done. God sees you inside and out, and He continues to extend His love and forgiveness to you.

"I write to you, dear children, because your sins have been forgiven on account of his name" (1 John 2:12).

"If we confess our sins, he is faithful and just and will forgive us our sins and purify us from all unrighteousness" (1 John 1:9).

Thank You, Lord, that You have forgiven my sins and cleansed me inside, fresh and new. Amen.

God's Forgiveness

If you've done things wrong (and we all have), the forgiveness that comes from God through Jesus can lift the guilt and the weight from your shoulders. The key to God's forgiveness is understanding that Jesus gave His life to pay the price for the things you've done wrong. There is no sin that God cannot forgive. God's forgiveness is made complete by asking Jesus into your life, by surrendering your life to Him.

Kay Arthur says, "It's no accident that God is speaking to your heart and drawing you to Himself. It's planned in the sovereignty of God. God doesn't want you to perish, Precious One. God wants to give you life. He wants you to pass from death to life. He wants to take you out of Satan's kingdom of darkness and bring you into God's kingdom. The way He does that is by saying to you, 'Your sins are forgiven.' Can you imagine what it's like to have all your sins forgiven? To have that load taken off of your back and to be set free?"

"So if the Son sets you free, you will be free indeed" (John 8:36).

"Everyone who calls on the name of the Lord will be saved" (Romans 10:13).

Kay Arthur offers a prayer that you can pray if you would like to be forgiven and free:

Jesus, I believe that You are God. I believe that You are the only Savior, that You are the one God promised who will give me eternal life. God, I want to be set free from my sin. I don't want to be a slave to sin any longer. I want to receive You as my Lord and my God. I want to be a child of God. Amen.

Five-Point Prayer of Forgiving

"If we confess our sins, he is faithful and just and will forgive us our sins and purify us from all unrighteousness" (1 John 1:9).

Rev. Harold Graham suggests that you ask the Holy Spirit to help you make a list of everyone you need to forgive; then list each person's offenses. Remember that some of these names will be from past situations not related to the breakup. This exercise will help make the forgiveness process complete.

Graham describes a five-point prayer of forgiving. Follow these steps for each name and offense on your list:

1. Confess the real problem, which is unforgiveness. Confess to God that you've been holding hatred, grudges, resentment, and disgust and that you've been holding that person in the bondage of unforgiveness. Then apologize to God for it.

2. Thank God that He forgives you.

3. Open yourself to the cleansing that comes from God. If you follow the first two steps, He will cleanse you of all unrighteousness. See 1 John 1:9 above.

4. Declare forgiveness for each offense listed.

5. Transfer ownership to the Lord Jesus Christ. Give your burdens to God: "Lord, these sins are too heavy for me to bear. I give them to You as Your property. Please nail them to Your cross so that I can't take them back anymore." Then give the Lord ownership of the person who hurt you: "Lord, I invite You to touch that person, convicting of sin and unrighteousness so that at an appropriate time, he or she will ask You for forgiveness and salvation."

"Rejoice not when your enemy falls, and let not your heart be glad when he stumbles or is overthrown" (Proverbs 24:17 AMP).

Lord Jesus, guide me through this prayer of forgiveness, and transform my life in Your name! Amen.

Reconciliation

Why Should You Consider Reconciliation?

When you hear the word *reconciliation*, your initial response might be, "No way!" Even if you feel that way, you should at least consider the concept of reconciliation.

Reconciliation is when a relationship is restored to good terms after having come apart. This does not necessarily mean a restoration of marriage; it can mean a cordial friendship where both individuals show respect and kindness to the other.

"Listen to what we have to say and listen to what God has to say before you emotionally react to the thought of reconciliation," recommends Dr. Jim A. Talley. "There may be some things here that will be of benefit to you long-term in your emotional and spiritual stabilization.

"You have to ask yourself, in five years from now when you look back on what you've done, can you really stand there with three things: a pure heart, a clear conscience, and clean hands before God? You cannot do that without dealing in the realm of reconciliation."

Most of the "right" things to do in the divorce recovery process have to do with making good choices and not giving in to fickle emotions. This is your life, and you have a definite say in how well you adjust, stabilize, and recover. Seeking reconciliation will benefit you both emotionally and spiritually and will enable you to stand before God knowing that you chose His way.

"Create in me a clean heart, O God, and renew a steadfast spirit within me" (Psalm 51:10 NKJV).

Without You, Jesus, it is impossible for me to have a pure heart and a clean conscience. Forgive me for my sins, and grant me wisdom as I consider the possibility of reconciliation. Amen.

Is Reconciliation for You?

Having been through the hurt and the pain of separation and divorce, you may have no desire to reconcile with your former spouse. Before you close your mind to the idea, consider what reconciliation means. Merriam-Webster's dictionary defines *reconciliation* as the act of restoring friendship or harmony. This does not necessarily mean the act of moving back in together and renewing the marriage vows.

Dr. Jim A. Talley says that reconciliation is "forcing yourself as a believer to come back to the minimum standard God expects of you, and that is the point of being friendly. Nothing below that level is allowed if you're going to walk with God and be one of His children who is obedient to the Word. God has given us the ministry of reconciliation. He expects you to do it; He wants you to do it; and He provides you the resources to carry it out."

In God's view, reconciliation is not an option; it is a necessity. Over the next several days, we will look at what reconciliation is, what it is not, and how it happens.

"Therefore, if anyone is in Christ, he is a new creation; the old has gone, the new has come! All this is from God, who reconciled us to himself through Christ and gave us the ministry of reconciliation: that God was reconciling the world to himself in Christ, not counting men's sins against them. And he has committed to us the message of reconciliation" (2 Corinthians 5:17–19).

Lord Jesus, when I hear the word reconciliation, I'm not sure what I think or how I feel about it. Teach me Your definition of reconciliation, and show me how to be a minister of reconciliation to the people in my life, including my former spouse. Amen.

First Stage of Reconciliation

Restoring a right relationship with your former spouse will need to be done over time and in stages. The first stage of reconciliation is friendship. There are four different levels of friendship. Keep in mind that you might not get through all levels, depending on your spouse's responses.

1. Acquaintances

2. Casual friends

3. Close friends

4. Intimate friends (a warm, deep-seated relationship that does not include sex)

"Reconciliation doesn't always mean moving back under the same roof," explains Laura Petherbridge. "I've met some divorced couples who are not going to get remarried, but they have reconciled their relationship. They are able to talk and communicate productively about the children. There is no bitterness or hatred between them anymore."

Second Peter 1:5–7 lists a series of qualities to build in your life that will lead to a strong and productive life and that will help you develop the desire to reconcile. The last two qualities on this list are brotherly kindness and love. To get to either of these points, you must first pray for and cultivate goodness, knowledge, self-control, perseverance, and godliness in your life. These godly qualities will lead you to a dynamic life in Christ and will enable you to understand the importance of reconciliation.

"Make every effort to add to your faith goodness; and to goodness, knowledge; and to knowledge, self-control; and to self-control, perseverance; and to perseverance, godliness; and to godliness, brotherly kindness; and to brotherly kindness, love. For if you possess these qualities in increasing measure, they will keep you from being ineffective and unproductive in your knowledge of our Lord Jesus Christ" (2 Peter 1:5–8).

Lord and Savior, with You there is reconciliation, friendship, and love. Help me to build my character one step at a time. Amen.

Second Stage of Reconciliation

The next stage in reconciliation, after building a friendship, is building a relationship. You might be in a situation someday where you can build a new relationship with your former spouse.

Juana and her husband, Terry, were separated for four years. During their separation they both came to have a personal relationship with Christ, and, as a result, they began to rebuild first their individual lives and then their relationship. This was a long, slow, and difficult process, but today they are happily married, and Jesus is the foundation of their marriage.

Dr. Jim A. Talley offers insights on rebuilding a marital relationship: "Decide to work on the relationship. Discuss what it is going to take to reconcile the marriage—what kinds of things you need to work off in the past, what kinds of things you need to prepare for in the future, and what kinds of issues need to be resolved."

Consider God's description of love:

"Love is patient, love is kind. It does not envy, it does not boast, it is not proud. It is not rude, it is not self-seeking, it is not easily angered, it keeps no record of wrongs. Love does not delight in evil but rejoices with the truth. It always protects, always trusts, always hopes, always perseveres" (1 Corinthians 13:4–7).

Father God, my former spouse and I have a close friendship with each other and with You. If it is possible, we would like to take our friendship to the next stage. We are willing to work hard and to seek Your guidance every step of the way. Amen.

Restoration of Marriage

Alice and her husband, Kim, were separated for six months. At one point during the separation, Alice thought, *This is hopeless. Kim can't even identify with the things I have problems with. It's like they don't exist in his eyes.*

After six difficult months that included seeing a counselor, becoming more involved in Bible study, experiencing spiritual growth, and really clarifying their thoughts, needs, and beliefs, Alice and Kim decided to try to reconcile the marriage. They made a commitment with each other to immediately find a church to belong to and a Sunday school class to regularly attend together.

Alice says, "You have to realize it takes two to make a marriage. The problems are not all one person's fault. Both of you have created the situation you're in. Both of you can create a new situation. If you have any kind of faith, you need to depend on that faith now and let the Lord guide your life."

Doug Schmidt says, "A meaningful restoration of the marriage would depend on the genuine repentance of both people—full acknowledgment of any irresponsible behavior, bearing the burden of any damage that behavior caused, a willingness to correct the behavior, and a readiness to ask for mercy, when it's appropriate."

God is the only One who can bring true reconciliation to your marriage, making the two people one flesh again.

"We're Christ's representatives. God uses us to persuade men and women to drop their differences and enter into God's work of making things right between them. We're speaking for Christ himself now: Become friends with God; he's already a friend with you" (2 Corinthians 5:20 MSG).

Dear God, even though reconciliation seems impossible to me, I pray that if there is any way we can reconcile, that we do so. Amen.

What If Your Spouse Has Remarried?

The Bible teaches in Deuteronomy 24 that if your former spouse has remarried, it is not appropriate for you to attempt to reconcile your marriage with that person. You should certainly take steps to restore your friendship, though, especially if you have children.

"Restoration can come whether the marriage is restored or not," says Roy. "My wife has remarried. I can't break that family up. But I can be restored in a relationship with her, her new family, and her husband in a way that brings healing. I'm never going to be restored to her as a husband, but I can be restored to her as a man, as an individual, and as a fellow believer."

When you choose to reconcile, that means you choose to have a godly response to the current situation and to any new situations that occur concerning your former spouse. Reconciliation is not easy, and it takes work and time, but the benefits will remain with you always.

"If a man marries a woman who becomes displeasing to him because he finds something indecent about her, and he writes her a certificate of divorce, gives it to her and sends her from his house, and if after she leaves his house she becomes the wife of another man . . . then her first husband, who divorced her, is not allowed to marry her again" (Deuteronomy 24:1–2, 4).

Lord of peace, I want what is best for both of us. I pray that my former spouse and I can remain friends and will both grow as believers in Christ, strengthened and wise through Your Word and as a result of our past experiences. Amen.

A Reason to Reconcile: Heritage

There are several reasons you should consider reconciliation. We will discuss eight reasons over the next eight days. The first reason to reconcile is because of the valuable heritage that you already have together.

"Once the separation occurs," says Dr. Jim A. Talley, "there begins to be a loss of all the positive memories and all the positive heritage, and an accumulation of all the pain and all of the negative. In order to get back into a balance and to really consider reconciliation seriously, you have to go back and remember some of the good things that happened. Every family and every relationship has a heritage that is valuable to be passed on to the children and to the grandchildren."

Alice shares, "We had always been each other's best friend, so we had a lot to build on if we could bring it back together."

When you think back to the time you were first getting to know your former spouse, the dating and the early part of your marriage, you likely have many fond memories. You have been through good times and bad times together, and the memories and traditions you have built together are your heritage. It is an important part of you.

"Indeed, my heritage is beautiful to me. I will bless the LORD who has counseled me" (Psalm 16:6–7 NASB).

Lord God, help me to remember the good times and not let the negative memories take over. Amen.

A Reason to Reconcile: Reduces Negative Stress

Reconciliation reduces negative stress in your life. Separation and divorce can cause a great deal of stress, which can continue until you have reached a point of reconciliation.

Sabrina D. Black says, "I have seen situations where people have reconciled in a positive way, coming back together or just becoming friends for the sake of the children and for the sake of future relationships. One thing that happens when people do that is they work through their pain. It is not an easy thing to do; it doesn't happen overnight. They have to get past the blaming.

"Once you start to work though some of those things, and you stop looking at the other person and start looking at yourself, you may see what God is trying to do in you and that it is easier to try to make things right. You don't see the person as the evildoer. You don't see the person with a sense of animosity. You start to see him or her as a person God loves just as much as He loves you. And you begin to see the image of God in that person just like the image of God that is in you. When your viewpoint changes, it is easier to reconcile and move forward. I have seen couples successfully do that."

Reconciliation involves an agreement not to pay back negative for negative, but to work toward living together in harmony. Make wise choices about how you relate with your former spouse.

"Fools mock at making amends for sin, but goodwill is found among the upright" (Proverbs 14:9).

Lord God, I never realized a separation or divorce could be so stressful. Please help me to be instrumental in bringing about reconciliation with my former spouse. Amen.

A Reason to Reconcile: Children Want It

Another reason to reconcile is because your children desire it. Your children may be dreaming, hoping, and working toward reconciliation. Melissa, whose parents divorced, says, "I was always hoping and praying to get my parents back together. That's what I wanted more than anything in the whole world." Be aware of how important this is to your children, and be careful not to brush aside their dreams. Show your children respect by letting them voice their desires and their concerns and by thoughtfully discussing each worry.

Reconciliation, in your circumstances, may mean friendship, or it may mean marital reconciliation. Either way, the children's feelings and needs should be taken into consideration. Divorce recovery expert Laura Petherbridge says that she meets couples all the time who "for the betterment of their family or kids are able to speak to each other in civil ways and do what's best for the children."

You are probably aware of how difficult this is in regard to your relationship with your former spouse. But anything that is keeping you from reconciling in friendship with your former spouse needs to be addressed and taken care of for the sake of your children. Teach your children by word and example how to reconcile with a person who has wronged you, even when you don't feel like reconciling. Teach them what God says is right to do.

"It's harder to make amends with an offended friend than to capture a fortified city. Arguments separate friends like a gate locked with iron bars" (Proverbs 18:19 NLT).

Dear Lord, I pray that my former spouse and I can reconcile for the sake of our children. Please work in both of our lives to achieve this. Amen.

A Reason to Reconcile: Economics

"It makes good economic sense to combine two households because two can live cheaper if they're living in the same household and dividing the rent," says Dr. Jim A. Talley.

There are economic advantages to bringing your family back together again. The fact is that the cost of maintaining one household is less than the cost of maintaining two. You might *need* to reconcile for financial reasons.

Dr. Talley continues, "I've had people say, 'But I don't want to go back into the same mess I came out of.' That's true. You take the same two miserable people, put them back in the same miserable spot, and you get the same miserable separation again. But changed people, change people. If neither one of you have married other people, you can rebuild a friendship and rebuild the relationship."

Marital reconciliation is always a possibility if neither person has remarried, and relieving financial stressors is one reason to consider reconciliation. By removing financial burdens, you can better focus your time and energy on rebuilding your relationship with God, yourself, your marriage, and your family.

"The wisdom of the wise keeps life on track; the foolishness of fools lands them in the ditch" (Proverbs 14:8 MSG).

Heavenly Father, I don't think I can survive on my income. This is causing me so much stress, and it's making my other problems seem even worse. Give me wisdom in the area of finances as well as in the emotional and relational areas of my life. Amen.

A Reason to Reconcile:
Attracted to Similar People

You may have thought or said at one point that you would never marry another person like your former spouse again. The fact is that people often find themselves attracted to similar types of people.

Dr. Jim A. Talley shares a story: "I once asked a woman, 'Why do you keep marrying alcoholics?' She said, 'I don't know.' I said, 'Where did you meet your first husband?' 'In a bar.' 'Where did you meet your second husband?' 'In a bar.' 'Are you divorced right now?' 'Yes.' 'Where were you Saturday night?' 'In a bar.'

"People tend to look in the same places, and they find the same kinds of people in those places. Your energy level and your mental capacity are so low that you're unable to discern character, and you're uncomfortable with anything different from what you had. You tend to choose the same kind of mate again because you are adjusted to the negative aspects of that character."

You are better off reconciling with your former spouse than putting yourself through the same situation you've just been through for a second or even a third time. You must try to get to the point where you are no longer looking for and finding the bad in your former spouse. Focus instead on what is good, and God will honor your actions.

"Why do you look at the speck of sawdust in your brother's eye and pay no attention to the plank in your own eye?" (Matthew 7:3).

Heavenly Father, open my eyes to truly see the kind of person I have been dating or thinking of dating, and open my heart to the idea of reconciliation with my former spouse. Amen.

A Reason to Reconcile:
Separation or Divorce Was Premature

Sometimes people in our society take the view that once a couple is separated, they will inevitably divorce. Separation does not always lead to divorce—it can lead to reconciliation! Think about your own situation and consider whether or not you might be moving toward divorce prematurely.

Dr. Jim A. Talley says, "I had a woman come to me and say, 'My sister and her husband have separated, so they're going to get a divorce.' I said, 'What about reconciliation?' She said, 'Oh no, that'll never happen. They're going to get a divorce.'

"Family, friends, lawyers, and others push the whole divorce issue; they don't say anything about reconciliation. Even if the divorce is final, you can reconcile to one another. Even if you're both married to other people, you can reconcile to the point of friendship. If neither one of you has remarried, you can rebuild a friendship, rebuild the relationship, and you can remarry each other. I've married a number of couples who have been divorced for as long as five years."

Don't give in to statistics, cultural norms, or pressuring friends. You do not want to live out the expectations of other people; you must create your own expectations. Consider reconciliation, and take it one stage at a time. With God by your side, there is nothing to fear if you choose to slow down and consider your options when others are pushing you to move too quickly.

"Have I not commanded you? Be strong and courageous. Do not be terrified; do not be discouraged, for the LORD your God will be with you wherever you go" (Joshua 1:9).

Lord God, help me not to let myself be pressured into making decisions too quickly when I know I'm not ready. Amen.

A Reason to Reconcile: To Stabilize Your Life

If you choose to reconcile, you will stabilize more quickly than if you remain at odds with your former spouse. Many people mistakenly feel that a new relationship with another person will be more stable than their former relationship and that they will stabilize more quickly in this relationship. This is often not true at all.

"You are able to stabilize faster if you go back to your former mate," says Dr. Jim A. Talley. "You do not have to rebuild a whole new relationship with another individual. It takes less time and effort and energy to make the marriage you are in work."

Laura Petherbridge says, "Why should you consider reconciliation? Number one, because God commands it; He wants you to be reconciled. Number two, because it is in your own best interest. If at all possible, it is definitely better to reconcile your present marriage than to remarry another person. When you are in the battle of divorce, it won't feel that way, but putting the time and effort into the present marriage will pay off. You will find that you've got a lot more ground to build on than you thought you had."

Choosing to try to reconcile God's way will help make you strong and secure within yourself. If you are worried that your inner turmoil will never end, listen to God's promise to you in the Bible:

"You will suffer for a while, but God will make you complete, steady, strong, and firm" (1 Peter 5:10 CEV).

Savior God, I want a stable life. My life has been rocky for a long time now. Please give me the wisdom to work toward the steadiness of reconciliation. Amen.

A Reason to Reconcile: God Desires It

God desires that you pursue reconciliation. He has given you the "ministry of reconciliation" (2 Corinthians 5:18). A ministry, in this sense, is a service that you provide to others out of a love for God. Reconciliation means to be in a right relationship with God first and then with your family and others. How are you living out the ministry that God has entrusted you? Are you serving God by pursuing a right relationship with others?

Wallace and Linda separated after ten years of marriage. Wallace says, "At one point we looked at each other and said, 'Good riddance.' We didn't want to be together; it wasn't enjoyable, and there was so much pain attached. So when the Lord laid the idea of reconciliation on my heart, and when I initiated it, it wasn't something moved out of a deep love for my wife; it was moved out of obedience to God. I wanted the Lord to work in my life to do what was right."

Linda says, "I didn't have any feelings for Wallace, but these words kept coming to my mind, *You have to keep your family together. You have to keep your family together. That means Wallace too.*"

Wallace and Linda chose to pursue reconciliation out of obedience to God, and they are now happily married and growing together in Christ.

"Now all things *are* of God, who has reconciled us to Himself through Jesus Christ, and has given us the ministry of reconciliation" (2 Corinthians 5:18 NKJV).

Lord God, You have given me the ministry of reconciliation. Show me how to live out this ministry. Amen.

Waiting

As unlikely as it may seem, your former spouse will probably consider reconciliation at some point.

"You may think your mate will never do that. Sometimes it takes a while; the longest I've seen is twelve years," says Dr. Jim A. Talley.

Rose Sweet says, "If you can't reconcile your marriage, then you can at least reconcile yourself to a right relationship with your former spouse, and that is one of forgiveness and one of peace. If you can't reconcile on that level, give it some time. Keep the door cracked because you never know how God is going to work in that person's heart. He is asking you to stay there and be patient and go about your life. When the time is right, He might move your former spouse's heart toward you, not necessarily toward remarriage but to mutual forgiveness and kindness, and you want to make sure that door is open. If it's five years from now, ten years from now, thirty years from now—how wonderful that you've left the door open for that beautiful gift for the both of you."

All things are possible with God. He is all-knowing and all-powerful, and His perspective is broader than anyone could imagine. Trust God, who desires reconciliation, and through whom it can be accomplished.

"For there is only one God and one Mediator who can reconcile God and people. He is the man Christ Jesus" (1 Timothy 2:5 NLT).

Almighty God, all things are possible through You. Lord, I want to believe. Teach me to trust in You. Amen.

Is Waiting a Waste of Time?

Some of you may feel that waiting for reconciliation is a waste of time. Dr. Jim A. Talley looks at it from another vantage point.

"The purpose of that period of time is for you to stabilize yourself spiritually, emotionally, relationally, and financially. Get your life together. Use this time for you. This is your recovery time," recommends Dr. Talley.

Juana says, "My life was still in turmoil, and I didn't know the answers, but I knew the One who knew the answers, and I was willing to wait for whatever God had for me. I did not have support from certain family members and friends. In fact, my mother would say, 'What are you waiting for? Why are you waiting for him?' I would say, 'Mom, I'm not waiting for him. I'm waiting on God.'" Juana used that time to read God's Word daily and to listen for God's voice.

Bobby says, "The best way I can continue to reconcile with my former wife is to love my daughter."

What areas of your life could you be working on while waiting?

"But grow in the grace and knowledge of our Lord and Savior Jesus Christ. To him be glory both now and forever! Amen" (2 Peter 3:18).

"So trust him absolutely, people; lay your lives on the line for him. God is a safe place to be" (Psalm 62:8 MSG).

Lord and Savior, this is a time in my life that I can devote wholly to You. I want to grow and mature and become strong through faith in You. Amen.

Practical Tips to Move Toward Reconciliation

Warren Kniskern recommends using another person as a mediator, or a neutral third party, to enable you and your former spouse to talk through issues without becoming hostile or hurtful. He recommends you choose a wise, capable-to-counsel, experienced person who can be objective and can help both spouses resolve the issues.

Lou Priolo offers another practical suggestion for moving toward reconciliation. He says, "When there is regular contact between you and your former spouse, you're going to have to talk with each other. You're going to have to solve conflicts together. The continued exposure can produce additional stress, but it can also be an opportunity for healing."

Both of the above suggestions involve interacting with your former spouse. Use wisdom in deciding if this is the best time for the type of interaction described above. If you aren't ready to speak with your spouse, write non-mailed letters to your spouse to help you see what's in your heart and to draw you closer to the point of reconciliation.

When interacting with your spouse, clear communication is important. Take time to sort out your thoughts and emotions, your beliefs and convictions. Learn to express these to other people in an understandable manner.

"Listen to the words of the wise; apply your heart to my instruction. For it is good to keep these sayings deep within yourself, always ready on your lips. I am teaching you today—yes, you—so you will trust in the LORD" (Proverbs 22:17–19 NLT).

Wise Counselor, You know how difficult it is for my former spouse and me to communicate. But I know You can reach the hardest of hearts. Please soften both our hearts so that we can break down some of the barriers between us and start talking and listening to each other. Amen.

Potential Pain

When considering reconciliation, you might be hesitant to open yourself up to the potential pain that could occur. This is a valid concern. Reconciliation is a process to begin when you are emotionally, mentally, and spiritually ready to go through it. This is something that you *and* your former spouse must grow into.

Doug Schmidt says, "If the person who has hurt you is moving toward genuine repentance, then reconciliation becomes a possibility. But, if the offender continues to deflect responsibility, then the appropriate response is to decrease your vulnerability to that person—even while moving toward forgiving him or her. True forgiveness does not always require reconciliation."

If your wounds are still raw and you haven't begun to stabilize your life, you might not be able to reconcile right away. Right now it is better that you seek to grow in faith and in the knowledge of God, learning and maturing as a single individual. Then, when you have begun to grow and stabilize and when you are ready to forgive, pray about reconciliation and actively seek it.

"We pray . . . that you may live a life worthy of the Lord and may please him in every way: bearing fruit in every good work, growing in the knowledge of God, being strengthened with all power according to his glorious might so that you may have great endurance and patience" (Colossians 1:10–11).

Holy Father, I pray that I will grow and be strengthened in You before attempting to make any major decisions or changes. I pray, too, for endurance and patience to wait until the right time to seek reconciliation. Amen.

Facing Reality

When attempting to reconcile with your spouse, the reality is that what you desire to happen may not happen.

"Reconciliation was something I had wanted more than anything in my life," shares Jan Northington, "and until I realized I was the only person who wanted this reconciliation, I still held on to it. Why did I wait as long as I did? Because I believe God called me to do that in obedience to what would be honoring to Him and to my marriage covenant. I did so also because I believed that if God could remake me and change me, He could also do the same for my husband. I did not give up that hope until I realized my husband would not allow God to do that in his life."

God has given us the free will to make choices in our lives, choices about what we believe and how we will live. God desires that we follow His paths and commands; He will bless us eternally if we do so. But many people turn from God and follow their own paths. Pray that your former spouse chooses God's will for his or her life.

"Since they hated knowledge and did not choose to fear the LORD, since they would not accept my advice and spurned my rebuke, they will eat the fruit of their ways and be filled with the fruit of their schemes . . . But whoever listens to me will live in safety and be at ease, without fear of harm" (Proverbs 1:29–31, 33).

Dear God, I want to reconcile with my former spouse, but I don't know if this is going to happen. Give me the wisdom to know when to keep trying and when to move on. Amen.

Is Reconciliation Possible?

You may think that reconciliation is impossible—especially marital reconciliation. Impossible? No. With God, all things are possible. As humans, we cannot see from God's viewpoint; we cannot see the future, and we cannot see or change hearts.

Dick Purnell says, "Let God take care of the future. If you worry about the future, you will get discouraged and depressed. Be patient. Let God rebuild it. Let God put that hope in your soul and your heart. Work on building a friendship together first. Like Martin Luther said, 'I don't know what my future holds, but I know who holds my future.' That's the hope you have."

You will want to be wise in all your daily decisions, especially in decisions regarding relationships and your life and future. The Bible says that wisdom comes only from God. A person can be highly educated and knowledgeable about many subjects, but a person can be wise only through God's enabling.

"Know also that wisdom is sweet to your soul; if you find it, there is a future hope for you, and your hope will not be cut off" (Proverbs 24:14).

The Bible also says that a blameless, upright man of peace has hope for a bright future. Can you say that you are a forgiven, righteous person of peace? Through Jesus Christ, everyone has the option of being that person.

"Consider the blameless, observe the upright; there is a future for the man of peace" (Psalm 37:37).

Father, I don't know what my future holds, but I know You hold my future, and I believe You are the God of the impossible. Amen.

Dating and Reconciliation

"The chance of reconciliation with a third party in the picture is zero," says Gary Richmond.

If you have any desire for marital reconciliation, even the smallest amount, you should not be dating another person. Your spouse will not think you are open to reconciliation if you are involved in a new relationship.

"I was certainly open to signs of reconciliation," says Terry. "It's just that I did not know which person I wanted to be with. I had muddied the water and brought another person, another relationship, into the picture."

If you are dating when you should not be, you are bringing potential hurt to this new person because you have allowed him or her to become emotionally attached to you when you were not truly available or ready for that attachment. If you are still married and the divorce is not final, then dating is not appropriate.

"To the married I give this command (not I, but the Lord): A wife must not separate from her husband. But if she does, she must remain unmarried or else be reconciled to her husband. And a husband must not divorce his wife" (1 Corinthians 7:10–11).

Lord and Savior, sometimes I get ahead of myself and make decisions based on feelings or desires. Help me to make wise decisions about dating and reconciliation in my circumstances, and help me to be God-focused today and not self-focused. I want what You want, Lord. Amen.

Making Changes in Your Life

Maybe you are willing to work on reconciliation to bring your marriage back together again, but your former spouse is not. Dr. Jim A. Talley suggests you first work on your personal stability and growth.

He says, "If your drive is toward reconciliation and you're the same person that your former spouse left before, then you're not going to ever see any real accomplishments."

Wallace chose to make changes in his life by attending a Bible study and prayer group. As he began to grow in faith and spiritual maturity, his wife, Linda (whom he was separated from), noticed the changes in Wallace and decided to start focusing on God herself.

Linda shares, "I could see Wallace starting to change, and it was drawing me to him. I thought, *Lord, what is so different about him?* It was a time of the Lord drawing me to Him and also to Wallace. I could see the Lord in Wallace."

As Linda and Wallace turned their focus from their own desires to a personal relationship with God, their marital relationship began to be restored. Wallace says, "The ability to be restored into a full relationship with the Lord or with another person can only come through Christ."

Linda says, "My focus isn't on Wallace anymore. I mean, I love him dearly, but my whole dependence is on the Lord."

"Let us go on instead and become mature in our understanding" (Hebrews 6:1 NLT).

Living Lord, I want to grow and change and mature to be a healthy and whole person in You! Help me to be faithful to Your commands today. Amen.

What If Your Spouse Is Not Willing to Reconcile?

If your spouse does not want to reconcile with you, how long should you wait for a change of heart?

"How long to wait is one of the most difficult questions I'm asked in divorce recovery," says Laura Petherbridge. "Each person's situation is unique, and there is no formula. You must stay close to God and make sure you are not in a state of denial.

"In my own situation, I prayed that God would reveal to me whether to wait or move on. God provided a situation where I could comprehend my ex-husband's true desires in a powerful way that couldn't be denied.

"I knew God was saying, 'Laura, it's okay. He has left. He doesn't want the marriage anymore. You can move on.'"

Seek to reconcile your relationship with God first. If you surrender your life to Jesus and commit yourself to learning more about Him and living for Him, you will be able to hear what He is saying to You. Seek God first in all situations, and learn to listen. God knows what is in your former spouse's heart, and His Spirit will guide you to make the right decision about when to wait and when to move on.

"By him [Jesus,] God reconciled everything to himself. He made peace with everything in heaven and on earth by means of his blood on the cross" (Colossians 1:20 NLT).

Jesus, I commit my life to You. As I spend a quiet moment with You right now, help me to hear Your words of wisdom and obey according to Your Word. Amen.

Do You Want to Reconcile?

You might be the one who is hesitant to reconcile. Your response to the suggestion of reconciling with your former spouse might be, "I can't do it. My former spouse hurt me, betrayed my trust, and has not given me any reason to trust him or her again." Yes, reconciliation is God's first choice for a marriage, but reconciliation requires two committed and repentant hearts focused on seeking God's will for the marriage and understanding that rebuilding the relationship will be a difficult process.

Laura Petherbridge explains: "Your heart should always be praying, 'Lord, teach me how to reconcile with this person.' Many couples receive counsel to move back under the same roof too quickly. This is unwise because if they don't dig down and discover the root of the problems and begin dealing with what broke up the marriage, it is likely to happen again. Sweeping serious issues under the rug and pretending nothing significant has happened is not reconciliation. Trust takes time to build. Ask God to give you a heart that is willing to reconcile, but always pray for the truth to be revealed. It's amazing what God will allow to come into the light when we diligently seek the truth."

Be committed to prayer and Bible study, for God is the only One who knows what's in the heart of an individual, and He is the only One who can change hearts. God can teach you how to reconcile, and He will teach you about trust.

"Guide me in your truth and teach me, for you are God my Savior, and my hope is in you all day long" (Psalm 25:5).

Holy Father, I have hope because of You. Teach me what it means to trust, and give me the desire to reconcile with my former spouse. Amen.

Do You Need to Reconcile?

Perhaps your former spouse wants to reconcile the marriage, and you feel guilty because you do not think remarriage is the best choice at this time; in fact, you think it might not *ever* be the best choice. Yes, God has called each person to the ministry of reconciliation, and He commands you to forgive your former spouse, to repent of your wrongdoing, and to seek reconciliation.

He does not command you to remarry your former spouse.

"If your heart is right with God," says Dick Purnell, "and you don't have a sense that this is God's direction, follow God's will. Just because your former spouse wants to reconcile does not mean you have to. You have to follow God's purpose and God's will in your life."

What is important is that you are actively seeking spiritual growth and that you are drawing closer to God in prayer, Bible study, and fellowship with other believers. As you grow closer to Him, you will be better able to hear His voice and know His direction for your life.

"What does the LORD your God ask of you but to fear the LORD your God, to walk in all his ways, to love him, to serve the LORD your God with all your heart and with all your soul, and to observe the LORD's commands and decrees that I am giving you today for your own good?" (Deuteronomy 10:12–13).

O Lord my God, I want so much to do what is right. I want to obey You and walk in Your path for my life. Please give me wisdom and a clear mind to know whether or not marital reconciliation is what You desire for me to do. Amen.

Is God Leading You to Attempt Reconciliation?

"To make this really work, it takes two willing hearts. But even if there are not two willing hearts, at least one willing heart plus God is a majority, and amazing things can happen," says Bob.

In the Bible, Hosea's wife had been unfaithful to him numerous times and with numerous men. Despite the blatant rejection of Hosea's wife to Hosea, God wanted him to reconcile with her. Hosea obeyed God and reconciled with his wife. You, too, need to be responsive to God if He is leading you to reconcile. You need to learn to walk strong with God and to be able to recognize His will in your life.

The book of Hosea is a picture of God's love for all people, despite the fact that we reject Him and put other things and other people ahead of our relationship with Him. God desires that we love others with the same kind of love that He has for us. This is only possible through the help of the Holy Spirit. Pray today that you can learn to love like God and that you will be open to whatever direction God leads you in the area of reconciliation.

"The LORD said to me, 'Go, show your love to your wife again, though she is loved by another and is an adulteress. Love her as the LORD loves the Israelites, though they turn to other gods'" (Hosea 3:1).

Almighty God, where are You leading me? What do You want me to do? I want to walk in loving obedience to You. Amen.

Moving On and
Growing Closer to God

Healing Through God

Kay Arthur shares, "Having been divorced and having seen the pain and the consequences of being divorced in my own life and in the lives of my children, I can still say that there is healing. There is healing because God's name is Jehovah Rapha, the Lord God who heals. He is the God of second chances. He is the God who turns ashes into beauty and gives us a garment of praise instead of a garment of mourning and sorrow. With God there is healing for anything, even the trauma of divorce."

God's healing is not a superficial healing, where the outside may look great but the wounds on the inside are still bleeding. He can heal anything that has hurt you, and His healing is deep and eternal. Believe this and cling to this hope. Allow God to turn your "ashes" into beauty and to clothe you with a garment of praise. Pray for healing.

God makes this promise in the book of Isaiah. He promises to "provide for those who grieve in Zion—to bestow on them a crown of beauty instead of ashes, the oil of gladness instead of mourning, and a garment of praise instead of a spirit of despair. They will be called oaks of righteousness, a planting of the LORD for the display of his splendor" (Isaiah 61:3).

Healing, Lord, through You, I have the opportunity to transform my life. I can walk forward in healing and wholeness with You by my side. Amen.

Three Possible Outcomes

As you begin to emotionally stabilize, it is important to look at the future and decide how this experience of separation or divorce will affect the rest of your life. Keep in mind that it is your choice how this experience will affect your future. H. Norman Wright discusses three possible outcomes for the experience of separation or divorce in your life. Which will you choose?

1. Your life can change for the worse, which means you continue to let the situation control and dominate you. You become so immobilized and damaged by this experience that you go through life crippled emotionally, mentally, and spiritually.

2. Your life can stay the same. You aren't damaged, but you haven't really learned and grown through this experience.

3. Your life can change for the better. That means you eventually move away from asking God, *Why did this happen?* to the place where you can say, *How can I learn from this, how can I grow through this, and how can God be glorified through what I have gone through?*

Claim this Bible verse with the psalmist:
"It was good for me to be afflicted so that I might learn your decrees" (Psalm 119:71).

Dear Lord, this whole experience has been horrible, but it happened, and it's still happening. As I live today and as I look to the future, I pray that my life is changing for the better. I know this is possible because of who You are. Amen.

Does God Cause Divorce?

God does not cause divorce. Remember that Malachi 2:16 quotes God as saying, "I hate divorce."

"I did not see my divorce as coming from God or that it was His fault," says Rob Eagar. "It was just a situation where someone chose to end the relationship. I wanted my wife to stay. I desperately loved her, but I couldn't make her stay in the relationship.

"My divorce experience brought me closer to God because not only did I realize that He has promised to watch over me and take care of me, at the same time, I sensed how Christ feels when I have rejected Him. It gave my heart a deeper understanding of how Christ still loves me when I don't always listen to Him or when I sometimes reject Him. It gave me more respect for God and His involvement in my life and the depth of His love for me."

God's desire is that you and your former spouse would bond together in love and forever serve Him in your relationship. He hates divorce, and He would never cause it to happen. Your divorce is a result of people making choices outside of God's will. But you can choose today to remain in God's will and to follow His plan for your life. Use your trials and pain as stepping-stones that lead you closer to God and closer to His healing and power.

"They are darkened in their understanding and separated from the life of God because of the ignorance that is in them due to the hardening of their hearts" (Ephesians 4:18).

Almighty God, forgive me when I try to blame You. You are a holy and perfect God, who desires holy and perfect relationships for His people. Amen.

How God Uses Pain

Even though God did not cause your divorce or separation, He can use it for your good. Perhaps you have chosen paths in life that led you away from God. He can use the separation or divorce as a way to help point you back into a relationship with Him.

"When you want to have a close relationship with someone," says Cathy, "you spend hours of time with that person. That's how you fall in love with God. You get to know Him on a one-on-one basis. That's what happens when you're forced through your pain to spend hours of time praying for relief, help, and strength.

"I'm thankful I had to go through it. As horrible as it was, I would go through it again to be who I am now in relation to Christ.

"You couldn't have told me that then," continues Cathy. "I remember praying that I wouldn't grow anymore: 'Lord, this hurts too much. If this is for growth, I don't want to grow.' But I'm glad He loved me enough to let me suffer through that to be where I am now and to have the relationship I now have with Him."

The Bible says that every trial you face is an opportunity for God to show His goodness to you and for you to become more like Christ.

"We know that in all things God works for the good of those who love him, who have been called according to his purpose" (Romans 8:28).

Lord Jesus, as I cry out to You in my pain, praying for relief and help and strength, I pray that I grow to be a better person—strong, wise, and mature in You. Amen.

Understand God's Comfort

Going through separation or divorce can lead you to a greater understanding of God's comfort. God's Spirit will comfort you through the Bible, through other people, through circumstances, through church, and through answered prayer.

Laura Petherbridge shares how God comforted her through the Bible: "Philippians 4:5–6 was such a comfort for me, especially the words, 'Be anxious for nothing.' I tend to be an anxious person, and during my divorce my fretfulness was magnified. I think God wanted me to know that there wasn't anything to be anxious about. He had my past, my present, and my future in His hands, and there wasn't anything happening to me that hadn't been sifted through His hands first. He was assuring me that He was going to carry me through.

"I remember those words jumping off the page into my lap, into my mind and my heart: 'There's nothing to be anxious about.' Even though I didn't believe it, I kept repeating the phrase, 'Be anxious for nothing.' The verses gave me steps to follow: pray, petition (make a request), and find things to be thankful for. Little by little, those steps are what made Philippians 4:5–6 come alive for me. When you speak God's Word, it provides a solid place to stand when the ground beneath your feet begins to shake."

Let God comfort you through His Word.

"The Lord is near. Be anxious for nothing, but in everything by prayer and supplication with thanksgiving let your requests be made known to God" (Philippians 4:5–6 NASB).

Holy Spirit, You are my comforter. I am learning to walk in Your comfort and not to be anxious or fearful, but to be thankful. Amen.

Develop Perseverance

God can use your separation or divorce to help you develop perseverance.

H. Norman Wright says, "I've really learned to depend on the passage in James 1:2–3 where it says, 'Count it all joy, my brethren, when you encounter all trials, for the trying of your faith produces perseverance or patience.' The Scripture does not say, 'Count it all joy immediately.' It is a process, but eventually you get to that place where you make up your mind to regard your adversity as something to welcome or be glad about. It is a choice. In life, problems are inevitable. Joy is an option."

Perseverance is a positive character trait that will help you through life's current and future trials. Think about what you have been persevering in as a result of your separation or divorce. Are you persevering in raising godly children? Are you pressing on in learning about and choosing forgiveness? Are you making it a habit to meet with other Christian believers in Bible study and prayer? Perseverance is developed by proceeding forward no matter what the circumstances, and when you stumble and fall, perseverance involves getting back up again (often with the help of others and always with the help of God!) and pointing yourself in that forward direction once again.

"Consider it pure joy, my brothers, whenever you face trials of many kinds, because you know that the testing of your faith develops perseverance" (James 1:2–3).

Gracious Father, You are always here to help me in my spiritual and personal growth. Thank You for lifting me up and supporting me when I begin to falter and fall. Amen.

Understanding Forgiveness

The experience of separation or divorce can teach you about forgiveness—how to forgive others and how to receive forgiveness for yourself, both of which can result in great freedom.

"In forgiveness you become free and you are released," says Doug Easterday, "and then you can be right with God, and you have available to you all the provision of Jesus Christ at the cross. That is the wonderful benefit of forgiveness."

You need to forgive others and be forgiven yourself. This is a process you learn by experience. Recognize this period in your life as a time to learn about what forgiveness is, who needs to do the forgiving, and the benefits forgiveness brings. Take a piece of paper and answer these four questions to see what you have been learning. (It may help to review past messages on forgiveness.)

1. What is forgiveness?

2. Who needs to forgive whom?

3. What are the benefits of forgiveness?

4. Who models forgiveness for us?

"Be merciful, just as your Father is merciful. Do not judge, and you will not be judged. Do not condemn, and you will not be condemned. Forgive, and you will be forgiven. Give, and it will be given to you. A good measure, pressed down, shaken together and running over, will be poured into your lap. For with the measure you use, it will be measured to you'" (Luke 6:36–38).

Father, I will continue to look to You for guidance and instruction on how to forgive. This is something that cannot be done by human strength alone! Amen.

Sensitive to the Need for God's Forgiveness

Going through a separation or divorce can make you more sensitive to your need for God's forgiveness for the things you've done wrong in your life.

"What's so wonderful is God meets you right where you are," says Cathy. "It doesn't matter if you have any Bible knowledge; it doesn't matter if you have any inclination as to who He is, what He is, what He's about, and what He expects, because He loves you so much."

No matter how badly you may have behaved, no matter how deeply you may have hurt other people, there is no sin that will keep you from God's love. He loves you and wants to forgive you.

Dr. Craig Keener states: "No sin you could have possibly committed could have been too bad for the price God paid to cover that sin—the blood of His own Son. And no demonstration of love in this universe could have been greater than the price God paid to show you how much He loves you and how much He wants you to come back to Him and belong to Him."

Come to God. Confess your sins to Him. Allow Him to love you.

"You are forgiving and good, O Lord, abounding in love to all who call to you" (Psalm 86:5).

Wondrous Lord, I cannot fathom Your great love for me. Please forgive me for my sins. I want to turn away from my wrong behaviors and habits and follow You instead. Amen.

Learn to Surrender to God's Will

God can use your experience to teach you how to forgive others. Remember, God does not *cause* bad experiences to happen to people, but He can *use* those experiences to result in good.

It is only through the power of God that you will be able to forgive other people when they have hurt you and wronged you.

"I'm finding more and more that I really do want to forgive these two people who have been responsible for almost destroying me," says Harriet. "If that doesn't tell you the power of our Lord, then I'm not sure what will."

James says, "There are two things you can do: You either can glorify God or glorify yourself. When I decided that I wanted to glorify God, that was when I finally said, 'God, I give up. I quit. I throw up the white flag and I surrender.' And I heard a voice say, 'It's about time because I have been waiting for you to do that for thirty-three years.'"

God wants you to surrender to Him because it is when you completely surrender your life, your agenda, and your definition of right and wrong, better and best, that you will be free. Surrender brings freedom; it brings power, and it ensures victory!

"And the presence of the Lord was with them with power, so that a great number [learned] to believe . . . and turned and surrendered themselves to Him" (Acts 11:21 AMP).

Holy Lord, I have no strength left of my own. I surrender my life to You, knowing that Your way is right and best. I believe in the abundant, victorious life that is available to everyone who relies on You. Amen.

Restore Your Moral Value System

Some people see their moral value systems break down before and during a separation or divorce. The Lord can use your past experiences as a catalyst to help you restore your value system.

"I've talked with so many people who say, 'If you had told me a year ago that I'd be doing what I'm doing today, I would have called you a liar because I would never do that. I'm too moral a person,'" says Dr. Jim A. Talley.

Tim shares, "The path may look dark, and you can get angry and nasty. Your spouse can get angry and nasty and fight for things that are of this world—money, businesses, cars. But long-term, bottom line is that God will take care of you. God will show you the way to go. So you can look on the negative side, or you can look on the positive side. I choose to look on the positive side because I've seen where I've been and where I'm going."

Now is a good time to define or redefine your morals and convictions. What is truly important? Do your words and actions reflect your values? If they do not, what steps can you take to remedy that?

"Do not store up for yourselves treasures on earth, where moth and rust destroy, and where thieves break in and steal. But store up for yourselves treasures in heaven" (Matthew 6:19–20).

Lord God, I've gotten mixed up lately as to what is truly important in life. I've done things I'm not proud of, but You offer forgiveness to all who ask. Please forgive me. From now on, I'm going to walk forward, seeking to do things that please You and following Jesus' example in the Bible. Amen.

Understand Who You Are in Christ

"Divorce is an opportunity to deal with that deep reality of who you are, who made you, and what God wants for your life," says Howard.

It's natural to go through a period of self-examination during a divorce or separation. This is an opportunity for great spiritual and personal growth. God can use this experience to show you who you are in Christ. He has a purpose for you to fulfill in this world, so focus on living each moment through Christ, and your purpose will become more and more clear to you. You will find your true identity in Christ. If you look anywhere else, you will find the wrong things.

Dr. Robert Abarno says, "I'm opposed to divorce, but for the Christian a great amount of good can come out of it if it occurs. You can learn about yourself and your relationship with God. You should take the time to concentrate on who you are in Christ. You can grow in grace and in the knowledge of your Lord and Savior Jesus Christ."

Dr. Abarno encourages you to put into effect the Lord's commands in Matthew 22.

"Jesus replied: 'Love the Lord your God with all your heart and with all your soul and with all your mind.' This is the first and greatest commandment. And the second is like it: 'Love your neighbor as yourself'" (Matthew 22:37–39).

Lord Jesus, I love You, and I want to live my life as a reflection of all You created me to be. Amen.

Personal Testimonies

Sue and Rose share what they have learned from their divorce experiences.

Sue says, "One important thing I learned was the concept of being a whole person. I didn't know I wasn't a whole person, but I know now that it contributed to the downfall of my marriage. I'd been relying on somebody else to provide me with security and happiness. I found out that God is the only One who can provide what I need."

Rose Sweet shares, "Divorce, in a way, was the best thing that ever happened to me. God hates divorce and so do I, but He used it to draw me nearer to Him, to grow me up mentally and emotionally, and to deepen my spiritual relationship with Him. For that, I will be eternally grateful."

If you embrace your divorce experience as a learning process, you have the opportunity to find out more about yourself, redefine your beliefs, and learn how to develop strong character traits. You can also use this time to discover God's promises in the Bible. Search for His truths, and redefine your life based on biblical principles so that you will have a solid foundation to walk on and a peace beyond comprehension!

"Formerly, when you did not know God, you were slaves to those who by nature are not gods. But now that you know God—or rather are known by God—how is it that you are turning back to those weak and miserable principles? Do you wish to be enslaved by them all over again?" (Galatians 4:8–9).

God, when I am in a relationship with You, I am set free from the old way of life, the old life of bondage and despair. My hope is in You! Amen.

Renew Your Mind

This is also a time for what Romans 12:2 calls the renewing of your mind. "God is interested in your healing," says Dr. Archibald Hart, "and God uses the natural losses of life to renew your mind to make you a more complete person, a whole person. That renewing is an ongoing process. When you learn to use the losses of life for healing purposes, you renew your mind."

Bonnie Keen offers a practical suggestion that she has used to help renew her mind and keep it focused on the Lord: "I began to take Post-it notes, and write on them a Scripture or a truth that I knew about the Lord, and stick them up in my bathroom where I would go every day to get ready. I would leave them there. I'd look over at them when I needed to, and I would remind myself of the truth and of God's faithfulness. I put those everywhere I could to remind myself, and I kept them up for years. Slowly but surely, the doubting started falling away and I began to say, 'I'm going to stand on what I know is true.'"

"Do not conform any longer to the pattern of this world, but be transformed by the renewing of your mind. Then you will be able to test and approve what God's will is—his good, pleasing and perfect will" (Romans 12:2).

Lord God, change my thought patterns and behaviors to ones that promote healing and wholeness in me. Amen.

Grow Closer to God

"This time is a gift to just entrench yourself in God's Word," advises Juana, "because there will be a time later in life when you will be busier, and you will not have that time. This time is a gift; how are you going to use it?"

Use your recovery time as an opportunity to grow closer to God. You can grow closer to Him by reading the Bible and praying, by telling people about His work in your life, by helping or comforting other people, and by talking about and thinking about things that are pleasing to Him. Although there will be times when you will feel like it's not working, your efforts to draw near to God are never in vain.

Selma says, "I remember when my husband first left that there was day upon day upon day when I would read the Word and try to find something from God to me. And my time with God felt cold; it felt dead, like there was nothing there. A friend of mine said, 'Keep praying and keep reading; it'll come.' And it did."

God is always close beside you. Believe in that truth and trust in it. Remember that your feelings cannot always be trusted, but God can.

"Let us draw near to God with a sincere heart in full assurance of faith, having our hearts sprinkled to cleanse us from a guilty conscience and having our bodies washed with pure water. Let us hold unswervingly to the hope we profess, for he who promised is faithful" (Hebrews 10:22–23).

Lord God, I know I am drawing closer to You, and I am so grateful. Thank You for never giving up on me. Amen.

Understand Your Worth to God

Low self-esteem is a natural reaction to the rejection you've experienced. Instead of focusing on your shortcomings, focus instead on the fact that God can use the hard times to show you how much you are worth to Him.

Let God validate your worth. God created you as a single, valuable individual. Through the power of the Holy Spirit, you can walk sure-footed from this point forth—separate, unique, and whole—on a new path that leads to healing and victory. If you are a Christian, settle it in your mind that you are never alone. Your heavenly Father, who loves you extravagantly, is always with you. Feelings can come and go, but God has come to stay. He will never go away.

Dr. Myles Munroe states, "Your value is not determined by what people think about you, and you are not valuable because someone married you. You're valuable because God says you're valuable. Your value is independent of other people's opinions of you. So believe in what you are worth."

When God looks at you, He sees beauty and potential and humor and talent. He loves you so much that He gave His own Son so that you can live forever with Him.

"Very rarely will anyone die for a righteous man, though for a good man someone might possibly dare to die. But God demonstrates his own love for us in this: While we were still sinners, Christ died for us" (Romans 5:7–8).

Holy God, I am special, lovely, and loved by You. Thank You. Amen.

Understand God's Plan for Your Life

God can use your separation or divorce to help you understand His plan for your life. God created you for a specific purpose that only you can fulfill. In order to know where He is directing you and to hear what He is saying to you, you must draw near to Him, spend time developing that relationship, and start praying about how God can use you.

Dr. Myles Munroe says, "God created everybody for a purpose. You were not born for the purpose of being married; therefore, you must discover the dream God put in your heart. There's something He wants done on this earth that requires your life."

The story of Esther in the Bible is a beautiful story of a young, orphaned Jewish girl who, through God's sovereignty, was chosen to be queen. While Esther was queen, a plan had been put into effect to destroy all Jews in Persia. In the face of great personal danger, Esther was obedient to God and approached the king on behalf of the Jews. Because Esther was in that unique position, she was able to save hundreds of lives. The Bible says that God placed Esther in that royal position "for such a time as this."

Those words also apply to your life. There will come a time when God has planned for you to be in a certain place, at a certain time, and at a certain level of spiritual maturity to fulfill His purpose. He is preparing you "for such a time as this." Be ready!

"Who knows but that you have come to royal position for such a time as this?" (Esther 4:14).

Sovereign Lord, You know and plan the days of my life.
Please use my life for Your great plans that I cannot yet see.
Amen.

Can God Use Divorced People?

Some people feel that because they have been divorced or because they have made so many mistakes in their past, God cannot use them to be godly leaders, teachers, role models, or a help to other people. This is not true. Your past does not determine your future. Read the Bible to discover examples of God using people with unexpected pasts to do great and mighty works for Him.

In Hebrews chapter 11, God lists heroes and heroines of faith. This list includes a murderer (Moses), an adulterer (David), and a womanizer (Samson). These people moved beyond their failures and followed God. They were used to accomplish God's purpose in their generations.

Before Kay Arthur had a saving relationship with Christ, she was divorced, and she did many things that did not honor God. Today, she is a respected Christian speaker, author, and teacher through the grace of God.

She says: "God chooses the base things, the foolish things, the things that are despised, the things that are nothing, so that no flesh can glory in His presence. He knew what was going to happen to me before I came to know Christ, and He has used that as a platform for ministry. You can step forward into any service that the Lord has called you to."

God has chosen you for a specific service—take the challenge to walk forward in that!

"The base things of the world and the things which are despised God has chosen, and the things which are not, to bring to nothing the things that are, that no flesh should glory in His presence" (1 Corinthians 1:28–29 NKJV).

Holy God, I am willing to be used by You. I want to be a part of Your glorious plan in this world. I know I can be victorious through You. Amen.

Reach Out to Others

Now is the time to reach out and help others. Even though you're still recovering, God can use you to minister to the needs of other people.

You are in a unique position to help those who are hurting because you've been there. Do not be afraid to share openly what you have struggled with and what you have learned. Pray for opportunities to reach out, and be open to God's leading. Look around you today and consider who might need an encouraging word or a listening ear.

One day after his divorce, Roy was driving and prayed that God would use him. After passing by two hitchhikers in the course of a few miles, Roy said, "Okay, Lord, if there's another hitchhiker, I'll pick him up." Soon after, he was inviting a hitchhiker into his car. The man hitchhiking had just left his wife and family and was running from the situation.

Roy and the man talked, and Roy shared the importance of surrendering his life to Christ and receiving God's forgiveness and help. The man was interested and prayed to receive Jesus into his life. The man returned home.

A month later, the man called Roy. Roy says, "I could hear the laughter and the joy in his wife and children in the background—that's the grace of God."

Follow Roy's example, and be willing and prepared to help others in need.

"I give you this charge: Preach the Word; be prepared in season and out of season; correct, rebuke and encourage—with great patience and careful instruction" (2 Timothy 4:1–2).

Lord Jesus, it's time for me to stop looking at myself and my problems and start reaching out to help other people in need. Show me to whom I can minister today. Amen.

Fix Your Eyes on Jesus

The only stable thing in life is a relationship with God through Jesus Christ. The Bible says this can never be taken away from you. "For He Himself has said, 'I will never desert you, nor will I ever forsake you'" (Hebrews 13:5 NASB).

Bonnie Keen says, "There were many years when I thought God had turned His back on me. I would read in Luke: 'God is not slow to answer the cries of His people,' and I'd think, *Yes He is. He's very slow. He's taking forever. I'm drowning over here.* I began to realize that I needed to know Christ more intimately. So I began to study the life of Jesus like I never had before.

"I believe Jesus is the heart of God. He came into this world and found the most messed-up, wretched, broken-down people He could find to be with. God's never been afraid of the dirt and the mess people get into. God is saying to you, 'I created you. I know where you've been, and I know where you can go with Me.'"

Keep your eyes on Jesus; He is answering your prayers, and He's also urging you to draw closer to Him so that you can experience even greater answers than you could imagine.

"Let us fix our eyes on Jesus, the author and perfecter of our faith, who for the joy set before him endured the cross, scorning its shame, and sat down at the right hand of the throne of God" (Hebrews 12:2).

Thank You, Jesus, that You died on the cross for me, to save me and to heal me. Thank You that I can live an abundant life forever with You. Amen.

Trust

Having Christ at the center of your life is a matter of trusting Him. If you are having trouble trusting God, Dr. Craig Keener wants to assure you that "God is someone who's never going to forsake you or betray you. His love is perfect."

Dr. Keener says, "When I didn't know how to love and found it hard to believe in love in a world like this, I found in Christ someone whose love I could trust. He was the One who taught me how to love."

James, who has been through divorce, realized that God is the one sure thing in life. He says, "Having a wife was a blessing from God. If I had had kids, it would have been a blessing from God. The job I had was a blessing from God. But those things were taken away from me. At first, they were my identity, and my identity was gone. Now that I have a Lord and a yearning to know who He is on an intimate level, it doesn't matter what's been taken away from me. I know what the true guarantee is—Christ Himself."

The Bible says that God can be trusted. He will love you, be with you, hold you, care for you, supply your needs, and heal you. He will give you strength and will empower you to fulfill the purpose He has called you to do. There is nothing you can do to escape His great love. He will never fail you.

"It is better to take refuge in the LORD than to trust in man" (Psalm 118:8).

Dear God, I understand now that You will never let me down and that You know and want what is best for me. I choose to trust in You. Amen.

Accept His Gift

If you don't have Christ in your life, then you don't have the stability that comes through a relationship with Him, and you don't have the necessary resources to fully heal. The opportunity to have a saving, personal relationship with Jesus Christ is a gift from God. There is nothing you can do to earn or deserve it; it's a gift!

Dr. Craig Keener explains: "To have a personal relationship with God is available to you through His Son, Jesus Christ. God loved you so much that He sent Jesus to die for you on the cross, to pay the penalty for the things that you have done wrong against Him and against one another, the things that alienated you from Him.

"God let His Son pay that penalty in your place. Now, because the price has been paid, He can offer you a relationship with Himself as a free gift, and all you have to do is ask Him for it—ask Him to give you a new life. He'll give you a new purpose, a new destiny. He'll give you something worth living for."

Through Christ, you have the opportunity to unload all of the baggage from your past and present and move forward with a lightness and joy that come from within.

"For it is by grace you have been saved, through faith—and this not from yourselves, it is the gift of God" (Ephesians 2:8).

Lord and Savior, You love me and want to give me an eternal inheritance in heaven! You have paid the penalty for my sins, and I thank You for that. I repent of my sins—I turn my back on them and turn instead toward Your path for my life. Amen.

Steps to Christ

If you would like to invite Christ into your life, here are a few simple steps to follow.

1. Confess your sin. The Bible says that everyone sins. "All have sinned and fall short of the glory of God" (Romans 3:23).

2. Ask for forgiveness from God.

3. Move away from your sins (repent). "Repent, then, and turn to God, so that your sins may be wiped out, that times of refreshing may come from the Lord" (Acts 3:19).

4. Ask Jesus Christ to save you from the effect of your sin.

5. Give Jesus control of your life (as your Lord). "That if you confess with your mouth, 'Jesus is Lord,' and believe in your heart that God raised him from the dead, you will be saved" (Romans 10:9).

By taking these steps, you are inviting Christ into your life as Savior and Lord. *Savior* means you acknowledge that He died in your place to pay the price for your sins. *Lord* means that you give control of your life to Him. Maybe you would like to invite Christ into your life right now. It can be done with a simple prayer.

Dear God, I've done things that are wrong. I've sinned. Please forgive me for my sin, and help me to move away from it. I now ask Jesus to come into my life as my Savior, to save me from my sin and to be my Lord. I give You control of my life. Thank You for forgiving me. Thank You for giving Jesus to me. In His name I pray. Amen.

What's Next?

You've been through almost a year of devotions, and we sincerely hope they have helped you in your recovery from separation or divorce. You might be wondering, *What do I do now? What's next for me?* Over these last few days, we will offer some suggestions to keep you moving forward spiritually and walking in God's healing.

You might be interested in reading this book again. The next time you read it, you will find that it will speak to you in a different way than it did the first time because you are at a different level of healing. You will also be pleased to see where you have grown.

Another suggestion is to join or help out with a DivorceCare® or other Christ-centered divorce support recovery group; you will not only have the opportunity to receive biblical love and encouragement, but you will also be able to help those who are just starting out in their separation and divorce and are feeling lost, alone, and hopeless. You might consider joining a new Bible study group or Sunday school class. Be sure to take the time to build friendships with other mature believers in Christ! Another idea is to start a new help ministry in your church for single parents or for people with other needs. Or perhaps God is leading you to serve Him in another new and exciting way.

"I will bless you with a future filled with hope—a future of success, not of suffering" (Jeremiah 29:11 CEV).

Saving Lord, my future is in Your hands, and I praise You for that. Thank You for the healing I have experienced so far and the new directions in which You are leading me as a result of this experience. Amen.

Spiritual Mentors

If you have not already done so, finding a spiritual mentor will be a tremendous help and support as you move forward in your daily walk and spiritual growth. Your spiritual mentor should be a person who is a mature Christian, one who knows and studies the Bible, and one who understands the power of prayer. This person should care for you and desire that you grow in the Lord.

The best way to find a spiritual mentor is to pray that God will bring the two of you together and to actively seek out someone in your church. Then, make a plan with that person to meet together or have regular phone chats. Plan to pray together, ask questions, and discuss biblical truths that apply to the difficulties you are facing each day. This person should be one who encourages you to study your Bible, meditate on God's Word, and live it daily!

The Bible contains many, many examples of Christians helping one another to grow in the understanding and application of faith and the Scriptures. Aquila and Priscilla were faithful followers of Christ, mentored by the apostle Paul. Later, Aquila and Priscilla had the opportunity to mentor a highly educated man named Apollos. A good spiritual mentor is one who is strong in areas that you are not.

"When Priscilla and Aquila heard him [Apollos], they invited him to their home and explained to him the way of God more adequately" (Acts 18:26).

Dear Lord, lead me to a person who can help me grow in my relationship with You and who will teach me how to live a life rooted in You. Amen.

A Comfort Ministry

Part of your new purpose in life will be to comfort others with the comfort you have received from God. You might begin a "comfort ministry" to people who are facing struggles similar to those you've experienced.

H. Norman Wright says, "Build relationships at church. Get involved more with your relatives. Spend time giving to other people, perhaps ministering at different homes for children or for the elderly."

Steve Polen, as a result of his own experience with divorce, has been called by God to help others who are facing separation or divorce. He says, "Being involved in this kind of ministry has been the most significant thing in my spiritual life since I became a Christian because I can see a purpose in all my suffering. I can see that even though this was not the Lord's original intent for my life, my suffering was not in vain because God used it for the good of other people. My life has a solid purpose to it, and it's something that I would not want to part with."

Your personal ministry could be within your own group of friends and relatives, or it could reach out to others in your church, community, state, or even farther!

"Praise be to the God and Father of our Lord Jesus Christ, the Father of compassion and the God of all comfort, who comforts us in all our troubles, so that we can comfort those in any trouble with the comfort we ourselves have received from God. For just as the sufferings of Christ flow over into our lives, so also through Christ our comfort overflows" (2 Corinthians 1:3–5).

Lord God, You have been a comfort to me this past year.
May I pass on Your comfort to others who need it. Amen.

Serving in a Support Group

Laura Petherbridge went through a divorce several years ago. Today she is a speaker and an author, and she leads a DivorceCare® divorce recovery support group. She has discovered that reaching out and helping other people in separation and divorce is what God has called her to do. She says, "When people come to my divorce recovery group and stay for the long haul and hard work, they come out knowing themselves in a completely different way than when they came in."

You might not be ready to lead a divorce support group, but you can minister to others who are at an earlier stage of healing than you. Open your ears and heart to listen to God and to listen to others. Focus upward and outward.

Is it not to share your food with the hungry and to provide the poor wanderer with shelter—when you see the naked, to clothe him, and not to turn away from your own flesh and blood? Then your light will break forth like the dawn, and your healing will quickly appear; then your righteousness will go before you, and the glory of the LORD will be your rear guard. Then you will call, and the LORD will answer; you will cry for help, and he will say: Here am I.

If you do away with the yoke of oppression, with the pointing finger and malicious talk, and if you spend yourselves in behalf of the hungry and satisfy the needs of the oppressed, then your light will rise in the darkness, and your night will become like the noonday. (Isaiah 58:7–10)

Father, I want to listen to the needs and the cries of other people and help provide for them emotionally and spiritually. Show me where I can serve. Amen.

Walk Forward with Confidence

"I know that regardless of what this world has to throw at me, I'm going to be okay," says Harriet, "because I have the mighty fortress of God around me. There is still a lot of rebuilding to do in my personal life. Nothing is ever the same when you go through separation and divorce; it's like you have to rewrite the script of your life.

"I'll be forty this month, which is kind of daunting, but you know what? I know that forty is going to be great because God tells me that I have value. I know fifty is going to be great, and so is sixty. However many years the Lord allows me to have on this earth are going to be good because He's the driving force in my life now; He is the One at the center of my life now. He's the One I worship, not my spouse. And I know there are limitless possibilities for me."

Walk forward with confidence in God. He will direct your paths if you ask Him and surrender yourself to Him. He has promised in His Word that He is working all things together for the ultimate good of those who love and believe in Him. We congratulate you on all that you have accomplished this past year, and we know that your new, purposeful life will bring endless joys.

"The LORD your God is with you, he is mighty to save. He will take great delight in you, he will quiet you with his love, he will rejoice over you with singing" (Zephaniah 3:17).

Heavenly Savior, You have pulled me out of the dark pit of despair into a new life in You. I praise Your name, and I commit myself to walking forward wherever You direct me. Amen.

Live Victoriously

"I know that without the love of my heavenly Father, I would have been a statistic last year," shares Harriet, "but my Father loves me, and He's reaffirmed it in a thousand ways. So much so that today—a year after I found out that my perfect, wonderful, adoring husband was having an affair—I know that I'm going to live. I'm not just going to get by, but I'm going to live victoriously.

"At this point, I can look back at my experiences and truly understand in my heart that I am a stronger person now, and I am somebody who is worth knowing and worth being with regardless of whether my husband threw aside our love and marriage so carelessly. Every day the Holy Spirit reaffirms in me that I am somebody special, and it has nothing to do with whether or not I have a spouse because I'm God's child."

You, too, can live victoriously through Christ no matter what circumstances occur in your life. An abundant life in Christ is a life with deep roots and a strong foundation. The winds of life may blow strong and the waters may rise, but you can stand firm. Our prayer is that you will walk empowered by God's strength and confident of His love every day.

"Arise, shine, for your light has come, and the glory of the LORD rises upon you" (Isaiah 60:1).

Yes, Lord, my light has come! A new day is dawning, and joyful hope is now a way of life when I remain rooted in You. Thank You! Amen.

About the Authors

Steve Grissom is the president of The Church Initiative, Inc.

After having experienced the pain of divorce himself, Steve discovered that local churches, while willing to help, were not equipped with the right tools to truly relate to and help the person in divorce. In 1993, Steve and his wife, Cheryl, designed and developed a Christ-centered support group recovery program called DivorceCare®. Today the DivorceCare® program is in nearly 9,000 churches around the world.

In 1994, Steve founded The Church Initiative, a ministry that develops and produces video- and workbook-based programs for churches to minister to people in other life crises, such as divorce, grief, and addiction.

Steve's past professional experience began in the telecommunications and broadcasting industries. He founded several satellite communications companies and spent more than ten years in television news management.

Steve and his wife, Cheryl, live in Wake Forest, North Carolina. They have three daughters: Carrie-Christina, Shannon, and Heather.

Kathy Leonard is the editorial director for The Church Initiative, Inc.

Kathy has been writing and editing for more than fifteen years. After graduating with a degree in English from the University of Maryland Asian Division in Okinawa, Japan, Kathy moved with her Air Force husband, Tim, to England. There she wrote feature articles for the Air Force base newspaper and worked as a publicist/graphic designer. After three years, Kathy moved to North Carolina where she taught high school English and was later hired by The Church Initiative as a writer and editor.

As a result of her time spent at The Church Initiative, she has developed a heart for those going through the deep pain and overwhelming emotions faced by people in separation, divorce, and other life crises; she ministers to people through her writing. She is coauthor of *Through a Season of Grief*, a 365-day devotional for people grieving the death of a loved one.

Kathy and her husband, Tim, live in Palmyra, Virginia, with their two children, Jacob and Alanna.

About DivorceCare®

DivorceCare® is a divorce recovery support group program for people suffering from the pain of separation and divorce. With groups meeting in locations around the world, this program has ignited hope and healing in the lives of many. DivorceCare® is a thirteen-week, video- and workbook-based resource that combines sound biblical instruction with the dynamic of small group interaction. The groups are designed to be lay led, usually by people who have been through divorce.

DivorceCare® video sessions and group discussion times help people travel from hurt and despair to peace and hope. DivorceCare® brings more than thirty respected Christian authors, counselors, and pastors into the small group setting via video, as well as personal testimonies from individuals who have experienced separation and divorce.

About The Church Initiative, Inc.

DivorceCare® is published by The Church Initiative, Inc., a ministry that assists churches in establishing support groups and teaching groups for people dealing with life crises and other life issues. Other ministry resources by The Church Initiative:

- DivorceCare for Kids™, a program to help children whose parents are separated or divorced (www.DC4K.org)
- Choosing Wisely: Before You Divorce™, a marriage crisis counseling tool (www.beforeyoudivorce.org)
- GriefShare®, grief recovery support groups (www.griefshare.org)
- Facing Forever™, an evangelism and discipleship tool (www.facingforever.org)
- Chance to Change™, gambling addiction recovery groups (www.chancetochange.org)

To place an order or to receive more information, call 1-800-489-7778 or e-mail info@churchinitiative.org.

Order DivorceCare® Group Materials

DivorceCare® is designed to help your church develop a divorce recovery seminar/support group ministry. This program equips your church with Christ-centered, biblical resources for ministering to people who are suffering from the hurt and despair of separation and divorce. The DivorceCare® materials kit includes thirteen video sessions on DVD, a leader's guide, a leader training DVD, workbooks for use by group participants, publicity brochures, and posters.

Order DivorceCare® Audio CDs

The DivorceCare® audio CDs contain the audio tracks from each of the thirteen weekly sessions on seven CDs. With a set of DivorceCare® audio CDs, you can catch up on sessions you missed or find encouragement by listening again to those sessions most meaningful to you. You can also share them with friends and family members to help them understand what you are experiencing.

To place an order or to receive more information,
call 1-800-489-7778 or e-mail info@churchinitiative.org.

Visit DivorceCare® Online

Whether you are in the midst of a separation or divorce, leading a DivorceCare® group, or interested in sponsoring a group, you will find helpful information and resources at www.divorcecare.org:

- Where to find the nearest DivorceCare® group
- Recommended resources dealing with divorce recovery and related topics
- Free online daily devotions
- Additional information about healing from the hurt of separation and divorce
- A detailed plan of salvation
- More about the DivorceCare® ministry
- Information about The Church Initiative, Inc., which sponsors DivorceCare®
- A special leadership forum for DivorceCare® leaders and facilitators
- Advice on how to start a DivorceCare® group

Find a DivorceCare® Group Near You

DivorceCare® groups are meeting throughout the United States, Canada, the United Kingdom, Australia, South Africa, and other countries. Here is how you can find out more about these groups: Search the database at www.divorcecare.org and find the location of the nearest DivorceCare® group by zip code, area code, city, or country. Or e-mail your zip code to info@divorcecare.org to receive a list of the groups nearest you. You can also call 1-800-489-7778 or 919-562-2112.